illustrates how a shorter man embarks
on his journey

A
CHALLENGING
LIFE

a memoir

Shin Hanok

This book
is dedicated to My Grandparents:
Shin Chigap and Yunahn Chacci,
and
My Parents: Shin Yusuk and Ju Bunsang,
to my Wife: Morana,
and two sons: Stephen and Leo,
to my Grandkids:
Yoorina, Yoojina
and Millie,
and
Forthcoming Descendants

About the Author

Shin Hanok[1] was born in the countryside of Korea, a year before the outbreak of the Korean War on 25 June 1950. Faced with persistent hunger, he decided to move to Busan, the second largest city in Korea, to overcome these challenges. He continued his pursuit of tertiary education, completing a postgraduate degree to ensure a comfortable daily life

After dedicating 13 years of tireless effort to KEPCO, he made a significant decision to immigrate to New Zealand with his family on 27 March 1993. In this new land, he invested another 30 years to establish his place in the multicultural society. Throughout these periods, he transitioned between a couple of real estate companies eventually founding his firm in September 1997. However, survival in the competitive landscape alongside larger firms was far from easy.

He has been deeply intrigued by humanity's survival in the universe forever, avidly reading thousands of books. In 2020, he authored a book titled "*Will Humanity Be Eternal?*", in Korean, in 2022, he also published a memoir chronicling his life journey titled "*Grandfather's Memoir*". Most recently, at the end of August 2023, he released a science fiction novel in Korean, "*No One Knows Tomorrow*", exploring the hope for humanity's sustainability through artificial intelligence.

With seventy-five years behind him, his life has been a tapestry woven with both triumphs and tribulations. Now, he stands at a crossroads, compelled to contemplate the path he has traversed on his own. Despite his inadequacy height, he possesses the confidence that he has faced every adversity in his life's journey head-on and with great thoroughness.

....
1) In Korea, when addressing someone by his name, it is customary to begin with the family name first.

Readers' Previews

'Reading Grandpa's memoir, our sisters have been filled with profound sense of honor to exist in the same universe with him. We're immensely proud to be part of our grandparents' legacy.' – **Yoorin, Yoojin, and Millie**[2]

'What a wonderful story about a short and humble man! It's truly unparalleled, full of challenges, and compelling.' – **Santos Dominique, Businessman**

'His incomparable history is imbued with the tension of cultural conflicts in every corner, which in turn ignites his courage to overcome every form of adversity.' – **Kimberly Kai, Editor**

'A great grandfather! He has left invaluable messages about moral virtues to his grandchildren, creating a remarkable family legacy.' – **Dave Hartfield, Friend**

'First and foremost, this book is written in such simple language that anyone can easily read it. Yet, as we read, it never provides a moment for us to pause until the very end. Most readers find a sense of peace and comfort within its pages.' - **Don Paterson**

'His memoir resides within a melting pot of experiences, beginning with tender moments of childhood and journeying through the challenges of middle age. As time has passed, the storms have receded, giving way to a new sense of happiness that now returns to the forefront.' - **Ethnic News Editor**

....

[2] Shin Yoorin and Shin Yoojin, children of our first son, and Shin Millie, a child of our second son.

'Hanok is somewhat of an institution at City Branch, Barfoot & Thompson – he is a character and generates a lot of fun and laughter within a team. Over a year ago he came to me and said he was going to be stepping back and handing everything over to Stephen and Leo, his sons, and that I would see a lot less of him. I assumed that would be the case however it wasn't. He still comes into the office every day! The reason for this is he has been writing books about his life including here in New Zealand and Korea, his family, and his career in Real Estate. He sometimes prints copious amounts of content on the work printer – all in Korean so I have no idea what it is – but I hope to have a chance to read them one day as I am sure they would be funny and endearing as he is'- **Sandra Forrester, Office Manager**

Introduction

In the crisp January air of 2023, a seemingly ordinary lunch with a friend took an unexpected turn, transforming into a pivotal moment. On that fateful day, I found myself tumbling down a flight of stairs, an incident that led me to an unforeseen week-long stay in the hospital. The purpose was dual-fold: to mend the head wound resulting from the fall and to undergo a thorough heart examination.

Amidst it all, a cardiologist's proposal for a pacemaker installation lingered in the air, a decision I've yet to make. This sequence of events shattered the complacency I had held towards my health. Until that day, the specter of my health and the relentless march of time had failed to disrupt my sense of invincibility.

However, that day acted as an intense inspiration: a realization that prompted me to document my family's history before my presence inevitably waned from this world. This determination was kindled by the awareness that I hadn't sufficiently imparted our family's history to my children, leaving them with limited insight into their heritage.

The moment of birth stands as a universal threshold, a shared manifestation of tears that heralds the start of diverse journeys for each soul. While some tread along smooth paths, others navigate rugged trails, and most grapple with winding roads.

My journey has been far from straightforward. When I cast my gaze back, I contemplate the contours of a life defined by its unique challenges. Genetically gifted with a stature of merely 154cm, I was thrust into a realm where survival often meant grappling fiercely against those of average height. Thus emerged the necessity to insert insoles into my shoes: a stratagem designed to circumvent the sense of inadequacy that often escorts physical stature.

Stepping into public spaces became an act that invariably attracted curious gazes, an amalgam of intrigue and amusement veiled behind polite smiles. Women, too, swiftly deemed me an unsuitable romantic prospect, their judgments hinging solely on my height. Job interviews at times concluded with an abrupt dismissal owing to my stature. These responses weren't the fault of others; rather, they were facets of my reality.

As graduation neared, the dean of the law school recommended that I consider a position with Korea's National Security Department. But during the subsequent physical assessment, a rather amusing incident unfolded:

Nurse: "Sir, I've got a short one!" she announced to the doctor record-
* ing measurements.*
Doctor: "How tall is he?"
Nurse: "It's only 154 cm."
Doctor: "Oh dear! Well below our parameters."

Unsurprisingly, I had failed to meet the criteria for the position. This anecdote marked the inception of a series of encounters shaped by my height. Did these obstacles and displeasures chip away at my resolve? I can assert with unwavering certainty that I consistently replied with a resounding "No." Beyond the confines of my situation, surmounting challenges and standing adversity has become the bedrock of my life philosophy.

Despite its diminutive stature, my spirit looms large. I tread along a path filled with challenges and obstacles, but I don't falter. Each step I have taken is purposeful, and I've carried a heart full of courage and a mind filled with dreams.

As I journey through the world, I encounter towering mountains that seem insurmountable, but I find a way to climb them. I traverse vast, uncharted forests, where the trees reach for the sky, yet I forge a path through the dense foliage. I cross turbulent rivers, sometimes having to swim against the current, yet I never lose sight of my destination;

Along the way, the small man meets fellow travelers, and despite his size, he leaves a lasting impact with his wisdom, kindness, and resilience. He learns from each experience and grows not physically but in character. He understands that it's not the size of the man that matters but the size of his heart and the depth of his determination.

As my journey continues, I realize that the world is vast, and I am small in comparison, but that doesn't deter me. I know that every step I take, every person I meet, and every obstacle I overcome is a part of my grand adventure. And I travel on, proving that it's not the size of the traveler but the size of his spirit that truly defines my journey.

As a result, I hold a unique distinction – I'm the first in my family to accumulate more than three decades of life experiences spanning both the Eastern and Western hemispheres. Additionally, my children face the challenge of understanding their native languages, which gradually disconnects them from our family's roots. Acknowledging my crucial role as a bridge between the past and present, I've come to realize the importance of passing down our ancestral history to my children before I pass away.

I am inspired to impart essential moral values to my grandchildren who will soon confront a challenging world. Therefore, my goal is to convey to them 15 basic moral virtues. Few Western people criticize Asians for being too ethical in their way of life, but despite this, I want to make ethical morals the basis of existence for my descendants.

Every culture and society has its ethical values and principles, and it's important to respect and appreciate the diversity of perspectives. The most effective way to pass on these is through one's actions and the environment created for my descendants. It's a lifelong journey of nurturing and fostering a strong moral foundation for generations to come.

For readers who approach this narrative without preconceived notions, I promise an unvarnished glimpse into an unconventional life. Amid the occasional shadows that obscure my past, I remain resolutely focused on a brighter future. I aspire to cultivate a thriving rose amidst the decay, with the hope that the intricacies of my life's journey resonate deeply within your hearts. To all who embark on this literary journey, I extend my full heartfelt congratulations!

My Timeline

1949 July, Born in Dongta village, Southern Province, Korea
1959~64, Attends Woongok Primary School, Hamahngun
1965~67, Attends Bajeong Middle School in Busan
1968~70, Attends Busan High School
1972 Mar, Enters Busan National University
1973~75, Serves the Army for 3 years
1976 Mar, Back to Administration Department of BNU
1979 Mar, Completes Bachelor of Public Administration, BNU
1979~81, Attends Graduate for Master of Public Administration
1980 Marries Jo Moran on 30 March 1980
1981 The first Son, Chorok born on 10 January
1981~92, Wors at Korea Electric Power Corporation for 12 years
1988 The second son, Puronsol born on 19 March
1992 Founds Seil telecommunication as a subsidiary of KEPCO
1993 Immigrates to New Zealand with family on 27 April 1993
1993 Studies at Carrington Polytech
1993 Nov, Joins Vision Realty, Northshore, Auckland
1994 Dec, Shifts to Bailess Real Estate
1997 Sep, Founds Impression Real Estate
2000 Aug, Joins Barfoot & Thompson Real Estate
2004 Leo and his Mom leave NZ to pursue Football Career
2004~06, Pursues legal suit at High Court for commission dispute
2014 Stephen joins B & T as team leader of 'TEAM SHIN'
2015 Leo joins B & T under his brother's arm
2020 Publishes first book, 'Will humanity last forever?' in Korea
2022 Publishes second book, 'Grandfather's Memoir' in Korea
2023 Publishes third book 'No One Knows Tomorrow' in Korea
2024 Publishes 'My Challenging Life' a memoir in English
2025 Living Funeral Celebration
2039 Targets to live on

9

CONTENTS

Introduction 6

I Life Begins at a Single Point. 11

II Family Roots 20

III Growing Up 47

IV Tertiary Study 75

V Breaking Eggs 83

VI Crossing the Southern Blue 102

VII Affection and Regret 134

VIII Plan for Enriched Ageing 179

IX Messages to Grandchildren 191

X Where is the next Destination? 227

Acknowledgment 240

Our Family Genealogy 243

I

Life Begins
at a single Point

I
Life Begins
at a single Point

"From this distant vantage point, the Earth might not seem of any particular interest. But for us, it's different. Consider again that dot. That's here. That's home. That's us. On it, everyone you love, everyone you know, everyone you ever heard of, every human being who ever was, lived out their lives.

The aggregate of our joy and suffering, thousands of confident religions, ideologies, and economic doctrines, every hunter and forager, every hero and coward, every creator and destroyer of civilization, every king and peasant, every young couple in love, every mother and father, hopeful child, inventor and explorer, every teacher of morals, every corrupt politician, every superstar, every supreme leader, every saint and sinner in the history of our species lived there – on a mote of dust suspended in a sunbeam.

The Earth is a very small stage in a vast cosmic arena. Think of the rivers of blood spilled by all those generals and emperors so that in glory and triumph they could become the momentary masters of a fraction of a dot. Think of the endless cruelties visited by the inhabitants of one corner of this pixel on the scarcely distinguishable inhabitants of some other corner.

How frequent their misunderstandings, how eager they are to kill one another, how fervent their hatred. Our posturing, our imagined self-mportance, the delusion that we have some privileged position in the universe, are challenged by this point of pale light. Our planet is a lonely speck in the great enveloping cosmic dark. In our obscurity – in all this vastness – there is no hint that help will come from elsewhere to save us from ourselves.

The Earth is the only world known, so far, to harbor life. There is nowhere else, at least shortly, to which our species could migrate. Visit, yes. Settle, not yet. Like it or not, for the moment, the Earth is where we make our stand. It has been said that astronomy is a humbling and character-building experience.

There is perhaps no better demonstration of the folly of human conceits than this distant image of our tiny world. To me, it underscores our responsibility to deal kindlier with one another and to preserve and cherish the pale blue dot, the only home we've ever known."

<**Pale Blue Dot**: A Vision of the Human Future in Space. **Carl Sagan** wrote in his 1994 book>

Once upon a time, a life came into existence on a pale blue dot; a distant and seemingly unremarkable speck. However, let's delve deeper into the history that unfolded long before my birth. This journey begins with the Big Bang, an event that occurred 13.8 billion years ago, as astronomers theorize.

According to this concept, the universe initiated as a single point, then rapidly expanded and stretched, gradually reaching the vast dimensions it occupies today; this expansion continues even now!

The energy constituting all that exists in the cosmos we now behold was once compressed within an unfathomably minuscule expanse. Then, for reasons yet to be fully comprehended, this intensely hot and dense mixture began to expand at a staggering pace.

In the initial moments of the universe's existence, our grasp of the unfolding events is surprisingly robust. We understand that the fundamental concepts of time, space, and existence took shape in rapid succession.

The first entities to emerge were subatomic particles, including quarks. Following closely were larger particles such as protons and neutrons. Roughly three minutes later, the universe's temperature had cooled to around 1 billion degrees Celsius.

This cooling allowed protons and neutrons to unite through fusion, leading to the formation of nuclei, the charged cores of atoms.

However, after approximately 20 minutes, the universe's temperature dropped to a point where fusion was no longer feasible. What remained was a heated, turbulent mixture comprising electrons, hydrogen nuclei, and helium nuclei.

This phase persisted for roughly 380,000 years. As time progressed, the cosmos gradually cooled, allowing electrons to unite with nuclei, creating the very first atoms.

Subsequently, over hundreds of millions of years, the earliest stars came into existence, illuminating the darkness that pervaded. It took an even greater period for the universe to begin to resemble the configuration we observe today.

As extensive time unfolded, the formation of our solar system took place roughly 4.5 billion years ago. This event arose from the condensation of a dense cloud comprised of interstellar gas and dust. The collapse of this cloud, potentially triggered by the shockwave from a nearby exploding star known as a supernova, led to the emergence of a solar nebula: a whirling, spinning disk of material. Within this disk, gravity exerted its force, drawing in more and more material towards the center.

Eventually, the core's pressure reached an astonishing level, causing hydrogen atoms to merge and form helium, thereby releasing an immense quantity of energy. In the wake of this phenomenon, our Sun came into existence, amassing over 99% of the available matter.

In the outer reaches of the disk, matter was also coalescing. These aggregations collided, leading to the formation of progressively larger objects. Among these entities, some grew to a size where their gravitational forces molded them into spherical shapes, ultimately becoming planets, dwarf planets, and substantial moons.

Conversely, in certain instances, the conditions for planet formation did not materialize. An example of this is the asteroid belt, a collection of fragments from the early solar system that never managed to coalesce into a fully-fledged planet. Other smaller remnants evolved into asteroids, comets, meteoroids, and small, irregularly shaped moons. It was during this period that our Earth also came into being.

Another billion years elapsed, bringing us to a point around 3.5 billion years ago. During this period, the genesis of life emerged from the natural interactions of non-living matter, particularly in hydrothermal vents within the ocean.

Here, simple organic compounds played a pivotal role. Within the realm of scientific discourse, a prevailing hypothesis suggests that the transition from non-living to living entities wasn't a solitary occurrence. Instead, it was an extensive process characterized by increasing complexity.

This journey encompassed various stages such as the establishment of a habitable planet, the prebiotic synthesis of organic molecules, molecular self-replication, self-assembly, autocatalysis, and the emergence of cell membranes. Numerous proposals have been put forth, each representing a distinct facet of this intricate progression. Indeed, scientists have undertaken experiments that shed light on these processes. As far back as 1924, Oparin and in 1929, Haldane postulated that the initial molecules forming the earliest cells gradually self-organized from a primordial soup.

This idea gained momentum when, 23 years later, Miller and Urey conducted a chemical experiment in 1952. They aimed to illustrate how organic molecules might have spontaneously emerged from inorganic precursors under the prebiotic conditions posited by the Oparin-Haldane hypothesis. In their groundbreaking experiment, they employed a highly reducing mixture of gases to generate basic organic monomers, including amino acids.

Nevertheless, the current scientific consensus portrays the early atmosphere as weakly reducing or even neutral, thereby constraining the quantity and diversity of amino acids that could have been generated.

Yet, the introduction of iron and carbonate minerals - materials abundant in the primordial oceans – can produce a broader spectrum of amino acids. Subsequent research has explored two additional conceivable reducing settings: outer space and deep-sea hydrothermal vents. These environments also hold the potential to contribute to the formation of organic compounds.

It's a valid point that an intense focus on the origin and evolution of life could lead us to lose sight of the broader narrative we seek to explore: namely, the emergence of humankind.

To circumvent this, crafting a condensed calendar that compresses the 3.5-billion-year history of life, predating the advent of modern human ancestors, into a single hour, holds the potential to illuminate the subsequent progression towards Homo sapiens.

This approach indeed has promise. Life, having emerged 3.5 billion years ago, persists in its evolutionary journey without interruption, continuing its trajectory right up to the present day.

Certainly, let's embark on this accelerated journey: an hour-long sprint that encapsulates the vast expanse of life's evolution. Here's the timeline condensed to fit within this hour: at the outset, within the

15

first second, primitive cells emerge; as 51 minutes and 10 seconds elapse, a fish enters the scene; just 3 minutes later, at 54 minutes and 10 seconds, amphibians make their appearance; within the next 2 minutes, dinosaurs arrive and, after a brief 3-minute reign, depart the Earth; swiftly following at 56 minutes and 25 seconds, mammals arise, filling the void left by the vanishing dinosaurs; the clock reaches 58 minutes, unveiling the advent of birds; near the end of the hour, at 59 minutes and 56 seconds, apes like chimpanzees emerge, marking the earliest human ancestors; finally, at 59 minutes and 59.8 seconds, mere moments before the clock's completion, modern humans, homo sapiens, make their entrance onto earth, igniting the start of human history.

This rapid timeline underscores the remarkable and intricate tapestry of life's progression, culminating in the emergence of our species. In the compressed timespan of 3.5 billion years, compacted into a mere hour, the emergence and existence of homo sapiens in the final 0.2 seconds is a striking visual. Human beings born within these last seconds might seem insignificant in the grand scheme of things. But we remain unaware of the potential magnitude and greatness of this very moment.

Within this incredibly short span, humans have rapidly acquired a vast array of knowledge, encompassing the entire history of the universe. This includes the 13.8-billion-year timeline of the cosmos, spanning from the universe's inception to the birth of our solar system and earth, even encompassing the demise of supernovae. Amidst this accelerated learning, humans are keenly aware of their mortality; a realization that lends a poignant depth to their pursuits.

Yet, human nature isn't constrained by this understanding; instead, humans strive tirelessly to transcend their limitations. This peculiarity defines them as beings of ceaseless aspiration. The upcoming chapters will explore the history of Shin Hanok, a member of the homo species, as a journey unfolds against this grand backdrop.

The history of the universe embarked upon its journey from a single point 13.8 billion years ago. It's almost as if we ought to extend congratulations to the greatest entrepreneur for his successful venture into the 'offspring life' business: a venture that has propagated an amazing 8 billion descendants across the Earth.

East Asia, as of 2015, is home to a population of 1.63 billion homo sapiens spread across various countries. Notably, Chinese civilization stands out as one of the earliest cradles of human civilization. This influence radiates across diverse regions in the Asian area, selectively embracing aspects of Korean culture that harmonize with its local traditions.

Certainly, the foundation of this complex tapestry lies in Confucianism, nurtured by ancient Chinese philosopher Kong Qiu. Its principles have profoundly shaped political and social systems, crafting social frameworks for generations.

This revival took the form of being adopted as the basis for imperial exams and the core philosophy for the scholar and official classes in two Korean dynasties: the Goryeo Dynasty was founded by the prominent general Wang Geon in 918, with its capital in Kaesong. At the time, the population was around 3 million; and Buddhism was the main religion. However, Confucianism exerted strong influences on the Goryeo Dynasty in later periods.

To solidify monarchical authority and establish a centralized political order, the Gwageo civil exam was begun, drawing inspiration primarily from China's imperial exam system.

This institution continued to be a vital management of society in the subsequent Joseon Dynasty (1392-1910). It was enriched with three broad categories: literary, military, and miscellaneous exams; covering subjects such as medicine, geography, astronomy, and the social sector, primarily in Chinese characters.

These exams centered on evaluating candidates' writing abilities and knowledge of Confucianism. They revolved around memorization and interpretation of the Five Confucian classics, as well as composing poetry and prose. This focus on comprehension hindered the ability of applicants' creative ideas, imagination, critical thinking, and curiosity.

Originally conducted every three years, the literary and military exams implemented three stages: a qualifying test in the provinces, a second exam in the capital, and a final exam in the presence of the king: where successful candidates were ranked immediately.

The highest scorer in the literary exam earned a post of the 6th junior rank. If the top scorer already held a post, they were elevated by 4 levels. The second and third scorers received posts of the 7th junior rank, while the rest had to await vacancies.

The miscellaneous examinations had only the first two stages and did not involve ranking candidates. Right throughout history into modern times, education has remained a vital avenue for social status. Parents had invested substantial resources, believing that their child's admission to a prestigious institution laid the foundation for success.

Noble families aspiring for their children to pass the Gwageo exams were committed to supporting their children's education. Since then, possessing a family member who passed the Gwageo and served in the office within the last four generations was necessary to present oneself as a nobleman.

As a result, parents became deeply invested in their children's education, these sentiments continue in today's Korean society. Evaluation based on academic performance remains prevalent today: with attending a prestigious university often equated with success. Consequently, parents tend to drive their children to excel in the academy from a young age, leading to the prevalence of after-school cram schools, or "hagwons," and an intense study culture.

In contrast, the Joseon Dynasty was characterized by a hierarchical society where local households sent their children to study in Seoul to improve their chances of passing the Gwageo exam.

The historical context sheds light on the fervor with which scholars dedicated their lives to becoming students and passing the Gwageo exam. Success in this examination not only brought personal fame but also honored one's family.

This dedication to education remains a defining trait in modern Korean society, where individuals are often assessed primarily based on academic achievements. Reflecting on the ancestors who faced the challenges of the Gwageo exams can offer valuable insights and foster positive attitudes for present-day endeavors.

In the tapestry of life's evolution spanning 3.5 billion years, one remarkable feature stands out: the uniqueness of every individual. No two people are identical. This diversity stems from the genetic process known as sex, intertwining genes and creating individual differences, contributing to the human gene pool.

Consider this perspective: Each person has a lineage that doubles with each generation. Ascending 30 generations, roughly 1,066 years ago, would result in over 1 billion direct ancestors, a number exceeding Earth's population at that time. Thus, most people would share duplicated ancestors.

Around 5 million years ago, the common human ancestor existed as a hunter-gatherer in Africa. Genetic differences among different races are minimal, primarily involving genes determining skin color, facial features, and physique. According to studies, the genetic difference between two individuals is only around 7%.

Delving into the history of human genetic evolution, I explore the narrative of my direct ancestors. This exploration profoundly impacts my life and continues to influence my children in the present, with implications for future generations.

The Gwageo system prevalent in the Goryeo and Joseon dynasties plays a pivotal role in this exploration, marking the inception of my family's journey. This historical connection serves as a tether bridging our family's past to our present reality.

As a descendant of my direct ancestors, I inherit the legacy of ancestors who pursued excellence, shaping my perception of a thriving life and a rich familial heritage. The educational and prosperous legacy passed down through our lineage remains vital in my pursuit of fulfillment.

II

My Family Roots

II
My Family Roots

Now, it's time to explore my family's origins. The narrative of human history is undeniably much shorter than the expansive tale of the entrepreneurial endeavor that began with the inception of life in the universe as recounted in the previous chapter.

The latter venture spans well over 3.5 billion years, while the former is confined to a mere several hundred thousand years, primarily taking place on the African continent.

Let's begin my family's story by digging into our ancestral heritage, tracing it back through human genetics. Mitochondrial Eve stands as the most recent matrilineal common ancestor of all living humans. To put it simply, she is the latest woman from whom every living human can trace an unbroken lineage solely through our mother and her maternal line, reaching back until all lines converge at one woman.

The male counterpart to "Mitochondrial Eve" is the "Y-Chromosomal Adam," the individual from whom all living humans can trace our paternal lineage. Through millions of years of evolutionary progress, I was born and continue to walk on the same ground that bears the imprints of the ancestral paths charted by Mitochondrial Eve and Y Adam, and their subsequent generations.

At the age of 5 or 6, my eldest brother undertook the responsibility of teaching me how to read, write, and understand the genealogical records of the spicy Shin family[3]. These records were written in Chinese, through which I could unravel extensive entries that documented births, deaths, marriages, burials, as well as the lineage

....

3) There are three Shin Families in Korea: *the Spread Shin Family* has a large number of families in the whole of Korea in 2015, with 741,081; *the Mind Shin Family* has a number of 51,865; and *the Spicy Shin Family I belonged to* has a population of 187,731.

of ancestors and descendants. These accounts also provided insights into their respective social position within the hierarchical structure. Even after King Sejong of the Joseon Dynasty had invented 'Hangul' (Korean) in 1446, these records continued to be documented in Chinese. Over 580 years, Hangul was eventually integrated into the existing records, but the core pattern remains the same.

These genealogical books hold a wealth of information: beyond just our family's history, they house glimpses into their lives. Reflecting on this, I now understand why my older brother was so eager to impart this knowledge of the genealogical records to me.

Confucius, born in 551 BC emphasized five principal relationships in society (called five classics): between ruler and minister, father and son, husband and wife, older brother and younger brother, and friend and friend. Among his teachings, the concept of Filial Piety held great significance in daily life. He advocated that children should honor their parents, younger ones should respect elders, and people should coexist harmoniously to foster peace.

This concept is deeply rooted in the understanding that harmony starts within the family, which is reflected in the traditional saying "Family is everything." He also taught that our bodies, hair, and skin are gifts from our parents and should not be harmed, laying the foundation for the concept of filial piety.

Following Confucius's teachings, ancestral rituals became a way to demonstrate respect for one's ancestors and were adopted as a practice of filial piety. These teachings gradually spread throughout Asia.

Since the Goryeo Dynasty introduced Confucian classics, these ancestral ceremonies held twice a year during Seollal (Lunar New Year) and Chuseok (Harvest Festival), became significant events. Outdoor rituals were also performed at gravesites or community shrines.

In my childhood memories, I recall collective ancestral rituals that involved the entire village, taking place once every three years. After I got married in 1980, I brought my wife to participate in our ancestral ritual in the village. Witnessing the unity and respect among Shin family members for our ancestors filled me with a sense of pride. This hidden intention of my older brother was apparent; he wanted to showcase our family's unity, and the impact of that day's experience remained with me for a long time.

Typically, in the inhouse ceremony, the rituals were dedicated to the four most recent generations; great-great-grandfather, great-grandfather, grandfather, and up to the father.

However, recent times have seen significant changes. It is very common to conduct rituals for only two or three generations, and in some instances, people limit the ritual to their immediate parents. Additionally, rituals known as Gijesa in the house, part of the three typical rites, are often conducted in the evening rather than after midnight, as hosts prioritize convenience.

There's a preference for holding ancestor rituals in the house of a younger son, even though it was traditionally held in the oldest son's house. These revised rituals continue to play an essential role in the modern lives of Koreans.

Whenever I visited my older brother's house in Busan with my children, he would seize the opportunity to impart to me the proper practices, much as he had been taught by our grandparents. This dedicated passing down of traditions is the reason I can still vividly remember these rituals and family customs; ones that I intend to pass on to the next generations.

During these rituals, my brother would demonstrate how to read from the genealogy book and how to pay tribute to our ancestors. He would change into decent clothes after bathing and sit down to guide me through the ritual procedures.

He showed me how to write prayer papers to place on the ancestral portraits, where the ancestors were symbolically thought to sit. Before the rituals, we'd prepare prayer papers, along with various foods and drinks, laid out on the table in front of the portraits.

The entire family would gather in front of ancestral portraits and bow twice in a respectful manner, offering foods and liquors as symbols of honor and remembrance. These rituals are conducted with a sense of reverence and devotion; If it's possible, we do this in a quiet and solemn atmosphere to maintain the sincerity of the whole occasion.

Upon completing the rituals, family members would come together to share a meal, enjoying food and drinks while reminiscing about the ancestors and expressing hopes and wishes for future generations. These rituals not only pay homage to our ancestors but also nurture a feeling of togetherness and ongoing bond among the descendants. Having searched into the essence of these rituals and comprehended their importance to our forebears, let us shift my focus to our direct lineage of ancestors and explore their lives and contributions to the tapestry of my own family's history.

My Family Tree

(**Founder**)   Shin Gyeong – 1 child
(Born in 1107, Song Dynasty)

⬇

(24th Gen) 7th great-grandparents   Shin Yeojuk+Ju PP, Park AA [4] – 2 child
(1660 ~ ?, Scholar, two wives)

⬇

(25th Gen) 6th great-grandparents   Shin Woocheul+Choi SS – 3 child
(Deputy Minister?)

⬇

(26th Gen) 5th great-grandparents   Shin Ilhwa + Bang KK – 2 child
(1728 ~ 1768)

⬇

(27th Gen) 4th great-grandparents   Shin Sunggon+Gwak XX – 1 child
(1746 ~ ?)

⬇

(28th Gen) 3rd great-grandparents   Shin Yungang+Cha YY – 1 child
(1774 ~ ?)

⬇

(29th Gen) 2nd great-grandparents   Shin Gyeungwoo+Park ZZ – ?
(1797 ~ 1875)

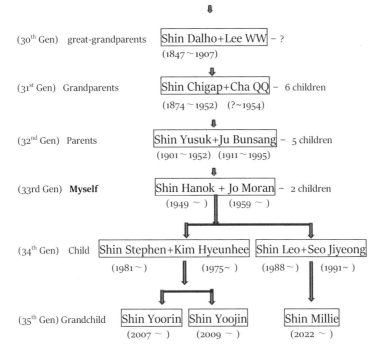

(30th Gen) great-grandparents   Shin Dalho+Lee WW – ?
(1847~1907)

(31st Gen) Grandparents   Shin Chigap+Cha QQ – 6 children
(1874~1952) (?~1954)

(32nd Gen) Parents   Shin Yusuk+Ju Bunsang – 5 children
(1901~1952) (1911~1995)

(33rd Gen) **Myself**   Shin Hanok + Jo Moran – 2 children
(1949 ~)   (1959 ~)

(34th Gen) Child   Shin Stephen+Kim Hyeunhee   Shin Leo+Seo Jiyeong
(1981~)   (1975~)   (1988~)   (1991~)

(35th Gen) Grandchild   Shin Yoorin   Shin Yoojin   Shin Millie
(2007 ~)   (2009 ~)   (2022 ~)

Shin Gyeong, born in 1107 during the Song Dynasty in ancient China, is the founder of the *Spicy Shin Family*. He journeyed to the Goryeo Dynasty in 1130 as part of a cultural exchange program between the two dynasties and subsequently passed the Gwageo exam in 1138 during the 16th year of King Injong's reign in the Goryeo Dynasty.

....

4) In the past, women's family names were typically not recorded in genealogies. instead, genealogies primarily focused on tracing the male line of descent. Therefore, when discussing genealogy, terms like G2-grandparent referred to great-great-grandparents, indicating the second generation beyond the grandparents. This tradition of emphasizing the male lineage in genealogy has shifted over time, and today, there is a growing recognition of the importance of documenting and preserving both male and female family histories. **The above genealogy is attached at the end of this book.**

His ability to write about Confucian classics in Chinese characters likely contributed to his quick success in the Gwageo exam; this word underestimated my ancestor's ability; but it might be true. After passing it, he served as a deputy minister with responsibilities in the cultural and artistic sectors. The details of his lifespan are unclear, but he was laid to rest in Gaeseung, the capital of the Goryeo Dynasty at that time.

Following him, his descendants continued to excel in the Gwageo exams and held high-ranking posts in official duties or as advisors to the king under the Goryeo Dynasty.

Shin Wunmin, the second-generation after originator, passed the exam at the age of 23 and became the chief advisor to the king. He managed the royal library and served as a researcher in Confucian philosophy, providing advice to the king on various matters.

5) Shin Mongsam's tomb is found at Pohang City in 1918. The annual tribute is held annually on the 5th of May.

Shin Youngge, a grandson of Shin Gyeong, passed the exam at the age of 26 and was appointed as another chief advisor of the royal academy in the palace. Shin Mongsam[5], the son of Shin Youngge and the fourth-generation descendant, passed the exam at the age of 23 in 1189. He was designated as a chief advisor to the king and his tomb was discovered in Pohang City in 1918.

He had four sons in the fifth generation: Shin Gwakge, Shin Cheunge, Shin Hyenge, and Shin Juge. All of them passed the exams and were appointed to high-ranking positions. Shin Juge, the youngest of the four, eventually became a minister during the Goryeo Dynasty.

Shin Baekryeun, the sixth-generation member of the family, was born in 1202 during the reign of King Shinjong. He also passed the exam and was appointed as a special advisor in the palace academy. His final resting place is in the Youngsan area.

This lineage demonstrates a remarkable tradition of academic and official excellence, with succeeding generations making significant contributions to the service of the Goryeo Dynasty.

Shin Hee (7th Generation): born in 1222, during the reign of King Gojong of the Goryeo Dynasty. He passed the Gwageo exam and was appointed as a deputy auditor. Burial Place was Jangmamyeun, Kyung-nam Province. His tomb is listed as a cultural property, which indicates its historical and cultural significance.

Shin Jihwa (8th Generation): born in 1241, during the Goryeo Dynasty. He went to the Song Dynasty in 1266 and was positioned as the chief scholar in both the Song and Yuan dynasties. This suggests that he held a prominent intellectual and scholarly role in these dynasties. He was said to be buried in Gyohwa, which is known as Paju today.

Shin Yoonhwa (Brother of Shin Jihwa): he was posted as a general and was involved in negotiating the border between the Goryeo and the Mongol Empire in 1260. He successfully completed the negotiations and returned to the Goryeo. These historical accounts provide a glimpse into the lives and achievements of members of the Shin family during the Goryeo Dynasty.

If you have any specific questions about this information or if you'd like to explore more about the Goryeo Dynasty or related topics, feel free to ask me about it. I'm ready to teach you our family genealogies.

Shin Cheon, the ninth generation, passed the Gwageo exam in 1294. It's the 20th year of King Chungnyeol, Goryeo, and appointed as the vice Auditor of the Kingdom.

Shin Hyeok (Shin Cheon's brother) became the post of vice minister for Art and Administration. Also, in the reign of King Chungmok, during the Goryeo Dynasty, Shin Ye (Shin Hyeok's grandson) was sealed into a local governor.

Under the reign of King Gongmin, Shin Boo (Shin Ye's younger brother), was promoted to high officer. Shin Inson (the grandson of Shin Boo), was appointed a special advisor of Imperial Academy during King Sejong. In the reign of King Sejo, Shin Seukjo (son of Shin Inson) was appointed to the position of vice minister.

Shin Don, a prominent figure in the Goryeo Dynasty, stands out as a significant ancestor who left a profound impact on history. A Buddhist monk and scholar during the reign of King Gongmin (May 1330 to Oct 27, 1374), Shin Don's legacy is characterized by his groundbreaking reforms and steadfast dedication to societal betterment. In the 1360s, backed by the unyielding support of King Gongmin, Shin Don assumed the role of Supreme Prime. This position allowed him to initiate a transformative role aimed at rectifying the plight of individuals who had been forced into slavery. One of his notable achievements involved reestablishing the land system, an endeavor that sought to restore lands that had been unjustly taken from their original owners.

Shin Don's influence extended to various aspects of governance. His duties as a potent reformer prompted improvements in the kingdom's exam system. He also exhibited keen discernment by appointing accomplished scholars like Lee Saek, Jeong Mongju, and Jeong Dojeon as palace servants. These individuals, driven by their convictions and brilliance, contributed to advancing the kingdom's affairs.

Shin Don's journey, though marked by determination, was not devoid of challenges. His visionary reform plans drew the wrath of numerous adversaries, and he found himself surrounded by insincere flatterers who often failed to grasp the true essence of his ideals. As a result, the firm support he had once enjoyed from King Gongmin began to falter, leaving him in a state of isolation to susceptibility. Tragically, his arduous journey had reached a sudden end when King Gongmin ordered his execution in 1371.

Despite this distressing outcome, history is in the midst of a reevaluation of Shin Don's legacy. Recognized as an ancestor who wielded immense influence as a political and social reformer six centuries ago, Shin Don's contributions are being revisited with a renewed grasp of his visionary ideals and their profound impact on Korean history.

From the eighth generation, the Spicy Shins underwent division into five subclans: Deukjepa, Chodangpa, Sangjangkunpa, Buwonpa, and Panseupa. Among them, the first three were established in the Youngsan province, Kyeungsangnamdo, while the latter two were in the Youngwol province, Gangwondo, northern part of Korea.

During the Goryeo Dynasty, the lineage of Shin Gyeong thrived, giving rise to a myriad of gifted descendants who distinguished themselves in the realms of politics and academia. Frequently, their prominence was solidified by their success in the rigorous Gwageo exam system.

Attempting to compile an exhaustive list of their names and successes could prove to be as challenging as following in their formidable footsteps. Nonetheless, their continuous influences seamlessly could persist into the Joseon Dynasty, leaving an unfading mark on pages of history.

During the Joseon Dynasty, the Shin family continued to distinguish itself. The lineage produced a remarkable total of 53 Gwageo exam successors, a testament to their dedication and prowess in the field of academics.

Moreover, seven ministers emerged from the Shin Family, further solidifying their weight and contributions to the local governors, royal advisers, and state officers. This enriched legacy underscores the enduring influence of the Shin family throughout centuries of Korean history, both in the realms of scholarship and governance.

In the modern era, the illustrious lineage of the Spicy Shin Family has continued to produce outstanding individuals across a diverse array of fields including economy, politics, arts, and entertainment.

Shin Gyeokho: an eminent figure in the business world, he served as the chairman of the Lotte Group. Under his leadership, the Lotte Group transformed from a humble venture selling chewing gum to children in Japan in 1948 into a global conglomerate. With over hundred business units spanning various industries such as hotels, retail, fast food, manufacturing, finance, chemicals, ICT, construction, and entertainment, the Lotte Group today employs around 60,000 individuals. After his passing, family disputes arose between the brothers' members regarding ownership and complex power battles.

Shin Seokjung: born in 1907 during Japan's reign, he emerged as a prominent Korean poet. He began his literary journey at the age of 24 as a contributor to 'poetic literature,' a monthly magazine focused on poetry. His unique style centered around idyllic themes, carving a distinctive place for himself in the world of literature.

Shin Aera: born on 7 March 1969, stands as a notable Korean actress. She made her debut in 1989 and has since portrayed leading roles in TV dramas. Beyond her acting career, Shin Aera and her husband, popular actor Cha Inpo (married in 1995), have embraced charities. Both of them engage in active volunteer work at orphanages and welfare centers, while also making substantial contributions to like combating child abuse, addressing school violence, and brotherly aid to underprivileged children.

Shin Sangwoo: a prominent politician, established his commitment to move through a journey marked by activism and service. Strong involvement in students' uprisings during his time at Korea University preceded his transition to journalism as a reporter for the Busan Ilbo. He later made his mark in politics, winning National Assembly elections four times despite the challenges posed by the Park Chung-hee military regime. Notably, he supported Roh Moohyun's successful campaign for the 16th presidency of South Korea. During his lifetime, he served as a vice-chairman of the Democratic and Peaceful

Unification Advisory Council for a year. His legacy was tragically cut short by liver cancer on January 26, 2012, at the age of 76.

These distinguished individuals from the Shin Family continue to exemplify the legacy of excellence and fulfillment that has defined our lineage throughout history. It is truly captivating to search into the rich tapestry of the Shin family's history.

In today's era, the Spicy Shin family boasts a substantial population, as registered by the 2015 census which seen around 190,000 members scattered across the country. Among these, my own direct clan finds its place within the Sangjangkunpa clan. This branch primarily found its home in the Youngsan mountain of Kyeongsangnamdo province, situated in the southern region of Korea.

The roots of my immediate family's journey can be traced back to the 24th generation, represented by Shin Yeojuk, my 7th great-grandfather. It was during the latter half of the Joseon Dynasty, around the 1660s, that Shin Yeojuk established our lineage in my hometown, Dongta. This era of Joseon was characterized by a robust central monarchy centered around the king, with governance overseen by civil bureaucrats and military officials.

In pursuit of positions at these institutions, individuals needed to successfully navigate the rigorous Gwageo test, which divided literary, military, and miscellaneous subjects. Those who had excelled in earned the position of Yangban, signifying a ruling class comprising scholars and military officers.

However, a majority of the population, roughly 80% to 90%, fell into the category of commoners. They encompassed farmers, artisans, and merchants, many of whom struggled to make ends meet.

Neo-Confucianism exerted significant influence during this period, contributing to the male-dominated nature of society. Women's roles were relegated to silence, with limited interaction with unrelated men. Purity to their husbands was of utmost importance, and widows were barred from remarriage: a transgression that would disgrace the family.

The early settlers of my family in my hometown were primarily farmers. Their first challenges involved clearing densely wooded lands to establish homes and cultivate fields for crops. Fencing the land was also crucial. In those days, staple foods such as rice, barley, wheat, sweet potatoes, cabbage, and garlic played a vital role in the sustenance. Livestock, including cattle, dogs, and pigs, provided assistance in farming activities and a source of nourishment. Amidst the scarcity of resources in the early days, settlers learned to adapt and utilize native foods. They crafted recipes using local meats like cattle, wild rabbits, and pheasants. Wild fruits, flowers, and nuts were discovered to be edible, while abundant fish and stream crabs supplemented their diet from nearby ponds.

As the settlers established themselves in their home village, their focus shifted to raising families. The next generations of the Shin family were born into a world where hard work was a way of life.

Shin Woocheul, the first son of Shin Yeojuk and the 25th generation ancestor, had toiled alongside his parents. Responsibilities included fetching water, washing dishes, aiding in laundry, collecting firewood, and tending to cattle. Children, both boys and girls, participated in the farm chores. Girls were tasked with knitting, sewing, cooking, cleaning, and caring for younger siblings. Boys sometimes assisted their fathers in construction work. Devoid of formal schools, most children did not have the privilege of attending.

The remarkable journey of the Spicy Shin family through these generations exemplifies resilience, adaptation, and the pursuit of better lives in the face of challenges. The legacy of my family unfolds their generations, revealing the lives and experiences of those who came before me. Their journey takes us to my great-great-grandfather, Shin Kyeungwoo, who was born in 1797. He found companionship in marriage with Park ZZ from Milyang Village. Despite the challenging circumstances of the time, he lived a remarkable 78 years, a testament to his resilience and strength.

Moving forward in my ancestral lineage, my great-grandfather, Shin Dalho, comes into focus as the 30th generation. Born in 1847 and passing in 1907, he lived a meaningful 60 years. However, the details of his life remain somewhat elusive due to the limited documents and the prevailing circumstances of the time.

The period in which my great-grandfather lived was marked by societal constraints, particularly given the closed nature of the society and the Japanese Empire's influence over the Joseon Dynasty. These challenges, compounded by a lifestyle heavily centered around farming, left little room for leaving detailed records or messages for future generations.

My journey into the stories of my ancestors continues, shaping the path of my family's history. my great-grandfather, blessed with two sons, marked the beginning of a lineage that would carry forward their values and wisdom.

My grandfather, **Shin Chigap**, one of the two, emerges as a significant figure in my ancestral annals. Through the lens of my mother's recollections, I began to grasp the tapestry of my heritage even as I was in my infancy.

Shin Chigap was a man of deep curiosity and intellect. He immersed himself in the study of Taoism and Confucianism, ancient philosophies from China. His fascination with the 'Tao Te Ching,' penned by Laozi around 400 BC, revealed his profound interest in a text that touched upon various schools of thought, including Legalism, Buddhism, and Confucianism. This text, renowned for its influence on art and academia worldwide, served as a wellspring of inspiration.

The teachings and morals gleaned from these philosophical pursuits found application in the lives of those around him, including his own family. He took himself on the role of an educator, imparting classical knowledge and the virtues of noble individuals to the children of my village.

While he initially harbored ambitions of participating in the Gwageo exams, over time, his focus shifted, and he chose to remain a scholar to the confines of the village. The pages of these related books were never far from my grandfather's grasp. In an era where knowledge and the art of living were often transmitted through written words, he stood as a beacon of enlightenment.

Despite his strict demeanor, he exhibited generosity toward his family, avoiding disputes over family holdings. His interactions with the family were distinguished by special enthusiasm, and he dedicated focused time to playing, conversing, and reading with me and my siblings. Directly passing on family histories and legacies, he left an indelible mark on my understanding of my heritage.

My grandfather emerges as a figure of not only intellectual pursuit but also of profound kindness and harmony within my family. His rapport with his partner stood out as a testament to their peaceful order.

In my mother's accounts of my childhood, the absence of arguments or battles between grandparents in front of the family illustrated the respect and unity that characterized their partnership.

In the midst of my mother's busy household duties, my grandfather made a deliberate effort to connect with me. Even as a baby, he would cradle me on his lap and read to me, fostering a sense of closeness and curiosity from an early age.

While I may not fully recall those moments, it's evident that he aimed to instill in me an interest in the knowledge of Taoism and Confucianism that had captivated him. On one particular day, my grandfather gathered the entire family together to share the story of the 'Frog at the Bottom of a Well,' a tale found in Taoism.

Through this story, he sought to impart a valuable lesson. The narrative emphasized the idea that our understanding of the world is limited, drawing parallels to a frog confined to the bottom of a well. Just as the frog's perspective is restricted to the well's boundaries, humans too possess a narrow view of the world unless they venture beyond their own experiences.

My grandfather's dedication to sharing wisdom and fostering a sense of wonder if I underscore the depth of his commitment as a teacher and guide in my life: The story we shared about the turtle and the frog at the bottom of a well paints a vivid picture of the frog's limited perspective and the turtle's broader understanding of the world:

The tale unfolds with a turtle making its way to the well and encountering a frog dwelling within. The frog, taking pride in its well, begins to boast about its seemingly convenient and versatile surroundings. It describes how it can hop along the well's edge when restless, rest against the wall when tired, and cool off by swimming in the water.

In response, the frog invites the turtle to join it in the well, unaware of the limitations of its habitat. The turtle, wise and aware of the bigger world beyond, declines the invitation.

Instead, the turtle suggests that the well is too confined for both of them and proposes that the frog visit the turtle's home in the sea. The turtle highlights the expansiveness of the sea compared to the strained space of the well. It mentions the sea's stability even in times of flooding or drought, emphasizing the contrasting capabilities of their respective environments.

Curious about the frog's reluctance to explore beyond the well, the turtle inquires why the frog doesn't venture out to experience another world.

On another day, my grandfather made an unusual request of my mother, urging her to fetch a chisel from the toolbox. The purpose behind this strange demand was nothing short of remarkable: he intended to free himself from the constraints of a bothersome corn on his foot; meticulously performing the task of removing it with his own weathered hands.

As my mother stood witness to this unexpected scene, her eyes shuttered with a mix of apprehension and awe. The ordeal unfolded with my grandfather's steadfast focus, etching a vivid image in my mother's memory; a blend of determination and grit, leaving behind a tableau of tools and crimson marks.

His character bore the weight of both strength and rigidity, the threads of his interactions with neighbors often tinged with an aura of aloofness and self-assuredness. His convictions were unhesitating, immovable even in the face of differing viewpoints.

Just as Confucius himself grew finicky about meals, leading his wife to leave him, my grandfather's strong adherence to this ideology seemed to kindle a similar discernment that tainted his perception of women. In modern parlance, one could say he was predisposed to misogyny, casting a shadow that dimmed the prospects of my two sisters. Under the weight of his prejudice, they were denied the threshold of education, and barred from crossing the hallowed boundaries of formal schooling.

Yet, amongst these recollections, the memory of my grandmother dances in my mind's eye, preserved in the fragile amber of my earliest years. Though debilitated by a stroke, rendering her bedridden, she was a constant recipient of my mother's tender care.

It was during these moments of practice and interaction that my young self would accompany my mother into the room, drawn by an invisible thread of curiosity. Despite her confinement, my grandma's face was a canvas of warmth, etching smiles that illuminated her struggle. She shared our family's storied traditions, imparting them to me with a worm air of pride, an unspoken testament to her enduring connection with our lineage.

The years rolled by, and the day arrived when my grandfather's earthly journey reached its end. In the hush of late-night hours, my mother assumed the role of solitary mourner, orchestrating a private ritual to honor him. I stood by her side, a witness to the interplay of reverence and grief, as the familiar contours of our home transformed into a sanctuary for remembrance.

Later, as the sun dipped below the horizon, I found myself beside my grandfather's final resting place: a tranquil hill overlooking the serene embrace of a local reservoir. Regrettably, the books and possessions that had been his strong companions throughout his life met a somber fate, consumed by the flames as a testament to his final wishes. As I matured, those cherished artifacts that had been integral to his existence remained elusive, forever hidden from my gaze.

As I journeyed loathly to Busan for middle school, a vigilant relative stepped in to tend to his grave, an annual ritual of mowing the lush grass, a testament to our enduring familial bonds.

Within the tapestry of my lineage, my grandparents were blessed with six children: three sons and three daughters. My father, Shin Yusuk, held the mantle of their eldest son, born in the year 1901.

However, his aspirations were destined for a different path; one that diverged starkly from the agricultural roots that had shaped his family for generations. My father's disposition was a departure from his father's stern demeanor, for he found solace not in the toil of farming but in the company of cards and the allure of gambling.

Unbeknownst to him, his inclinations cast shadows that would fall heavily upon my mother's shoulders, as the burden of the family's wellbeing rested squarely on her.

In the realm of my arrival, as my father's youngest offspring, jubilation reverberated through our abode. Yet, this elation proved fleeting, dissolving like mist in the morning sun. My father's tendency for gambling, it seemed, was an unbreakable cycle; one that my mother attributed to the dearth of alternative diversions available to men in that era, aside from the seasons of rigorous farming labor.

What began as a modest gathering of companions for games of Hwatoo, a card-based gamble, soon spiraled into a consuming habit, days blending into nights as they indulged in this newfound pursuit.

And so, in the annals of our family history, these threads of memory weave a mosaic that captures both the resilience and frailty of my lineage. As I pen these reflections, I find myself transported across the canvas of time, retracing the contours of a bygone era, reliving moments that have shaped my identity and understanding of the world around me.

When I was nearly three years old, I recall my father returning home with a visibly angry expression after a bout of gambling. A few days later, he passed away at the age of 52 due to natural causes, leaving me with only faint memories of the incident. His untimely demise was a sorrowful moment in my life.

Regrettably, I can only piece together fragments of my father's passing. His gambling habits had squandered the fortunes he had inherited from our ancestors, a tragic outcome that cast a shadow over our family. The weight of financial responsibility fell solely on my single mother's shoulders, as she worked tirelessly to provide for us, assisted by two dedicated in-house servants.

As a result, my childhood was marked by an absence: a void left by my father's lack of presence and influence. Raised by a determined single mother who, by necessity, took on both parental roles, I yearned for the guidance, discipline, and masculine influence that my father should have provided. His absence became a source of my own vulnerability and shortcomings.

In the absence of a father figure, I found myself assuming a peculiar role - that of caretaker for my own father. I felt compelled to establish rules and boundaries, taking on a responsibility that should have been his. This role also extended to fostering a sense of security; I instinctively grasped that my parents needed all the support they could receive to navigate the complexities of parenthood. However, the support I sought couldn't be gleaned from my father.

Even in his physical absence, my father's genetic legacy has exerted a formidable influence, including contributing to my genetic short stature. These intangible threads carry traces of his character, subtly but undeniably shaping me with distinct attributes that could develop a unique blend of traits, bearing a semblance of his presence even in his physical absence.

My first uncle, Shin Musuk, entered the world in 1913, but his time here was short-lived as he departed in 1945 at the tender age of 32. He was wed to a daughter of the Kim family and left behind a daughter of his own.

Amongst six siblings from my grandparents, my second uncle, Shin Unsuk, born in 1916, embarked on a unique journey. He married young, finding a partner in Aunt Jeong. Seeking to glean advanced techniques and cultural insights from Japan, he ventured there, only to be met with the tumultuous backdrop of Japan's conflicts with China and Korea from 1931 to 1945, a period predating my own birth. Despite these challenges, he endeavored to manage a medium-sized watch factory employing around 200 workers. The watch factory had experienced some success, evident in the scattered broken watches I encountered strewn around my childhood home.

Life mimicked a roller coaster for my uncle and aunt, with soaring highs followed by plummeting lows. Tragedy struck in 1946 when a group of envious fellow employees, consumed by jealousy over their achievements, pushed both my uncle and aunt off a bridge to their deaths. They were a mere 31 years old at the time and commuted to work together by bicycle. Their bodies were never recovered from the water, leading to the somber realization that my uncle and aunt were laid to rest without their physical remains in their hometown, Dongta, in Korea.

In my childhood, my mother frequently recounted how my second uncle shared a personality and a fervor for learning akin to that of my grandfather. With this in mind, she may have harbored hopes that he would play a paternal role in our lives, perhaps as a solution to her dissatisfaction with my father.

In the time preceding my mother's passing, she consistently urged me to pay tribute to my uncle and aunt biannually during the main holidays: Harvest Day and New Year. I heeded her requests dutifully, for they had no children of their own who could carry out this tribute.

During my childhood, three aunts stand out vividly in my memory. The first aunt, married to Mr. Bae, resided in the neighboring village of Gadong. The second aunt found her partner in Mr. Seo and settled in Changwon village. Meanwhile, the third aunt exchanged vows with Mr. Hwang and established her home in Sukjeon village.

It's worth noting that my second and third aunts played a special role in my life, as they graced my wedding ceremony on the 30th of March, 1980. You can find further details about this momentous event in the latter of this book.

My mother, **Ju Bunsang**, was born in 1911 and raised in a well-respected family, blessed with prosperity, from Hamahn Village. This village had once been a prominent hub of the Aragaya, one of the six Gaya Federations, which thrived for 519 years from 42 AD to 561 AD. This era left behind numerous ancient tombs that dot the landscape to this day, a testament to its bygone affluence and vitality.

Within the Ju Family, a notable figure emerges in the form of Ju Sebung. He held a distinguished position as a civil officer during the

Joseon Dynasty, boasting high scholarly achievements. In 1542, he founded the pioneer civilian academy known as Baekundongseowon, situated near the entrance of Suksusa Temple in Yeongju City, Korea. This institution later underwent a name change in 1550 to become SosuSeowon. Remarkably, its original structures have been preserved through the years, earning it the status of National Treasure of Korea number 55.

During that era, the rigid contours of societal norms cast a shadow that enveloped women; confining them within narrow boundaries. The very act of reading and writing was a privilege extended solely to men; a door firmly shut for women like my mother. Furthermore, the conventions of propriety constrained interactions between women and unfamiliar men, creating an environment permeated with solitude.

Her wedding day, a significant juncture in her life, also epitomized the stark realities of the era's social confines. It was on this day that her eyes first locked with my father's, a bitter illustration of the scripted encounters dictated by tradition.

As the threads of matrimony wove her destiny, she embarked on a journey that led her away from her cherished hometown, severing her connection to the land of her birth. With resolute steps, she embraced the role defined by convention, embracing her new identity as a member of her husband's family, tethered to their abode by the unyielding strands of custom. The world she had known gradually dissolved into memory; its essence etched in the fragments of recollection that would later paint the tapestry of her life.

They brought forth four sons and two daughters, their lineage stretching back as the 33rd generation descendants. Sadly, their second son's life was cut short shortly after birth.

The confines of a closed society deprived my mother of an opportunity to record her life through written words. So, she often expressed her lament over this, underscoring that if she possessed the ability to read and write, she would have penned countless volumes chronicling her own life's journey. In reverence to her unrealized aspirations, I am dedicated to crafting her narrative on her behalf, a promise I intend to fulfill before my own life's voyage concludes.

Despite the challenges of being a single mother after our father's passing, my mother displayed remarkable strength as she raised two daughters and three sons on her own. She held a steadfast belief that her children should forge their paths; a principle she instilled without resorting to nagging or physical punishment. Instead, she empowered us to confront our challenges independently.

During the years she dedicated to nurturing our growth, my mother prioritized the concept of 'face' (a value deeply rooted in Confucian traditions) she had imbibed from her upbringing. The keeping of our face (known as Chemyeon in Korean) holds massive significance in our culture; serving as a means to safeguard reputation and uphold respect. Her constant admonition to hold our heads up rather than bowing down became a steadfast command; she urged us to maintain our self-esteem and dignity.

With an unfaltering commitment, she fostered an environment where our siblings' potential could flourish without constraint. She stood as a stalwart figure, ready to rescue us from adversity and provide for our needs. Through her guidance, we learned to approach daily challenges with a decided resolve.

Being the youngest of three sons and two daughters, I was the recipient of special treatment from my mother in every aspect of my life. When she ventured to distant markets, she brought me along to expose me to the realities of the outside world. This experience served to broaden my perspective and connect me with the wider world sooner than my peers.

In the eyes of my mother, the family was the cornerstone of everything. She was steadfast in her conviction, consistently displaying the family motto, "The family is the source of everything," prominently posted on the home's main door since my childhood. This constant reminder underscored the pivotal role that family played in our lives and further shaped our understanding of its significance.

The chronological order of my siblings' births traces the path of our family history. The eldest, Shin Hankuk, was born on 4 January 1933; followed by my elder sister Shin Hansun in 1936. The next in line, my second brother Shin Hansi, came into the world in 1938 but regrettably left us shortly after birth. The cycle continued with my third brother Shin Hanpil in 1940; then my second sister Shin Haengja in 1943. Our youngest sibling, Shin Hanok, joined us on 10 July 1949. Today, among us, two sisters and I remain standing on this earth, a testament to the passage of time and the bonds that hold us together.

My eldest brother, Shin Hankuk, was fortunate to have public access up to high school. But my two sisters and the second brother were denied this privilege. Yet, they managed to acquire the skills of reading and writing through their own efforts.

A courageous and resourceful elder brother embarked on a solo journey to Busan, Korea's second-largest city, with dual purposes: to pursue his further education and contribute financially to the family. Despite the geographical separation, he made frequent returns to our hometown to provide care for his mother and his siblings who remained there.

My eldest brother embarked on his own journey with marriage to Bae Yoonja in 1960. Together, they welcomed a son and two daughters into their family. Their first daughter, Shin Bunkeum, arrived the year after their wedding; followed by another daughter, Shin Misun, a year later; their youngest son, Shin Youngsu, was born in 1967 after much effort. He has since become a distinguished figure, currently holding the position of a professor at KAIST in Korea.

My second brother, Shin Hanpil, was a multi-talented person who excelled in singing, sports, martial arts, and social interactions. He stood as my role model during my childhood. He aided me in preparing for oratory contests at school, contributing to my victory. Singing was a particular forte of his; he consistently secured the first prize in song festivals held in nearby villages. His musical talents were such that he eventually became a judge for the festival.

Our home perpetually buzzed with activities, often populated by his friends and neighbors airing grievances. He had an infectious energy that drew people in, and he thrived amidst the crowds. I tried to emulate him as I matured, but I recognized the distinct nature of his talents. He married a woman named Mrs. Han, and together they had three sons: the first son, Shin Jinsan was born in 1972; the second one, Shin Youngjin in 1973; the last one, Shin Youngmin in 1975.

Two remarkable women graced our family as my sisters, each with her distinct qualities that enriched our lives. The dynamics within our family were uniquely influenced by their personalities and bestowals. My older sisters were undoubtedly devoted to our mom. As she navigated the challenges of being a single mother, they supported her endeavors and adapted to the shifting dynamics. Among them, my eldest sister, Shin Hansoon, exhibited a striking resemblance to our mother.

Her presence was so reminiscent of our mother's that it wouldn't be an exaggeration to consider her a surrogate in some ways. Despite enduring significant losses, including her husband Kang Bongsul, and her son Kang Jongku, she kept her strength and perseverance. Living with her daughters Okja and Mija, she proved herself a steadfast matriarch.

In contrast, my second sister, Shin Haengja, possesses a uniquely relaxed disposition. With a demeanor that exudes a sense of calm, she seems capable of planting an apple tree single-handedly if the earth were to disappear.

Unlike our older sister, she's blessed with five daughters who take turns caring for their mother and father, Hwang Hwanggu, who is enjoying his retirement and the loving care of his five daughters. During my visits to Korea, I make it a point to see my two sisters, as the precious moments spent with them are invaluable.

Within my own family, my wife and I are blessed with two sons who collaborate under the banner of 'Team Shin' in a real estate firm. Our eldest son, Shin Stephen, and our second son, Shin Leo, mark the 34th generation of the Spicy Shin Family. We also take great pride in our three grandchildren, who carry forward as the 35th generation. The first son's line brings us two granddaughters, Yoorin and Yoojin, while the second son's line introduces us to Millie.

The below photograph capturing my wedding on 30 March 1980, holds a myriad of meanings for me. It stands as a portal to the past, evoking reflections from every angle. My Queen Morana, a pillar of strength in her own right, appears in the photograph. While I find it challenging to encapsulate her essence within this memoir, I will make sure to touch upon her presence periodically, acknowledging her significance in my life.

At times, she expresses her concerns that crafting a memoir might become a source of vanity for my ancestors and families. Naturally, there are instances where such manuscript might unavoidably be included. Nonetheless, the aim behind documenting my history, as previously mentioned, is to ensure that I pass on our family's roots to my descendants before my time ends. Moreover, it would be an endeavor to highlight the immeasurable dignity of life, acknowledging that my descendants are born with a probability of 1 in 400 trillion following me.

@Second Row, sitting from left to right: third aunt, second aunt, and my mother: Ju Bunsang, my mother-in-law, my father-in-law, mother-in-law's sister.

@Third Row, standing from left to right: my second sister-in-law, my first-in-law, my second sister: Shin Hangja, my niece, short groom: myself, my Queen: Jo Moran, four relatives.

@Fourth Row, standing from left to right: my two nieces, my old sister: Shin Hansun, another relative, a boy, standing behind the queen: sister-in-law, three relatives.

@Fifth Row, standing from left to right: my second brother with glass Shin Hanpil, three standing relatives.

@Back Row, standing from left to right: four relatives, behind me with a flower on chest my oldest brother: Shin Hankuk, two of my brothers-in-law, and six relatives.

45

Our immediate family photo was taken on 24 May 2014, on Shin Leo and Seo Jiyeong's Wedding Day: from left of the first row, the first standing: Shin Yoorin, the first granddaughter, myself, My Wife: Jo Morana, and second granddaughter: Shin Yoojin. From left, on the first standing of the back row, our first son: Shin Stephen, our second daughter-in-law: Seo Jiyeong, our second son: Shin Leo, and our first daughter-in-law: Kim Heunhee. The third granddaughter from Leo and Jiyeong: **Shin Millie is under here**

III

Growing Up

III
Growing Up

My hometown
was
a small mountain valley
where all sorts of flowers bloom
peach, apricot, azalea
and colorful flowers
I have missed
the moment I was playing with my friends

My hometown
was
covered with all sorts of flowers
where weeping willows were dancing
by the wind
when it blew from south of Blue Field
I have missed
the moment I was playing with my family in it
I have missed
You!

Korean Poem, 'Hometown'

As I grew up amid my family's inheritance, I found myself steering the intricate tapestry of traditions, values, and challenges that had been woven by generations before me. The legacy of my ancestors, both inspiring and at times confounding, served as a backdrop to my own journey of growth and discovery.

The influence of my grandfather's intellectual pursuits and strong convictions cast a long shadow over my upbringing. Even though I never had the chance to lay my hands on his books or witness his study sessions, the stories that lingered in the air were a reminder of his passion for knowledge and wisdom.

His steadfast commitment to both Taoism and Confucianism has left an imperishable impression on me, molding my comprehension of the intricate facets of the world and emphasizing the significance of firmly adhering to my own principles.

Yet, the rigidity of his beliefs also posed challenges. The bias against women's education cast a shadow over my sisters' lives, denying them opportunities to expand their horizons. This duality of wisdom and prejudice was a constant reminder that even those we revere may harbor limitations that we, as the next generation, must strive to overcome.

Amidst the intricate tapestry of these familial dynamics, it was in my grandmother's unwavering resilience that I discovered solace. Even though confined to her bed, her spirit remained unextinguished, radiating a deep affection and pride for our family's rich heritage. Through the stories and wisdom, she imparted, lovingly relayed to me by my mother's careful guidance, I came to understand the significance of upholding our legacy while together embracing the advancements of the present.

However, the echoes of my father's gambling habits reverberated through our household. His choices placed additional burdens on my mother, who valiantly bore the responsibility of managing the rest of the family's well-being. The contrasts between my father's escapism and my grandfather's intellectual pursuits made me acutely aware of the choices we make and their impact on those around us.

As I came of age, I sought to strike a balance between honoring tradition and forging my own path. The stories of my ancestors served as both cautionary tales and sauces of inspiration. The lessons of The Frog in the Well taught me the importance of expanding my horizons and seeking to understand beyond my limited perspective.

Embracing education, I aimed to break the cycle of prejudice that had kept my sisters from learning. With the support of my mother and the values instilled in me, I pursued knowledge and growth, striving to become a bridge between the past and the future.

Looking back, I recognize the layers of complexity that define my family's history. From the stern wisdom of my grandfather to the resilience of my grandmother, and even the flaws of my father, I see the mosaic that has shaped my identity. With each passing day, I continue to draw upon the lessons of those who came in front of me, learning from their triumphs and mistakes as I navigate the path ahead.

As I reflect on the memories of my hometown over 75 years ago, a vivid scenery of sights, sounds, and emotions comes rushing back. My mind's eye paints a picture of a bustling home, vibrant and alive with the presence of people who have long since become cherished recalls.

The memory of my hometown, blanketed in an array of colorful flowers and adorned with graceful weeping willows, evokes a sense of nostalgia that takes me back to carefree days of playing with friends amidst the dance of nature's elements.

The date etched in history, on 5th March 1930, marks the union of two souls: bride Ju Bunsang, aged 19, and groom Shin Yusuk, aged 29. Traditionally, their marriage was orchestrated through a good process guided by cultural norms. In an era where mingling between men and women was restricted from an early age, and women's education was a distant dream, arranged marriages were the norm.

The role of a wedding planner was pivotal in bringing together two individuals who had never crossed paths before their wedding day: tasked with facilitating a union that would shape the destiny of their offspring. Marriage, in those days, was a meticulously planned affair before the official wedding, involving proposal letters exchanged between families and meetings of parents and relatives to negotiate the terms.

The groom would travel to the bride's home, carrying essential items for the ceremony on horseback. On the auspicious day, both families would gather to officiate the event and introduce the betrothed couple, after which the groom would escort the bride to her new home.

The societal divisions of the time were still evident, with the Yangban, an aristocratic class, distinguished by their vibrant and elaborate attire made from high-grade silk fabrics, standing in contrast to the Pyeongmin, the working class, donning more subdued colors. The formal wedding attire, including the Chima (wrap-around skirt) and Jeogori (jacket), reflected the significance of the occasion, adorned with intricate designs and fine embroidery.

Cultural symbolism was deeply embedded in every aspect of the wedding. Hand lanterns illuminated the path from the groom's house to the bride's, wooden duck carvings and cranes symbolized peace, fidelity, and prosperity, while wedding geese foretold a long and happy marriage. The couple's formal ceremony, attended by neighbors and friends: culminated in a joyful wedding march, marking their first steps together as husband and wife.

The festive atmosphere extended beyond the ceremony, as neighbors gathered for days to celebrate the newlyweds. The wedding feast featured a sumptuous spread of ritual Korean dishes from Ddeokguk (rice cake soup) to Bulgogi, marinated grilled meat.

Amidst the revelry, the couple's wedding night came on, a mixture of anticipation and shyness hanging in the air. As they retreated to their chamber, the youthful curiosity of their peers led to lighthearted prying, leaving the couple with a blend of embarrassment and shared laughter.

These memories of days gone by, the love stories woven through generations, and the traditions that produced lives, remind me of the enduring power of culture, family, and human connection. As I look back on the vibrant landmark of my family's history, I find myself not only a party in their story but also a guardian of their legacy.

During my parents' marriage, the Korean Peninsula was under Japanese rule from 1910 to 2 September 1945, when Japan surrendered in World War II. At this time, many people were mobilized by Japan for various wartime efforts, including the war against China and World War II. Factories supplying war materials also relied heavily on labor, causing widespread suffering and scarcity in households that engaged in these activities.

My hometown, Dongta village, has dramatically changed in 70 years since I left; factories were placed and roads and many houses were removed.

I was born in 1949, blessed as the youngest son into the 33rd generation of the spicy Shin family in a small rural village called Dongta. The village comprised around sixty households, primarily belonging to the Shin family, but also a few households from other clans like the Lee family, the Ku family, and the Chun family.

Dongta was located in Hamangun, Gyeongsangnamdo, South Korea, and was about 15 kilometers away from the main center of Chilwonmyeon. The village was surrounded by a vibrant natural landscape, with colorful birds singing in the trees, various flowers blooming, and weeping willows swaying in the breeze. The seasons brought their own charm, with matured yellow persimmons being a highlight during their season.

Jangchunsa, a temple in the vicinity, added a spiritual aspect to the area. Approximately sixty households of the Shin family had formed a peaceful community, as captured in the photo you shared above. When I entered the world, my dad was deeply engrossed in gambling for a period. Gambling, you see, is a game where only a few come out victorious, while the majority end up losing. My father found himself among the latter, eventually passing away when I was merely three years old.

My mother shared with me the worst incident during that time: my father once attempted to compel her to sell her hair for money to be used in the games, driven by the rumor that such an act would lead to guaranteed victory. No one intervened, and eventually, he depleted the entire family fortune and met his end. It seems he lived life on his own terms.

After my father's untimely passing, my eldest brother bore a significant societal burden. This shaped my early years, where I spent most of my time with my mother, and the remaining siblings: a second brother, and two sisters. Back then, countryside markets convened twice a week, approximately every three or five days. These markets were located about 20 to 25 kilometers away from home.

On market days, my mother would balance, on foot, a wooden bundle on her head as she made her way to the market to sell them for our family's necessities. If she couldn't sell everything, she wouldn't return until late at night. I would sometimes leave the house to meet her midway.

On fortunate days, I'd find her before passing through the chilling area near our village, rumored to be haunted by the spirits of deceased ghosts. Unfortunately, on less lucky days, I'd steel myself to pass through with the sole thought of reuniting with my mother on her journey back.

Upon her return, I sometimes fell ill, and my mother's caring hands came to the rescue. She'd have me lie down on the floor and would bring a brass bowl filled with rice and water, along with a kitchen knife.

She'd place the knife in my mouth along with the water and rice, reciting a spell: "My hands are Midas Hands, cold is going away from him." Strangely, the pain would vanish without a trace, as if the discomfort was banished by her touch.

In the evenings, after dinner had been cleared away, my mother would sit at the loom, becoming a storyteller from the heavens. Her hands moved with such rapidity as she worked the loom's drums that they became a blur. From her lips flowed "stories of fairies and woodcutters", tickling my ears until I fell into a deep slumber:

Once upon a time, a fairy descended from the heavens and decided to take a bath in a well. As the fairy bathed, a woodcutter happened to catch sight of her and noticed her clothes left unattended. Swiftly, he seized the opportunity and snatched away her clothes, concealing them from her view. When the fairy emerged from her bath, she was unable to locate her clothes, and in her vulnerable state, she was left with no option but to stay with the woodcutter.

In time, their companionship grew into love, and they were joined in matrimony. Soon enough, they were blessed with the arrival of a son and a daughter, and their family thrived in the embrace of happiness. Days were spent relishing the joys of a contented family life.

However, a fateful day arrived when the woodcutter, in a casual exchange of stories from the past, inadvertently revealed the secret of the hidden clothes. Startled by his confession, the fairy realized that her clothes were still hidden away. Swiftly, she located her garments and discreetly placed her son and daughter beneath them. Then, with a heavy heart, she made her way back to the heavens.

The reason for her departure lay in the failure to heed her parents' advice. He had been instructed not to disclose the location of her clothes until they had welcomed three children into their lives. Alas,

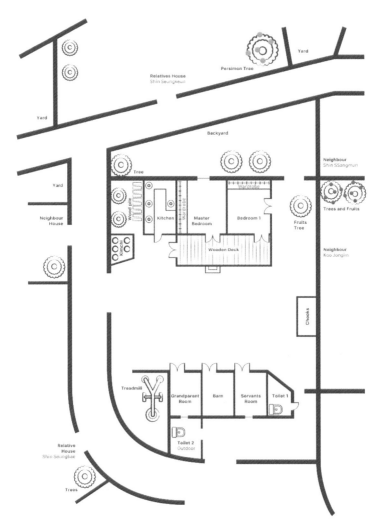

My home layout was stored in memory for over 70 years; On my last visit, it's removed.
The above Illustration is created by Kemelyen Studio, in New Zealand

the woodcutter's careless words had shattered that promise, and the fairy's return to the heavens marked the end of their time together on Earth.

My mother had a weekly routine of stitching clothes. One such day, I accompanied her to mend my grandma's worn-out pants. As I curiously lowered my head to catch a glimpse of the pants, my grandma's hands quickly reached out and gently touched my cheeks, saying, "My dear boy, why do you want to see your grandma's old pants?" Her reprimand left me feeling embarrassed, and I hastily left her room.

These memories belong to a time before I entered primary school. When I explored our home, I stumbled upon intriguing objects: broken watches and wooden clogs. Opening the drawers in the room, I discovered numerous broken watches scattered around. I used them to practice assembling and disassembling, a knowledge I later learned had originated from my uncle's watch factory in Japan.

There were also many wooden clogs scattered about the house. These clogs served various purposes, from water containers to sharpening sickles, or simply as playthings wearing it for me to dance around in for fun. These items, although seemingly mundane, held the connection to our ancestors, specifically my great²-grandparents and great-grandparents. My mother told me that these relics had been passed down through the upper generations, though they were not regarded as particularly valuable.

In the 1960s, as a child growing up, my interactions with others on the street often began with the question, "Sir, have you eaten something?" This sympathetic inquiry identified the reality that many people in the village might have missed meals due to poverty. If the answer was affirmative, we would engage in daily life conversations. These talks typically concluded with well-wishes for good health, acknowledging the shared struggles of poverty and hunger that united us all.

Let me paint a picture of the layout of my house from over 75 years ago (see above drawing). As I entered the house, the crock platform stored kimchi in porcelain pots on the left. Passing this point, we encountered a spacious kitchen with three cauldrons.

Next to the kitchen, there were two spacious rooms, and just before them, a generously proportioned wooden floor stood ready. Towards the rear of the primary dwelling, an expansive yard stretched out, which had once borne an array of fruits. Eventually, my mother decided to present this yard to our village, transforming it into a vibrant playground.

During those years, the heating system relied on burning wood. The traditional 'Ondol' system, commonly found in Korean architecture, involved underfloor heating using the heat from wood smoke to warm the underside of a thick masonry floor. The main components included an Agungi (firebox or stove) accessible from an adjoining room, a raised masonry floor with smoke passages, and a freestanding chimney providing a smoke out.

At night, we would all sleep on the warm underfloor, layered with quilted cotton mats and blankets; our home was usually illuminated by oil lamps or lanterns. These oil lamps emitted a unique ambiance and were commonly used before the advent of electric lighting.

In the lower part of the house, you could find a treadmill to pound grain, often being used by neighbors free of charge. Besides my grandma's room, there was a variety of storage space, a main toilet, and a room for in-house servants.

In front of the lower area also featured a medium-sized fruit yard and an outdoor toilet. Outside toilet visits during the night were challenging for me due to my fear of encountering ghosts, whispered about by neighbors.

At night, the second bedroom on the upper part of the main house, where I slept with my second brother, turned into a hideout for my brother and his friends. They would gather in the middle of the night, making noise and enjoying chicken stews made from pilfered chickens. In those days, pilfering chickens from neighboring villages wasn't uncommon. The so-called "chicken thief experts" knew how to quietly approach the chicken coops at night. These experts were adept at capturing chickens without causing too much commotion.

Now, as the sun rises on the day of December 2020, I find myself reflecting on a recent dream I had last night. In this dream, someone important, who will be discovered later, visited my hometown with her son:

On that day, I found myself needing to use the outdoor toilet in front of my grandma's room. As I stepped outside, I heard noises coming from the small backyard. In my dream, this yard had transformed into a sauna room.

Curious, I peered into the room and saw a lady and her son bathing in the sauna. I immediately questioned their presence and asked why they were there without permission. She explained that she had found the room open and decided to use it for a bath with her son. She apologized for not asking me first and seemed genuinely remorseful.

I scolded her for not seeking permission before entering, and she quickly attempted to smooth things over. She asked if they could stay a bit longer to finish their bath and informed me to purchase the front house for herself and her son.

Despite my insistence that they leave, she began to prepare to move into the front house. As she made her way out, my son Leo appeared at the entrance. He looked tired, leaning against the floor as if he had been resting. Before waking up, I urged him to take a bath in the room, ending the dream on a curious note.

As I woke up, I found myself once again immersed in memories of my hometown. The dream felt so real, much like my actual experiences. It wasn't the first time I had dreamed about this kind of thing during the early hours of dawn. As I recalled the past before getting out of bed, a realization struck me: the woman who visited my house in the dream must have been the same woman I met on the day I entered Busan National University, which was on 25 March 1972.

Throughout my childhood, our home was a perpetual hub of activity. Brother's friends, neighbors, unfamiliar lads, relatives, and military personnel from the nearby US military base in Jinhae City frequently congregated at our house, especially after their hunting escapades in the mountains behind our village.

They would bring back roe deer, pheasants, wild rabbits, and even boars from their hunting trips, along with their own provisions and supplies from the military base. My family would have lively crowding and parties at our home, and once they departed, our neighbors would continue the festivities with the leftover food. My mother didn't mind the constant influx of visitors; she believed that being surrounded by people brought joy and happiness, and my brother and sister shared this sentiment.

My oldest brother, independent and ambitious, left for Busan at a young age to chase his dreams. My second brother was naturally sociable and had a knack for making friends, bringing them home without hesitation. My two sisters and I had no objections to this lifestyle, simply following the lead of my brother and mother.

A traditional Korean cuisine primarily consisted of rice and various soups or stews, often accompanied by side dishes known as 'Ban-chan.' These could include spicy cucumbers, lightly boiled spinach, or black beans seasoned with garlic, green onions, chili peppers, and ginger.

However, the staple of Korean cuisine was kimchi with a rice bowl, which came in various forms, consisting of fermented vegetables such as cabbage, cucumbers, and Korean radishes brined with a mixture of seasonings. Other side dishes included Namul, with steamed or marinated vegetables seasoned with vinegar, garlic, chili peppers, soy sauce, and sesame oil. There were also "Jeon," similar to pancakes, made from savory ingredients like potatoes or scallions.

Over the years, Western influences began to shape the younger generation's food preferences. Fast food and convenience foods started to gain popularity, particularly among the youth who were drawn to the familiar tastes of Western cuisine. Grocery stores and restaurants began to offer items like cereal, breakfast pastries, and standard egg dishes that were reminiscent of what one might find in American street food. This shift represented a change in eating habits and reflected the growing influence of Western culture on Korean society.

In my childhood, rice held a higher price tag than barley, leading many to consume barley as their primary food. Barley was a preferred staple because it was independent of specific climate and water conditions compared to rice.

While rice cultivation required long, hot summers and clayish soil to retain moisture, barley could thrive under a broader range of conditions. Additionally, barley yielded more per unit of farmland, making it a practical choice. As a result, barley was the daily choice for most people, and the idea of eating rice every day was a distant hope, with only two opportunities each year: New Year's Day (Seollal) and Harvest Day (Chuseok).

As these dates approached, the entire country seemed to be in motion, with millions of cars traversing the nation as descendants embarked on journeys to visit their own country to pay tribute to their forebears. Two special tribute days were the most significant event in our tradition. Unlike Western celebrating New Year's Day, on the 1st of January, my generation adhered solely to the lunar calendar.

On Seollal morning, as the offspring, we would perform the usual New Year's bow (Sebae) to our elders within the family. In return, the elders would offer us money as a tribute. It was believed that sleeping on the last day of the year would cause one's eyebrows to turn white, so many would stay awake throughout the night.

The main event of Seollal and Chuseok involved paying tribute to ancestors and sharing a meal together. Families would prepare tables laden with rice, fruits, meats, and stewed dishes. After paying respects to our ancestors, the family would partake in a bowl of rice cake soup, Ddeokguk, while sitting around the table. It was a custom that by consuming this soup, one would age by a year. I distinctly remember dreading this soup as a child, as I wanted to avoid growing older.

New Year (Seollal) usually occurs in late January or early Feb on the second new moon after the winter solstice. It marks the first day of the Korean calendar and is celebrated over three days: the day before Seollal, Seollal itself, and the day after.

Another important day is Chuseok, celebrated on the 15th of August on the lunar calendar. Families and close relatives would gather to clean the grasses around their ancestors' graves or cemeteries, which had overgrown over time. And they paid their tribute usually at the old son's home. Chuseok differed from Seollal in that children didn't bow to the elders in the morning. Instead, in the evening it was marked by various activities such as kite flying, Korean wrestling contests (Ssireum), fireworks, and traditional folks' dances.

One such dance was the Ganggang Suweolrae Dance, and there was also a musical performance called Pungmullori, featuring drums, gongs, and chamberlain. One well-liked activity was Korean traditional wrestling (Ssireum). The earliest evidence of Ssireum dates back to the Goguryeo Dynasty period; it gained popularity among the populace during the Goryeo and Joseon periods. Besides, another favored pastime was a Korean traditional board game called Yut-nori, which fostered family togetherness, providing an avenue for enjoyment and strengthening bonds among all members.

As the year came to a close, villages would organize song contests, and my second brother was often invited to judge these competitions due to his singing prowess. Although he frequently emerged victorious in the competitions, his position as a judge served as a shrewd means to engage him while affording others opportunities to showcase their talents. On this occasion, I would partake in these contests, securing second or third place despite possessing skills comparable to the leading singer's position. My brother's sense of dignity prevented him from awarding me the first place, yet I took immense pride in his role as a judge.

A vivid memory comes to life, painted in the hues of my second aunt's annual tribute day. On that occasion, my mother guided me on a journey to my aunt's distant dwelling, nestled in the folds of Changwon province, a place woven with both distance and sentiment.

While my mother and aunt were busy preparing tribute foods, hunger led me to the barn to search for food. My mother scolded me for taking food without permission, although my aunt offered me more. My mother took the food away from me to prevent me from becoming spoiled.

When I was around three or four years old, I was joyfully horsing around with my mother on a neighbor's floor when I accidentally fell to the ground. I suffered a deep cut on my forehead, which bled profusely. Given the considerable distance to the local hospital in Chilwon, around 20 km away by foot due to the absence of taxis or bus service, I was given first aid to stop the bleeding with cigarette ash. The scar on my face from that incident remained etched forever, although it went unnoticed by others for over 75 years.

A love affair between a man and a woman within the Shin family, which I can't forget, occurred in our neighborhood. It's a challenging and sensitive topic to openly discuss. Nevertheless, the circumstances of the time revealed the intricacies of a closed society and its cultural norms. In our village, the interconnectedness of the Spicy Shin family's residents was notable, with only a few exceptions from other families.

This close bond extended to the surname system in Korea, backed by the Tang Dynasty in ancient China. This gradually designed for male surnames system accepted by the Silla Dynasty in Korea, while strictly prohibited marriages between individuals of the same surname within the same home. Even when a woman married, she did not adopt her husband's surname. Violation of this revered tradition was viewed as serious consequences, equating such individuals to social outcasts.

In such an incident within our village, this social norm was challenged. This unfortunate case of rape occurred between a man and a woman from the same Shin family. The close-knit nature of the community meant that news spread rapidly. An unidentified informant brought the incident to the attention of the entire village by spreading cow fodder around the village well, signaling the occurrence of a significant event. The village director subsequently launched an investigation, leading to the expulsion of the perpetrator from the village. Such actions reflected the importance of retaining social norms in the fabric of village life during that era, even though they may differ drastically from the current level.

Around the time I entered primary school, my mother decided to open our backyard for use as a communal playground by our

62

neighbors. After school, both boys and girls would gather there, often playing soccer or volleyball barefoot. However, a few young lads ventured into an empty house in the village, where their playful actions took a more mischievous turn. These encounters, although noticed by giggles from the observing girls outside, remain as colorful memories etched in my mind.

As a testament to the energy and vibrancy of my youth during those days, my arm bore the small tattoos of 'King' and 'Friendship,' marks of camaraderie, and shared proof with my peers. Alongside these visible symbols, I carried a scar on my face, a reminder of an accident that occurred when I was three or four years old. Despite the potential difficulties and adversities that featured those years, I perceived my family, school, and friends as a strong support network that provided me with a sense of resilience.

Experts researching adverse child experiences have underscored that individuals during their adolescent years may have encountered adverse or traumatic events in their upbringing. During my own puberty period, I was fortunate to have a strong sense of family unity and a nurturing educational environment. My siblings were pillars of support, aiding me in navigating through any difficulties that arose. Looking back, it is this network of love and understanding that fortified my resilience during my formative years.

As I entered primary school, a new chapter of my life began. Despite the delay in starting school due to the birth registration issue, I was excited with my classmates in learning and growing. My experiences have shaped me into a self-reliant and resourceful person, always finding ways to entertain myself and others with the limited resources available.

My mother played a significant role in providing me with a sense of safety and happiness. Living next to the backyard allowed me to explore and enjoy the fruits and nature that surrounded me. I had the freedom to play with my friends, fostering a sense of fellowship and adventure.

One of my daily responsibilities was taking care of a cow, which involved feeding and tending to it in the fields and farming yards. This routine taught me responsibility and a strong work ethic from a young age. I was grateful for the occasional ritual foods shared by our next neighbor, the Koo Jongim family, which lightened the load of my daily tasks. It was certainly a reminder of the importance of reciprocity and community bonds.

As I reminisced about my childhood, I recognized my inclination toward self-learning and creativity. With limited resources at that time for entertainment, I often made my own toys and games, not only for myself but also for my friends and relatives. This knack for creativity and leadership qualities led me to become a group leader in various activities, including being the class monitor when I finally entered primary school.

Starting school was a significant milestone for me, as it marked the transition from childhood to the world of education. However, due to the birth registration issue, I began primary school at the age of 10, which was older than most of my classmates.

Entering primary school brought new experiences and challenges into my life. On the first day, I received an unexpected invitation from a female classmate in the school area to visit her house and play. This was my first taste of the world outside my immediate surroundings, and I followed her home, where I met her stepbrother who was also my classmate, Kim Taesik. We spent time together, losing track of time, and I returned home quite late.

Despite this, my mother's concern was only for how my first day of school had gone. Soon after starting school, I was appointed as the class monitor, a position I held throughout my six years in primary school. While I was a couple of years older than my classmates due to the birth registration issue, my height was similar to theirs, I didn't feel inferior. However, this would change when I entered middle school.

I requested our teacher that our village girl, Shin Kija would be appointed as the vice class monitor, and we worked well together. She took a leading role in many matters, especially when it came to interactions with girls.

In the first year, our school organized an exhibition to showcase our learning progress and achievements to our families and community members. This event featured various activities, including a play of Aesop's fable "The Hare and The Tortoise." I was chosen to play the role of the Tortoise, and Ahn Sunnam, a girl from another village, played the Hare. Our close collaboration during rehearsals sparked jealousy among other girls in the class. Its fable conveyed the moral of the story: slow and steady wins the race.

During my primary school years, there came a day when I crossed paths with a charming girl from Yangchon as I usually made my way to and from school. It was love at first sight for me, and I took the initiative to connect with my classmate Shin Kisun, a friend of our home. She arranged to meet us at an empty, dimly lit house where we spent delightful moments sharing stories and exchanging details about her family. However, as I moved to Busan for middle school, we lost touch, and I found myself missing her. The memories of our time together remained dear to me.

During this time, my mother often visited the local temple, Jangchunsa, to pray for our family's well-being and help with temple chores. She had a strong connection to the temple, especially because my elder brother had restored its murals.

However, a new temple governor arrived to replace an existing one, and I had a disturbing encounter with him. One day, I went up to the temple with his rumored son, and he lured me into a room. Then, he engaged in an inappropriate action by touching my private area. Despite this disgraceful experience, I chose to keep it a secret from my mother.

During the summer school break, I paid a visit to my elder sister who had married Kang Bongsul in the Kamcheon village. I cherished wonderful moments with her and her family, relishing their kindness and forging strong bonds. When the time came for me to leave, I couldn't bear the thought of parting with my sister. I hugged her tightly multiple times, tears flowing. Eventually, I bid her farewell and made my way back home, recounting my journey to my mother. The act of parting from a close family member, even for a short period, evokes a mix of emotions: a bittersweet longing and a heartache.

After my trip to see my elder sister, my mother sent me to my older brother's house. On the bus journey, I bought a bundle of apples and enjoyed them as I gazed out the window. This was the first time I had ventured so far from home, and my stay in Busan allowed me to explore the city and adapt to urban life. Upon returning, my mother welcomed me warmly, expressing her delight at my safe return.

Spring brought a school picnic during my third grade, where mountains and fields were adorned with vibrant flowers like forsythia, azaleas, cherry blossoms, and camellias. These picnics became more than just school events; they turned into festive family gatherings that brought together siblings, youngsters, elders, and all the neighbours.

Jangchunsa Temple was often chosen as a destination for school picnics. People brought lunch boxes and sat together eagerly for their lunch. However, a quarrel broke out between two individuals, and a crowd gathered to witness it.

Surprisingly, one of the fighters was my second brother. Although my brother was typically adept at handling such situations, he appeared to lack confidence this time as the opponent showcased his strength by performing flips in front of us.

Observing this, I stepped forward and issued a challenge to the opponent to fight with me. But my brother discouraged me from doing a fight saying, "Let's give it another chance." This incident imparted a lesson to me about the importance of family bonds and unity, stressing the notion that 'blood is thicker than water'.

School sports day was another occasion that united teachers, students, parents, and the community. We were divided into two groups, the Blue and White teams, and we cheered for each side during various activities. Flags of different nations waved in the sky as students shouted in excitement. From short races to javelin throws, the event was full of energy. I often participated in the 400-meter relay, being the last runner for six years. While winners received medals, participation itself was a reward. The event typically marked the end of the school year.

In fourth grade, our school had a soccer match against another school, but there was no left winger available. The teacher noticed my skills during informal matches and assigned me to play that position. This was my first official soccer game, and it marked the beginning of my love for the sport. Soccer ran in our family's blood, and my eldest brother had brought home colorful flags from a local soccer competition. My own younger son Leo later played soccer at the international level: he played in Germany, Japan, Australia, and NZ.

I had a deep passion for reading and would frequently lose myself in the school library. Then, one day, a new woman librarian, arrived who captured my attention. I discovered that I was lingering in the library just to be near her. My peers of the same age also began to join in, helping to organize books and seeking her guidance. We came up with playful ways to engage with her, sharing moments of laughter and joy.

Each experience during my school days, from trips to sports events to new hobbies, contributed to my growth and understanding of the world around me. Continuing from where we left off, my natural progression into a leadership role began at an early stage. I took on the role of class monitor from the very first day of primary school. As the years went by, my leadership abilities became more apparent, and by the time I reached fifth grade, I achieved another milestone by being chosen as the head boy out of several candidates.

During school assemblies, I organized the students to stand in formation before the principal and teachers arrived on the field. I directed commands to the students, ensuring they followed protocols like "Attention," "Salute to the principal," and "At ease." Little did I know that this skill would come in handy later during military training in December 1972 when I was appointed as a room leader during my military service at Nonsan Camp. I efficiently managed and oversaw all the commands during training.

In our family's customs, when a son-in-law visited his wife's family, the mother-in-law traditionally provided him with nutritious chicken soup or dishes to wish for his health and the production of many offspring. However, my brother-in-law preferred squid soup with bean sprouts, which my mother enjoyed cooking for him. I also had the opportunity to enjoy a bowl of it alongside him.

He once playfully teased me and offered me a thousand won while we were eating; I secretly hoped he would visit often. Little did I know that this teasing action would later encounter serious trouble, given today's standards and laws.

Reflecting on my childhood, my mother aimed to instill five essential rules of living in us siblings, encouraging us to practice ourselves every day. Since my mother couldn't do it herself, she had my eldest brother write these rules on mulberry paper and paste them on the toilet wall. The family mission statement: "Family peace is the foundation of all things" adorned the master room door. The rules were as follows: First, always hold your head high; second, water flows from high to low; third, adapt to change; fourth, humans leave their names and tigers leave their skins; fifth, practice the virtue of moderation daily. When neighbors visited us, my mother taught us to greet them first and see them off at the entrance.

Though my mother hadn't received a formal education, she possessed profound knowledge about children's discipline due to her background and ancestral teachings. Research shows that effective teachings for children come not solely from charismatic parents, but also from the children interacting with one another. Face-to-face interactions and equal communication play a significant role.

In response to my mother's hidden rules, I had the opportunity to choose my own punishments for any misdeeds, which enhanced my internal motivation to avoid wrongdoing. By selecting my rewards, I became more intrinsically driven to uphold my mother's moral virtues.

As I continued my primary schooling, a pivotal moment arrived when my eldest brother surprised me by bringing a hat and uniform for middle school. The prospect of higher education had never crossed my mind until then, and I was overwhelmed with happiness and gratitude. I clutched the uniform and hat to my chest that night, feeling an immense sense of joy. This opportunity was a turning point that would lead me down a path I had never imagined.

It was this act of kindness that propelled me to where I stand here today. His support and guidance undoubtedly shaped my journey. but I hadn't properly expressed my gratitude to him during his lifetime, a fact that still weighed on my mind. Instead, I thanked my sister-in-law several times for his generosity.

Upon entering middle school, I joined the night class at Bajeong Middle School in Busan. This was a private school run by Nam Kiyeol, established as part of a poverty relief program. Most of the students were from poor families or were orphans. They worked during the day as scavengers and attended school at night. I met fellow students, Kim Doosu, Son Seongjo, Lee Manhee, Jo Malre, Lee Changgyo, and Lee Woonchan, others on the first day.

I quickly established strong friendships with them. There was one cherished teacher, Koo Taebong, who particularly stood out. From the first sight, he went out of his way to support and care for me, offering assistance whenever I needed it. His guidance extended even beyond middle school, as he helped me find part-time teaching and counseling jobs during my high school and university years.

Despite my efforts to locate him recently, I discovered that the school had closed due to low enrollment. I regret that I might never have a chance to see him again.

During my time at the night class, I wasn't particularly focused on studying. I would rather find more enjoyment in spending time with friends and exploring the mountains, fields, sea, and islands. We watched movies and had fun in various ways.

It wasn't until a year had passed that I entered a poem contest held at the school. Surprisingly, my first-ever poem was awarded as the best, giving me a profound emotional experience. This recognition ignited a passion for poetry, and I began participating in various poetry competitions with the guidance of our high school senior. Although I faced failure in many competitions, I was eventually invited to take part in a citywide poetry contest hosted by the Education Board in Busan.

As I sat in my room trying to remember the poems, I had memorized the previous night, the title "Fishing Boat Filled with Fishes" emerged on the blackboard. Without hesitation, I began crafting a new poem by interweaving lines from the various poems I had memorized. The result was a poem that earned a special award in the contest. I received the award from the esteemed poet Yu Chihwan and the experience left me deeply moved.

During my first and second years of middle school, I spent much of my time socializing with friends, not yet fully understanding the potential within me. Despite this, my natural aptitude for learning helped me achieve outstanding academic records across all subjects, my esteemed teacher Koo Taebong's continuous support and recognition of my abilities led him to promote that I transfer to the day class for the following year, and the opportunity that held the promise of a brighter future.

In the third grade of middle school, I transitioned to the day class and entered a new phase of intense study. The school had established two special target classes, C and D, designed to prepare students for admission to prestigious high Schools: Busan or Kyeongnam High School in Busan.

I was placed in the D class, which aimed to enroll both schools, under the guidance of teacher Cha Sangyul, who oversaw maths. The students in the classes engaged in rigorous study, often bringing two meal boxes to school and studying until 8 pm, with the goal of achieving exceptional results. I was among four classmates who had successfully passed the admission test to Busan High School In 1968, an achievement that filled me with pride.

During this time, I also experienced moments of doubt about my stature. Despite my academic successes, I couldn't help but feel self-conscious about my height when comparing myself to my classmates. I found myself resorting to strategies to appear taller, such as inserting insoles into my shoes, but these attempts did little to alleviate my insecurities.

As my middle school years began, my determination to succeed in my studies persisted, and I diligently prepared for the entrance exam to Busan High School. I remember receiving the good news that I had passed the exam, and my enthusiasm grew as I anticipated the start of this new chapter. I visited the school before my first day and met a fellow student named Kim Dongjin, who introduced himself. Little did I know that this chance encounter would mark the beginning of a lasting friend that continues today, even across distances and years.

The first day of high school was on 4 March 1968. I was at 5th from right, 2nd row. In the Middle-seated, class teacher Kim Dongchan.

On 4 March 1968, I commenced my high school journey in classroom #5, under the teacher Kim Dongchan. Each assigned individual ID numbers based on height, with the lower numbers indicating taller stature. Fortunately, I was able to secure the 55th position out of 60 students. This achievement was partially attributed to my creative solution of wearing army shoes with hidden insoles, which helped me appear taller.

This strategic choice was made to avoid being tagged as the shortest student in the class. I consistently wore these modified army shoes, maintaining the illusion of height until they were eventually replaced by my second brother's new shoes. He had acquired them during his service at the Katusa camp.

During my first summer break, a fellow classmate, Ju Keumdon approached me to learn soccer skills. I gladly shared my knowledge, and to my surprise, he dedicated himself to practice, rapidly improving his skills. The camaraderie of playing soccer and spending time with friends continued to captivate me, often drawing me away from coring solely on my studies.

However, a serious challenge emerged during my first year of high school. My eldest brother was hurt in a car accident, resulting in brain damage and impaired vision. This led me to put my part-time job of teaching a younger student on hold. Instead, I took on taking care of my injured brother in the hospital while juggling my studies.

Luckily, his condition began to improve through several surgeries and treatments, I found myself with more freedom as his caretaker duties lessened. However, I could no longer stay at my brother's house, which led me to seek out the part-time teaching job that I had paused due to his accident.

This time, I needed to find a student to teach within their own home by dwelling. Through the help of my beloved teacher Koo Taebong again, I was introduced to a family that owned a briquette factory. They had two sons and a daughter; I was assigned to teach the older son, who was struggling with his performance in school. Despite his initial academic struggles, I established an ambitious objective for him to excel in his studies. Over time, with my guidance, he made remarkable progress, significantly enhancing his records before my eventual departure.

A few days before I departed from him, as I engaged in a teaching session with him, a peal of laughter wafted through the air from a group of ladies outside the room. Their whispers carried my name: instinctively I saw the reason behind their laughter; the insoles I had inserted in my shoes to gain a bit of extra height. A rush of shame surged within me in response to their discovery.

In the days that followed, I decided to notice my imminent departure from their home, citing the need to prepare for my university entrance exams. However, really beneath the surface of this explanation, a more profound truth remained hidden: a truth rooted in my personal feelings of inferiority of my height. The true driving force behind my departure wasn't solely my ambition to pursue a university exam, but rather a deep-seated unease stemming from my perceived short stature.

Upon leaving that house, I found strength and growth alongside one of my closest friends, Choi Sunghyun. Our deep connection was built upon a shared passion for soccer and a genuine admiration for each other's unique qualities. Choi Sunghyun, who, genetically could have seemed like something of a genius, appreciated my innocent traits and unwavering dedication to soccer.

Through our friendship, I learned that soccer could be played not only with physical abilities but also with strategic thinking. He possessed an extraordinary memory for all football history, player names, skills, and records, making him a walking encyclopedia of the sport. His intellectual dexterity seemed almost AI in nature, and he demonstrated his genius by excelling in school records as well. Our friendship was characterized by playful challenges, such as finding the longest names in the world and racing to see who could reach the school first in the morning.

In addition to soccer and academic pursuits, he and I often ventured to our favorite beach, discussing topics related to beauty, values, and moral virtues. Our talks would transition to gazing at the stars, singing songs, and connecting with a lonely trumpet player who shared his love story with us at Haewoonda Beach.

Our connection seemed to transcend normal edges as if we could feel each other's thoughts and movements even when apart. I would imagine him as a modern-day Faust, his deep thoughts mirrored in his eyes. As time passed, I sometimes regretted not dedicating more effort to studying during high school, as my focus was often divided between soccer, part-time jobs, and socializing.

As graduation approached, the university guidance teacher became busy helping students plan their futures. With no concrete plans, I relied on the school's recommendations for university options. The prestige of our high school was often measured by the number of students admitted to Seoul National University.

Consequently, the focus was on getting students into university rather than guiding them toward specific fields. Despite this, I was encouraged to apply to the Pharmacy Department at Seoul National University in December 1970, along with two others. Unfortunately, my efforts were not successful. Among the three students who took the test, only Do Kangryong managed to pass. In the subsequent year, I retook the exam and was admitted to Busan National University.

In February 1971, as my three years of high school came to a close, my classmate Park Jonggon and I embarked on a journey with virtually no money. Discreetly, we boarded a train from Busan Station to Milyang Station, eventually arriving at Youngsan village, where our friend Shin Bokgi, who would later retire as a Professor from Busan National University, resided.

From there, we relied on hitchhiking to make our way to Ulsan, sustaining ourselves through the kindness of drivers who shared their food with us. The penniless journey led us to Tongdo Temple in Yangsan Province and eventually to Ulsan, spanning approximately five days. This trip taught me valuable lessons about independence, the importance of money, and the endless possibilities that life's journey holds. It was a transformative experience that shaped my perspective on life and its challenges.

IV

Tertiary Study

IV
Tertiary Study

It's evident that I have a deep and reflective perspective on the social context of my upbringing and the values that were prevalent during my time. My observations on the male-centered society, the emphasis on education, and the aspirations of parents for their children's success provide valuable insights into the cultural and societal norms of that era.

My personal journey to tertiary education, from the challenges of entrance exams to enrollment at Busan National University, showcases my determination and resilience. It's also touching to read about the immediate connection I felt upon meeting the girl from MY Girls High School. The emotions and infatuation I had experienced are beautifully conveyed, and my reference to "Arthur Conan Doyle, The Return of Sherlock Holmes"[6] adds a poetic touch.

If I'd like, I could continue to explore my memories and experiences, perhaps diving deeper into how my university years unfolded, how my relationships evolved, and how I navigated the academic and social aspects of university life. My personal stories provide valuable glimpses into a unique time and place, and they can offer readers a greater insight into the dynamics and emotions that shaped those experiences. Arthur started a poetic touch:

From the first day I met you, you were everything to me. Every day of our meeting I loved you more, and many a time since have I kneeled in the darkness of the night and kissed the desk of that class because I met you first and your dear hands had touched it. We had never promised each other. You treated me as fairly as ever a woman treated a man. I have had no complaint to make. It was all love on my side and all

....
6) Love At First Sight Quotes, Goodreads.

friendship on yours. When we parted, you were a free woman, but I could have never again been a free man.

Reflecting on my past and sharing my stories can be a meaningful way to document history, capture personal growth, and offer insights that may resonate with others who have similar experiences. Whether I choose to write for myself or share my stories with a wider audience, my perspective is a valuable contribution to the collective narration.

From the following day, we sat side by side in the classroom only with eye contact and had continued for 9 months, before I parted her for army service at the end of freshman. Also, we usually took the same bus on the way to the city center.

Discussion between us on or off the bus led us to know gradually everything: her two brothers were my high school senior, her younger brother my school junior who was currently attended by her, and her two elder brothers were currently in the USA studying, and she had been visiting her parents every weekend, and so.

If I got classroom first, she came beside me and sat with a nod. On vice versa, did I do the same when she arrived before me at the classroom. As if we had been done long ago, no one in our class would interrupt us: if we parted inevitably, someone let us know where one of us was. Especially, one of my classmates, Yeo Sangbeum himself had declared that he would act as our secret guard.

Being with her, always felt I comfortable, but not beside her, was my heart filled with her. Being in the school, no exception, we both were seeking where the other was and sat next to each other.

On Friday, after class, before back home, she informed me that she was going to see her parents the next day. I requested her to sleep over with her parents, but she replied she wouldn't be able to stay because she had to look after her younger brother at home. I would suggest to her that I could be able to accompany her to her home station.

On Saturday, while I accompanied her to MY Station, lots of talks were exchanged between us on the train, and I waited for her at the station until she returned there. But on our back, we occasionally exchanged our words staring at each other in the train.

A few days later, it was English class. As an English tutor, Professor Lee Suyoung had recently returned from the USA, so, his pronunciation sounded like a native speaker: we were always looking forward to English class; English was my favorite class so I was sincerely looking forward to coming. Sometimes tutor came across a difficult sentence, and would call me deliberately to translate it: I'd love it.

However, at a certain point, she showed me she couldn't be able to understand some parts, signaling her distress; I spontaneously helped her understand those. I led her up in this way until the end of the first year: our fate hadn't left us alone; end of the semester I had to leave her for military service.

One spring day, our class was going on an outdoor picnic, with a bit of red face and full of heart, I took off the part-time-job home heading to the first meeting spot holding a camera in hand, but I couldn't see her even though the departure time was nearby; my swollen heart with endless hopes was gradually cooled off. We took off on an outdoor picnic thinking that she might see her parents on the weekend.

At the end of the first year, my parting time from her was drawing near. Our classmates joyfully supplied me with a drinking party to see me off the army service.

During those days, many young lads detested the idea of undergoing compulsory military service, as spending three years at the army order compound seemed like a significant waste of their precious time. However, my perspective on fulfilling my duty for the country differed. As a result, most young men resorted to various tactics to evade this service: deliberately causing harm to a part of their body; staging photos of themselves consuming toothpaste; enlisting the help of relatives to intervene on their behalf; leveraging their social background; exploiting their extreme height or short stature; playing the single-son card; using tattoos or scars as excuses; citing imbalanced eyesight; and countless other strategies.

Instead, I strongly believed that It's a conviction for a man born in Korea to join the army. Therefore, with no tricks, no hesitation, no promise, and without saying her goodbye, I would help but join in the drilling compound in the Nonsan Camp in December 1972.

The average height of Korean young men is, these days, 174cm, while my height, is only 154 cm which was not necessary to join the army, but I would like happily to go duty service. My real hidden intention was highly to show a Korean manhood who, although born too small, could also be able to serve in the army duty.

After two months of hard drilling, such as shooting, crawling, individual battle, group hooving, and so on, I was deployed to the headquarters of the 6th District in Seoul. Five trainers deployed there got into the truck and ran for several hours to get there.

Deployed in 6th District Headquarters in Seoul, I was 3rd from right, the first row.

On the way to the Headquarters, I started to wonder who the trainees were in this truck with. I was excessively surprised that all what I had gradually known while talking to each other, were children who had been enjoying great power: two trainees were sons of the generals in the army; another two were relatives of prominent persons in our society. But who was I? I was finally assigned to the 33rd Guard Group of the Headquarters, which was in charge of the security for the 6th District Headquarters Day and night.

6th District Headquarters where Major General Park Chunghee and his allies had conspired the May 16 military coup d'état on 16 May 1961. After my assignment here, I had never stood the front gate guard on

79

account of shortness except one day: when the whole 33rd guard group should go team training.

After being deployed, my job was managing military supplies for our unit under the supervision of the chief officer. This role was relatively good demanding than that of frontline duty.

As I settled into this routine, I had a week of vacation and intended to visit the university to see her. However, I learned that she had been prohibited from approaching anyone by an older cousin who was in the classroom. My close mate Sangbeum apologized for not protecting her for me during my absence. But I reassured him that it wasn't his fault; it was simply fate.

Returning to my barracks, I received an invitation from my high school friend, Choi Seunghyun to attend a party at the Engineering Department of Seoul National University. Excitedly, I went there hoping to see him, but I learned that he was facing difficulties in his romantic venture. Sadly, my trip turned out to be in vain, and rumors later circulated that he had made a drastic decision. Thereafter I never saw him nor heard.

Having spent three years in the military, I returned to Busan in September 1975 to find that much had changed, especially among my classmates. Many had already left school to seek jobs, apply for positions, and undergo interviews. Some were exempted from military service, while others served in local community positions for shorter durations. At this time, for the first time, I began to regret that I wasted three years in the army service, moreover, looking at the empty school she left.

On 5 March 1976, I returned to school as a sophomore in the Public Administration Department. Interestingly, on 29 November 2021, I woke up from a dream where I was searching for a classroom to study. A passing student had helped me with installing apps easily to find the classroom, but he then tricked me by swapping my phone for his old one. In my state of panic, another student recommended that I should report the incident to the office, and then I suddenly woke up. While I felt that this dream occurred 17 years ago, but in reality, it has been 47 years since then.

Back in sophomore, my main focus was to prepare for the civil servant exam, a goal I had set for myself since I first entered the university in 1972. Within a few months, another young student and I passed the first-round exam. This achievement drew attention from professors due to the difficulty of accomplishing this in such a short timeframe as a returning student. However, overconfidence hindered me, leading me to believe the second-round exam would be easier than it actually was.

Around this period, my uncle and aunt experienced a roller-coaster-like life during their prime in Japan, marked by soaring highs followed by plummeting lows. Meanwhile, I faced a distinct challenge due to my teeth. Genetic factors contributed to the deterioration of my teeth and gums. Without sufficient funds for proper dental care, I had to resort to extracting my teeth at an unlicensed facility. Consequently, this resulted in a severe gum infection, making it challenging for me to eat or open and close my mouth.

With the support of my close high school friend Ha Sangjo, I was fortunate to receive free medical treatment from a hospital run by the fathers of high school friends. Over approximately six months, my teeth gradually healed from their condition. During this time, my middle school teacher Koo Taebong played a crucial role in helping me secure a teaching job.

My teaching journey commenced as I began tutoring the daughter of the vice president of Dongmyeong Wooden firm, one of the prominent established companies in those periods in Busan. Despite the promising opportunities, my personal aspiration to succeed in the civil servant exam took a backseat due to the circumstances I was facing.

Nevertheless, the student I was tutoring exhibited an impressive academic performance. This achievement even led her brother to propose the idea of a potential business venture after my graduation.

Instead of the tempting prospect, I remained resolute in my focus on preparing for the civil servant exam. As my situation evolved, I transitioned to studying in the school reading room. Among my companions in the law school reading room were individuals who, like me, had faced repeated disappointments from the exam.

In a heartwarming gesture, they would organize a good gathering at a local tavern. This occurred during a period when a curfew was enforced. Following our late-night meal, we departed the restaurant around midnight, only to find ourselves intercepted by the police.

Intriguingly, a police officer had overheard our talks expressing discontent with the government and politicians. Seizing this time, he had been awaiting our exit. The consequence of our dialogue was an unexpected encounter with the law. We were detained, handcuffed, and compelled to spend the night in a prison cell. The subsequent morning brought a summary judgment and our eventual release. This incident served as a stark reminder of the substantial power held by even the most junior police officers during that era. It underscored the intricate power dynamics prevalent in society at the time.

V

Breaking Eggs

V
Breaking Eggs

Amidst life's trials and transitions, I found myself immersed in a period of profound transformation, akin to the process of breaking eggs. The path I had initially embarked upon had taken unforeseen twists and turns, revealing both adversities and unexpected opportunities.

The metaphor of "breaking eggs" perfectly captures the essence of this phase, where I navigated through layers of challenges, unveiling the delicate yet resilient facets of existence. As I look back on these experiences, I discern the intricate patterns that have woven the fabric of my journey, much like the mosaic formed by the fragments of shattered eggshells.

Over time on reflection, I've come to realize that life's meandering course is part of a grander scheme, sculpting us into the individuals we stand as today. Just as breaking eggs is an essential step in crafting something new, so too are hurdles and setbacks integral to our maturation and transformation.

My first fondling of "Damian" by Hermann Hesse occurred during my second year of high school. Nestled within its pages, a particular character in Chapter Five, Damian, captivated my attention. It was this very Damian who first coined the phrase "Time of breaking eggs." In those words, I discovered a profound resonance with my journey, encapsulating the essence of the challenges, growth, and renewal that define our lives:

"The bird fights its way out of the eggs. The egg is the world. Who would be born must destroy a world. The bird flies to God. The God's name is Abraxas."

This passage captures a powerful and metaphorical sentiment, suggesting that growth and transformation require breaking away from familiar confines. The image of a bird struggling to emerge from an egg evokes the idea of rebirth and evolution. The egg, symbolizing the world, represents our comfort zone or the limitations we are accustomed to. To embark on a new phase of existence, one must break these constraints, even though it means disrupting the familiar.

The notion that to be born anew, one must dismantle an existing reality emphasizes the transformative nature of personal development. This process can be daunting and unsettling, but it's essential for progress. The bird's flight toward God, represented by the name Abraxas, symbolizes a journey toward a higher state of being, a transcendent understanding, or a greater truth.

Hermann Hesse's passage speaks to the idea that growth and change demand leaving behind the old and embracing the unknown. It underscores the challenges inherent in evolution and the eventual rewards that await those who dare to venture into the unfamiliar.

During the time I was immersed in reading "Damian," my close friend Choi Sunghyun in Busan High School and I shared a series of fantastical dreams where we envisioned ourselves as the main characters of the novel: Damian and Sinclair. These dreams created an unspoken connection between us; let us sense each other's thoughts, emotions, movements, and even when we were apart.

It was as if our soul was intertwined, and the bond we shared transcended physical distance. I often imagined him as having the same contemplative and deep gazing as Johann Wolfgang von Goethe, the author of Faust.

As I delved into my younger years, many of my old wounds and pains started to heal. This period marked the first time I was able to gradually let go of the burdens that had weighed me down.

As graduation approached, I was presented with various job opportunities, mainly from smaller companies. However, none of them seemed to resonate with me, as I struggled to find the right balance between reality and my dreams.

The allure of the civil servant exam and the uncertainty of job interviews kept me wavering between paths, along with the option of pursuing a Ph.D. and becoming a university professor. Yet, my obsession with the civil exam continued to dominate my thoughts.

Ultimately, I made a decision that allowed me to address both my hunger for learning and financial concerns. I was able to start working during the day, selling cars while dedicating my evenings to studying. This arrangement could seem like a win-win solution. I joined Saehan Motors Company, a venture that emerged from the former GM Korea, during a time of rapid economic growth in Korea. This was a significant moment in my life, as it was here that I encountered two valuable figures: my superior boss and my future wife.

My director boss, Park Taeho, left an enduring impression on me. His altruistic nature and selflessness were evident in his actions, always putting others before himself. His kindness resonated deeply with me and her, and we even chose to live in his immediate as neighborhood. This experience led us to follow a Catholic path after our marriage, though we later chose a different spiritual path. Throughout the years, I continued to maintain a good rapport with him, visiting him whenever I returned to Korea.

As I worked at Saehan Motors, a dinner event that brought together graduates from school classmates, we voiced our complaints and wishes to our professors. During the discussion, an incumbent professor who had recently returned from Tokyo University in Japan shared his perspective. He remarked that during his time at Tokyo University, *students never complained to professors about management issues.* However, his condescending tone and lack of sharing of our students' circumstances frustrated me to the point that I couldn't bear it any longer. In a fit of anger, I hurled a boiling pot at him, an incident that would later earn me the nickname, "Boiling Pot." This outburst marked my first public expression of frustration against hunger, status, peace, injustice, discontent, unfairness, and social division.

Amidst selling cars and pursuing various paths, I continued my postgraduate studies in public administration. I felt like a reed swaying between different endeavors, a continuous cycle of shifting priorities.

One day, the dean of the law school, Professor Jeong Gwonsub, introduced me to a postgraduate woman student who worked as his assistant, suggesting that we might make good partners. This meeting led me to an invitation to her home, where I introduced myself to her family during a meal. However, my short stature became an obstacle once again, as her parents dismissed me as a potential partner for their daughter. This recurring rejection reinforced common torments that the short person might often face in their lives.

Despite my initial decision to forego marriage, fate intervened and introduced me to my eternal fiancée. She had applied for a job at our company, and the moment I laid eyes on her, I knew she was the woman I had been seeking. We both agreed to reverse the roles; I proposed to her. We had married on 30 March 1980, in a grand celebration attended by a couple of professors, family, friends, and colleagues from Saehan Motors.

Upon returning from our honeymoon, I had to leave the car sales company. The dean of the law school then recommended a couple of opportunities as I approached graduation: agency for National Security Department and Korea Electric Power Corporation.

Once again, during a physical test for the Agency for National Security, I fell short of the height requirement: this experience highlighted the disadvantages I faced due to my height. As I stepped into society, I had to continue encountering challenges associated with being short, a recurring theme that seemed to define various aspects of my life.

After my long arduous journey of hunger and darkness, I finally saw a path ahead of me: Korea Electric Power Corporation. My first step was to take on the Ph.D. course right after completing my postgraduate studies. Another choice was to become a tutor at Kyungju College (later changed to Sorabol College), a newly established institution in March 1981. The opportunity to become a tutor was contingent upon a successful interview with the college dean.

Simultaneously, I received a job offer from KEPCO, which was recommended by my law school dean. As the time came to decide between the two paths: KEPCO and Tutor at Kyungju College.

However, everyone around me, my wife, relatives, and friends, all leaned towards KEPCO. Their promise to provide us with a house for me was a significant factor. When it became clear that the opportunity at Kyungju College wouldn't materialize, I finally decided to join KEPCO.

On 5 March 1981, the day I entered the staff training center of KEPCO, the first act of my journey came to a close. The new chapter was beginning with KEPCO as my destination. I wrote a letter to my wife, describing my experiences in the training center and making a promise to her. I vowed to travel every highway along the way, and even more than anyone else had ever done. I intended to live a life that was whole and fulfilling.

Hello Darling!

I've safely arrived here. How's our baby doing with you? This marks the beginning of a whole new level of life for me: taking care of you and our baby before it's even born. Once our baby arrives, I'm committed to looking after both of you. I've been busy searching for baby names with the help of my friends and experts in naming, and I've come up with a couple of options. For a boy, I'm thinking of "Chorok," which means "Green," and for a girl, "Bunhong," which means "Purple." What are your thoughts? Have any ideas crossed your mind, Darling? I'm eagerly anticipating the moment when I can see you and our newborn baby in person.

With all my love,

From your sincere husband, on 5th January 1981

On 10 January 1981, I received a joyful reply from her, sent from the baby room in the hospital. She proudly announced the birth of our first son, Chorok, who later became Stephen after we moved to New Zealand.

After completing my training on 18th January 1981, I was assigned to the Kori Nuclear Power Plant located in Janganeub, Gilcheon Village on the outskirts of Busan. From the following day, I began working in the material depart, handling both offshore and onshore materials essential for units 5 and 6 (Kori 3 and 4). This marked a significant step for Korea's energy policy, as we transitioned from relying solely on foreign contractors to taking a more active role in nuclear power plant construction.

But these two units were being built by our hands. In those days, nuclear power had played a pivotal role in Korea's energy policy, with nuclear plants contributing to 29% of the country's electricity. The country has made strides to reduce dependence on imported fuels by focusing on nuclear energy. The nuclear power plants in Korea had a combined electrical generation capacity of 20.5 GWe from 23 reactors, representing around 22% of the nation's total electrical capacity.

My role as a material coordinator primarily involved collaboration with Roderick from Bechtel. Our responsibilities included handling insurance claims, managing inventory, ensuring quality assurance, tracking materials, reporting on faulty materials, and more. The practical experiences I had while dealing with foreign materials during this time significantly contributed to my work at KEPCO in the future.

After settling in at Kori Nuclear Power Plant, our family initially faced challenges finding suitable housing due to a shortage of available units. After much discussion with my wife, we managed to secure a small flat near the office, which later became a cherished space for our small family. We cherished moments like morning and evening walks on the beach, and engaged in activities such as catching grasshoppers in the fields and gathering clams on my days off.

Time passed, and the container houses that had become vacant as Bechtel employees expressed concerns about health were offered to new families, including ours. During my time at the plant, there were interesting incidents, like when a fellow newcomer and I crawled under a container to disconnect the cable of a Bechtel employee who hadn't yet vacated. This allowed us to access foreign broadcasts, a rare luxury back then.

Throughout this period of my youth, I engaged in lots of activities, from late-night drinking sessions with colleagues while discussing philosophy and participating in union activities. I actively expressed our dissatisfaction to the management and bosses, embodying the spirit of a young person eager to make a difference.

After my three-year stint at the Kori Nuclear Plant and passing the promotion test to secure third place, I was appointed as the secretary general of Yeongwol Thermal Power in Gangwon Province.

On 28 August 1984, three years and eight months after I first joined KEPCO, my wife, our three-year-old son, and I embarked on a journey of approximately 220km, crossing numerous mountains and fields, from Kori to Yeongwol. Yeongwol was a county in Gangwon Province with a historical spot. It was famously associated with King Danjong, the sixth king of the Joseon Dynasty, who was exiled and eventually murdered there in 1457 after being forced to abdicate by his uncle, later known as King Sejo. Arrived in Yeongwol, our family visited the sites linked to this tragic history multiple times, seeking to indirectly comprehend the unfortunate fate of King Danjong.

Upon settling in Yeongwol, I also discovered that it was the location where the Yeongwol Eom Family had been established during the Silla Dynasty. The founder of the Eom Family was dispatched from ancient China to Silla as an envoy alongside *Shin Kyeong*, whose story intertwines with the history of our Yeongsan Shin Family, discussed in Chapter I. Our Shin Family, in its eighth generation of descendants, was divided into five subclans, and among them, Buwonpa and Panseupa had settled in this Yeongwol province. Therefore, our arrival at Yeongwol Plant was welcomed by another clan of the Shin Family, sharing the same ancestors.

My tenure at the Yeongwol plant, spanning a mere seven months, was marked by significant endeavors. My primary mission, assisted by local staff Ahn Tasup, was to precisely trace and document the company's assets that had been lost or misplaced during the initial registration process. Subsequently, I took the crucial responsibility of officially registering these assets under our company's ownership.

During this period, numerous assets had fallen into the possession of individuals without proper authorization. In many instances, the most pragmatic solution was to secure personal endorsements from local village or community leaders, thereby facilitating the legitimate registration of these assets in the company's name.

Navigating these complexities, my duty demanded full attention to close detail and adept negotiation skills. By addressing these assets' ownership discrepancies and streamlining the registration process, I contributed to the company's efforts to establish a solid and verifiable root for its holdings. This experience underscored the complex network of relationships that frequently intersected with the significance of community cooperation in addressing such matters.

Another major responsibility was to daily oversee the Plant Director, who lived alone just above our apartment and was focused on searching for precious stones in neighboring villages that were soon to be submerged due to the construction of the Chungju Dam. My duties accompanying him or arranging transportation for his outings.

I also took it upon myself to eliminate unnecessary group dinners with bosses after work. Although these gatherings were initially seen as stress relief, they primarily involved eating and drinking and were costly in terms of time and money. This practice had started casually under the guise of stress relief upon my arrival at the plant. I was concerned about whether I had made the right decision to discontinue this practice, as some people were still interested in continuing it for stress relief.

During our time in Yeongwol, our son experienced a traumatic incident: he fell from a desk to the floor in his room and sustained a brain injury. He couldn't sleep and was in pain. This highlighted his isolation as there were very few children in the apartment complex to play with. He was sent to the nearest Yonsei University Hospital in Wonju for a brain checkup, and luckily, his injury wasn't serious. My wife and I took turns caring for him day and night until he recovered in about two weeks. Gradually, he returned to his normal routine.

When my wife started making Kimchi at home, unbeknownst to us, our staff's wives began gathering to assist her. As a young wife who had been married for only 4 or 5 years and was relatively new to the area, they brought gloves from their homes and helped her in making

Kimchi. This experience epitomized the close-knit human interactionns within the rural society of that time.

On weekends, we would take walks around the village, often we encountered these neighbors who greeted us with big smiles. As rumors spread about my impending departure, an elderly uncle Kim who was in charge of carpentry in my department, visited our home. He held my wife's hands, cried, and pleaded with her not to leave. Such affection and love were unique to our experience here.

Leopold von Ranke, a 19th-century German historian, once remarked that history is born through an ongoing dialogue between the past and the present. This idea, that history is a constant interaction between the facts of the past and the perspectives of the present, resonated with historians like E.H. Carr, who endorsed Benedetto Croce's assertion, "All history is modern history." This concept underscores the notion that historical facts may belong to the past, but historians exist in the present, thereby necessitating a continual dialogue between the two realms.

The purpose of revisiting my own past memories in the present is to bring fresh insights to them and find delight in reliving them. Even though our time at the Yeongwol plant was relatively short, reflecting upon those moments of contentment and satisfaction with our countryside life ignites a desire to prepare for a new future.

After leaving the Yeongwol plant, I received the sad news of the tragic death of a staff member who had worked under my supervision. He had generously provided us with fresh fish from Gwangju far from for a farewell party just days before we left. I couldn't help but wonder: if we hadn't left Yeongwol, what would have happened to him? Was it his fate?

Unexpectedly, as my assignment at the Yeongwol plant concluded, I was sent back to the Kori Nuclear Power Plant, where my career had first started. It was as if the journey had come full circle: I had left for Yeongwol on 28 August 1984, and returned to Kori on 26 March 1985, spanning within only 7 months.

Upon my return, I promptly acquired a used Hyundai pony and began remodeling it. I repainted it red, made technical alterations, changed the gearbox, and more. Once the remodeling was complete, I frequently would use the car to transport my family and staff to Haewoondae Beach for meals and relaxation. This marked the beginning of my efforts to establish my own style and identity.

Drawing from knowledge and wisdom, I recognized the significance of virtues in our careers, such as maintaining strong relationships, satisfying the workforce, and embodying compassion. These qualities contribute to a successful life, as they make us both likable companions and dependable workers.

As I assumed the role of materials manager for Unit One, I aimed to fulfill my responsibilities effectively in handling the inflow and outflow of materials to ensure the smooth operation of the power station. However, I realized that adhering solely to my own approach might lead to variant outcomes. Balancing these characteristics was crucial to our success, as it allowed us to adapt to the realities we faced while upholding our core values.

When I transitioned to the Gori Plant, manager Oh Byeongjin who was at the same level in the orgarnization, took the role of overseeing administrative support for the operation of the first power plant. On top of it, he was tasked with providing assistance to the boss, who had been relocated from Seoul to work at the plant. Under the boss, all four managers, myself included, operated as subordinates closely following his directives of him. This obedience was driven by the boss's authority to evaluate our performance, a critical factor in determining our prospects for future promotions.

As a result of this hierarchical structure, we occasionally participated in seemingly unnecessary group activities with our family, such as playing the card game 'Hwatu.' Amidst these dynamics, a silver lining emerged in the form of the opportunity to explore renowned tourist destinations on weekends as a group, accompanied by the boss. The boss preferred the company of his subordinates during these travels rather than being alone at home, resulting in mutual benefits for us.

Looking back, this period of my twelve-year tenure at KEPCO was likely the most unremarkable and uneventful phase. Yet, it appeared as though some higher power was observing these occurrences, prompting a shift in my responsibilities.

On 29 March 1986, I received a fresh assignment to the New Project Group at the headquarters in Seoul. This new role was primarily focused on thermal and nuclear projects. As the name implies, this group was dedicated to selecting foreign companies for new power construction projects initiated by KEPCO at that time. It was such an important task that members of this elite team were required to be proficient in foreign languages such as English, Japanese, and French within the company.

Of various tasks, my job was to support and look after the other staff who did the selection work: taking care of their unspecified meals and providing all the necessary support for the selection process; also played the same role as the mother of a single family. Everything was done except for the so-called bedding provider. The work for a team began at the building of Hankook Heavy Industry Company opposite the current Kyeonggi High School because it was far before the KEPCO Head Office Building in Samsung-dong was completed.

Also, the work was different from other employees in the form of a task force. Because this team had to hold frequent meetings in the morning and afternoon about the progress and performance of the task given to them, they often missed mealtime.

So, group dinner was usually between 7 and 8 pm. Although the meal started so late, it was common for the meal to last past dawn the next day as we ate and drank first, second, and third place, while talking to each other. Since this life continued until the project was completed, most of the personal family life was sacrificed: this was the reality of most of the working life in Korea in the mid-1980s.

I had to go home for a short sleep after one or two o'clock in the morning and went to work by 9:00 the next morning. Sometimes my breath could smell like alcohol, so I sat on the toilet seat and dozed off, and I ate lunch at the restaurant at 12 o'clock before I was ready to work; this routine repeated itself throughout the week.

After 9:00 one morning, security staff were checking employees arriving late for work. The moment I was about to get on the elevator, one of them stopped me in front of the elevator and asked which department I was in, so I came to answer with no hesitation that I was a Hankook Heavy Industries employee.

A little while later, he called and said, "I know who you are working for in the new project department." Shortly after that, I received a warning letter. The officer who had stopped me at the time also immigrated to New Zealand later and currently serves as a minister in a church.

Nearly approaching the completion of new projects, I had asked my boss several times for an opportunity to go abroad for job training. Overseas firms I would like to go to job training, had already submitted their bids for construction. However, it was often rejected. The reason was that after I went to training, there was no one who could handle my job as properly as I did; it's just a narrow-minded excuse. So, while working at KEPCO, I had never been to overseas' training, which was easily received by everyone; a four-character idiom that says that "after catching a rabbit, don't need a hunting dog, so burn it in a cauldron and eat it."

The uncertain trajectory of my career and the lack of substantial job training opportunities orchestrated by the boss compelled me to grapple with an ongoing question: "Am I genuinely positioned in the department I aspire to be in?" The echoing response was a resolute, "No." Even as I maintained a sustained passion for my work and dedicated myself wholeheartedly, regardless of my role, the external environment diverged from my dedication. This introspective realization underscored the disparities between my aspirations and the realities of my employment situation.

Despite my unshakeable energy and loyalty to my work, it became apparent that the environment I was in did not resonate with my true desires and ambitions. This discord led me to question whether I was fulfilling my potential and whether the path I was on truly aligned with my goal. Thus, I initiated a search for an alternative path that would eventually unveil itself.

The 100th Anniversary Celebration of the electric power business was waiting for me next: this event seemed like a vital milestone that aligned with the company's mission of supplying electricity efficiently to meet the needs of people. The event not only commemorated the long history of power supply but also symbolized enduring partners cultivated over 100 years with international collaborators. The fact that this celebration was taking place at the end of the ninth President Han Bongsu's tenure indicated a well-prepared and meaningful event.

Attending this celebration could offer me a chance to engage with colleagues, industry professionals, and international partners. It could also provide insights into the direction of the electric power industry, the technological advancements achieved, and the future goals of KEPCO. It was only a 7-day event that started on 1st November 1987, but top-levels of president and chairperson from world power companies such as EDE, INPO, CEGN, TPL, EGAT, ENEL, O/H, PNL, etc. were invited to this event.

Thus, it was a monumental event for KEPCO to fortify the existing relationship and continue the good rapport between both companies. Although it was a week-long occasion, it involved a large-scale project with numerous tasks that needed to be done in advance, such as flight schedule, lodging arrangement, tour schedule, vehicle arrangement, and brochure production.

As the event began, I guided them around famous tour attractions around Seoul: historical sites from the Joseon Dynasty to the Folk Village, and Seoul skyscrapers. I noticed their prejudices gradually disappearing from their faces as they realized that Korea might not be the small country they had imagined in the Asian suburbs.

This experience left me with a sense of pride as one of the event organizers. As a result, I was honored to receive two awards from the company as recognition for effectively executing this task.

Following this event, there seemed to be a sign of the birth of our second child: Puronsol (which means green). While my wife was pregnant, she had a good dream. Also, in 1988, the coming Seoul Olympics was being held, creating a festive atmosphere for people around the world. It was a year in which people all over the world were encouraged to have children as it marked the year of the 'Golden Dragon,' an event celebrated every 60 years.

From the beginning, my wife and I had planned to raise one child. However, due to the earnest demands of our relatives and families, we decided to have a second child. Amid these collective energies, Shin Puronsol entered the world, letting out his first cry at an obstetric hospital in Seoul on 19 March 1988. As he grew up, he too would have to embark on his journey of life, alongside mine, a journey that wouldn't be without challenges.

On 25 March 1988, exactly two years after I entered into the New Project Team, I received a new assignment: to join the Organizational Improvement Team under the flag of Director Kown Youngmu. Mr. Kown was perceptive about KEPCO's predicament and recognized that overcoming the impending challenges in the power business with an outdated organization would be a formidable task. With this foresight, he assembled the Organizational Improve Team by handpicking talented individuals from various fields.

I was chosen as an organizational specialist due to my academic subject. As the efforts for organizational improvement to gain its momentum, team members began to assess inefficiencies and wastage within the organization through hands-on field research in their respective domains.

Meanwhile, my focus shifted towards studying and analyzing the successful organizational models and ideal structures from other developed countries. I compiled my findings and reported them to my superior. Given the massive scale of organizations like KEPCO, I suggested introducing lower-level team structures and task force-type organizations tailored to each unit's characteristics. This proposition received a positive response, likely due to my postgraduation subjects in the organizational study.

Encouraged by positive feedback, I embarked on a data-gathering mission, visiting large domestic firms such as Samsung, Hyundai, LG, and other government-funded enterprises. The thorough research I conducted yielded suggestions for different organizational models. While a few of my suggestions were partially put into action, the majority were discarded due to leadership changes.

Looking back on the phase of my career at KEPCO, I ponder whether this job marked the peak of my creative and cognitive capabilities. From an academic standpoint, a team is a collective of individuals united to achieve shared objectives. Each member is interdependent and can be recognized as a cohesive unit by himself and the observer. Teams coexist within larger organizations, like KEPCO, and engage with other teams and the organization as a whole. Teams offer organizations a means to gather input from members and provide a sense of participation in the pursuit of organizational goals. Besides, teams offer flexibility in assigning members to projects and facilitate the formation of cross-functional groups.

In June 1991, immediately after wrapping up my job with the OI team, I was at this time transferred to the General Planning Department, essentially another planning group within KEPCO. At this juncture, you might be curious about the reasons behind my journey through different assignments within KEPCO, as I've narrated thus far. I must confess, it's a real question that captivates my curiosity as well.

My new duties involved a project related to hydroponic cultivation utilizing late-night power. The concept behind the late-night electricity system was to optimize electricity usage by supplying excess power generated during nighttime at lower rates, thus diversifying demand. This idea stemmed from the concern of Ahn Byunghwa, the former president of Pohang Steel, about efficiently utilizing surplus electricity during his time as the president. It was a concept he was eager to implement upon taking up the presidency at KEPCO.

The project was initiated based on his interest, who had previously held the position of president at Steel Company. The electric facilities were planned to supply for the peak consumer usage, resulting in a power surplus during nighttime. His innovative idea was harnessing this surplus electricity for high-yield crop cultivation. This notion emerged from contemplating ways to utilize the idle nighttime power.

I, helped by assistant Mr. Kim, initiated the pilot phase of the project at a distribution center located in Siheung, a vicinity close to Seoul, intending to expand nationwide upon a successful base. The target product of our endeavor was hydroponic cultivation, which, in its essence, wasn't overly intricate. With a basic grasp of farming principles, one could competently oversee the process. My routines involved commuting to Siheung daily, accompanied by Kim who supported me in various physical tasks. Upon completion of this project, I decided to offer a permanent position to this assistant within the subsidiary Hansung Company Ltd, a venture fully backed by 100% KEPCO investment.

Following the principles that were outlined in Newton's Principia, the fundamental tenets of natural philosophy that he introduced at the age of 45, even those with a basic grasp of classical physics could have intuited that my tenure at KEPCO was approaching its conclusion. As I alluded to my pursuit of an alternative path, set in motion upon the completion of my tenure with the New Project Team, it became evident that change was on the horizon.

There was a day when I found myself standing in a shop at the Yongsan Electronics Market in Seoul, engrossed in contemplation over how to navigate the burgeoning field of computer business at KEPCO. My mind was brimming with thoughts about the forthcoming ICT. Though vague, it was a longing that indicated a certain degree of foresight, even though I lacked specific insight or information on the subject. It was a sign of my keen cognitive ability to anticipate future trends.

The 1990s marked the dawn of the ICT revolution, characterized by the rapid emergence of mobile phones, pagers, high-performance computers, and most significantly the World Wide Web. Information telecommunication technique was progressing with remarkable speed.

In Korea, Sambo Computer recognized this trend ahead of Samsung and entered the market.

Particularly, the ICT sector spearheaded almost unbelievable changes. Technological advancements in music, for instance, moved beyond imagination. The shift from traditional CD players to streaming was inevitable. The introduction of Sony's Walkman in place of cassette players instantly thrilled the younger generation. The IT technology trends that began during this period transformed how we eat, drink, see, and listen.

Newton, revered as one of the eminent figures in the annals of scientific thought, expounded on determinism in his seminal work "Principia," postulating the independence of time and space, asserting that they exert no influence upon each other. This insight, though unfamiliar to me at the time, might have held a profound magnitude on that day I stood at the Yongsan Electronics Mart.

Nonetheless, within the elite group of KEPCO, an exceptional cadre of individuals recognized the implications of these technology shifts from the outset. Naturally, I was aligned with this forward-thinking group. Countless talks among these experts culminated in a realization: division of the computing sector from the power supply business could synergize with the core objectives of the power enterprise and elevate overall efficiency.

With this conviction, we should embark on a mission to persuade the Ministry of Energy and Resources, a pivotal government agency, to establish *the computing division* as an independent entity. This endeavor bore fruit in the creation of Seil Communications, initially a venture wholly invested by KEPCO, on 23 January 1992; just a year before my preplanned relocation to NZ as part of my alternative path.

By 2004, this company underwent a transformation and rebranding, emerging as KEPCO KDN. Its exclusive focus on KEPCO's ICT operations resulted in the provision of comprehensive ICT services throughout the electric power system worldwide. What had started as a modest enterprise in 1992, burgeoned into a workforce of 2,800 employees, driving critical functions in electric power systems worldwide.

In moments of retrospection, I occasionally ponder whether I should have remained within this remarkable firm rather than embarking on my migration to New Zealand. I hope the growth, impact, and transformative journey of KEPCO KDN stand as a testament to the dynamic interplay of technological foresight and corporate evolution. However, I'd rather be proud of my decision to move along.

VI

Crossing the Ocean Blue

VI
Crossing the Ocean Blue

The annals of humanity tell the tale of migration, A saga woven into the fabric of time. My forebearer, Shin Gyeong, journeyed from ancient China, During the Goryeo Dynasty, he arrived upon this realm, scattering his descendants who took root in this new land.

In distant epochs, the progenitors of all humankind, emerging 200,000 years ago from the heart of Africa, ventured forth in quest of hospitable terrain, navigating the currents of climate change, their odyssey marked by the ebb and flow of time.

And so it was that on 27 April 1993, guiding my family along the path of migration, we embarked on a voyage to New Zealand's embrace, finding a haven on foreign shores, where new beginnings awaited our embrace.

For as long as existence unfurls its tapestry, humanity, like a nomad, shall forever journey, seeking a realm more promising to reside, a pursuit eternally intertwined with our essence.

And here, on the fertile soil of New Zealand, our family forges a foundation for happiness, constructing a haven, brick by brick, a testament to the enduring spirit of migration, a sanctuary born from our dreams and toil.

As my family stepped onto the grounds of Auckland Airport on 27 April 1993, autumn rain fell gently, the temperature reminiscent of early spring in Korea. However, it was indeed autumn: a sorrowful reminder of NZ's exact contrasting climate. In this Antipodean haven, New Zealanders savored the tranquility of the year's most settled weather. They reveled in sun-soaked days, amidst golden leaves, pursuing their outdoor activities like hiking, cycling, and kayaking. The temperature ranged from 10 to 21 degrees Celsius. Positioned at 36 degrees south latitude, Auckland stood opposite Seoul's location at 37 degrees north latitude.

Emerging from the terminal with luggage in tow, fellow immigrant colleagues arrived earlier enveloped us in warm embraces. Their applause, cheers, handshakes, and heartfelt greetings transported us back in time. As we embarked on the car journey to our staying spot, my anxiety was palpable. Seated in the right-hand driver's seat, my companion's unceasing stream of advice filled the air. My children and wife, brimming with excitement, absorbed the newness around them.

The panoramic views outside the car window only amplified my awe, affirming that this place matched the images I had encountered in immigration seminars. A sense of relief washed over me, and I expressed my contentment: this was our new homeland.

Our lodging for the first night was graciously provided by a colleague in Torbay, north shore of Auckland, who had guided me to attend an immigration seminar and currently helped us settle in. Guess who he was. This gesture of kindness sheltered us as we sought more permanent housing.

A common question that accompanies its immigration emerged: "What prompted your move?" Answers varied from education for children, to improving health, and to embarking on new challenges. My answers encompassed all these factors.

One day, seated at my desk in Seoul's head office, I reminisced about my journey. It struck me that if I hadn't embraced new challenges in life, I might have lost the opportunity forever. Moved by this realization, I reached out to a friend for advice. His reassuring words echoed in my ears: "Don't worry about tomorrow, just go on it."

That weekend, my friend guided me to an immigration seminar focused on New Zealand. The moment I stepped into the seminar and gazed at the screen before me, the decision to immigrate crystallized immediately in my mind.

The following weekend, I eagerly brought my wife to the seminar along, and she embraced the idea even more fervently than I did. With no prior site tours, my dream embarked on the journey to New Zealand on 27 April 1993. The person who guided me at that pivotal moment was now driving us to his own house: former manager Oh Beungjin. We had worked together at the Nuclear Plant Operation Unit One in Kori. He, too, had made the journey and found success in this new land. Our paths continued to cross in this foreign city.

The next day, our family was relocated to a motel in Mt. Albert, embarking on a search for rental housing. We joined forces with my nephew's earlier settled family in this pursuit. Despite our best efforts, every application to move in was rejected due to the presence of our two children. After a month of searching, we finally secured a three-bedroom, one-bath in Glenfield, north of Auckland. The first night was a challenge: no blankets to keep us warm, the wind whistling through the open door, and the cold rendering sleep elusive.

We were improvised, huddling under blankets borrowed from our nephews, igniting newspapers and wood chips in the fireplace. That night, the entire family's shared ordeal etched itself into our memory. Throughout that year, the rain persisted, save for four fleeting days since our arrival. As we sought a proper rental home, the rain continued its dance, matched by a gradual drop in temperature.

Yet, the camaraderie of our immigrant colleagues who had arrived earlier buoyed us through the chilly days: they took turns inviting us for dinners and drinks. Amidst our efforts to secure a rental home, I faced the need to learn English. The immigration boom had already gripped New Zealand, closing English courses at the nearby universities. A community college in the high school became my haven for language acquisition, with my wife joining me.

Simultaneously, I enrolled in real estate and computer courses at Carrington Polytechnic on completion of community college. After six months, armed with a real estate agent license, I began my journey as a real estate agent in November 1993: a path I continue to tread even three decades later.

I began my career as a broker at the Torbay office of Vision Real Estate on the north shore, of Auckland. I had chosen this office after thoroughly conducting research, during which I noticed that their signs were prominently displayed in neighboring areas during my drives over several days. This company's signboards were especially prominent in this area. Recognizing the significance of signboards as a 24/7 promotional tool, I decided to join this office. The visual impact of these signboards became a powerful marketing strategy for agents and the company alike.

As I stepped into the office, the receptionist greeted me with a warm smile, saying, "Welcome on board. You must be Shin Hanok, right?" Her friendly demeanor left a lasting 'impression' on me from our very first meeting. Little did I know that this encounter would later inspire me to choose the name for my own real estate firm when I established it a few years down the line, on the last day of November 1993.

This office was managed by Robert Hodgson, with June Freeman managing director providing oversight. After a brief interview with the manager, I was ready to dive in and began my work the following day. Interestingly, the receptionist happened to be the manager's wife, and their son was also part of the team, responsible for handling the signage for the company.

As anticipated, I quickly acclimated to my role in the office. During this period, the New Zealand government had opened its doors to the world, resulting in an influx of immigrants from various corners of the globe. This surge in population naturally drove a bustling real estate industry. Despite being a novice in the New Zealand real estate scene, my sales performance steadily improved day by day, leading to a boost in my confidence. Agents were tirelessly showcasing properties on the market, often shuttling from their motels where prospective buyers were staying.

As you likely know, in real estate transactions, it's the seller in New Zealand who bears the commission. However, this commission is only earned by the agent when a sale is successfully completed. Its structure was straightforward: 4% on the initial NZ $300,000 of the sale price, and 2% on the remaining amount, plus the Goods and Services Tax (GST). For instance, if a house was sold for $1,000,000, the works would be as follows: 4% of $300,000 equals $12,000, and 2% of $700,000 equals $14,000. The total commission paid by the seller would be $29,000, comprising $26,000 plus the 15% GST.

However, it's important to note that the agent doesn't retain the entire commission amount. Instead, it's divided between the agent and the company, usually following a certain ratio that takes into account the individual sales performance. Initially, this amount often starts at 50:50, but it could be adjusted upwards depending on the agent's achievements and contributions.

Indeed, the profession of a real estate agent appeared enviable due to its potential for substantial earnings. But attaining success in this industry necessitated overcoming personal challenges and dedication to own continuous self-improvement; a dash of luck was occasionally required as well. Above all, steady and tireless efforts were the keys to achieving success.

My achievements during the intense 13 months at Vision Realty were not solely the outcome of my own endeavors but also a result of the sacrifices made by my family.

Adapting to a foreign country after the age of 40 presented its own difficulties, requiring dedication and tenacity. To understand the local perspectives, I thoroughly watched and assessed the behaviors of both young and old agents within the company. I would like to participate in various company events and even follow the routines of my colleagues during the 2nd and 3rd rounds.

Every week, the managing director convened a strategic sales meeting attended by all agents. The meetings served as a platform to discuss a wide range of topics, from miscellaneous matters to regulations, permits, and changes in laws pertinent to brokers. The meeting was followed by presenting the previous week's sales numbers and new listings for the current week.

Following this, the agents embarked on the 'Caravan': a visit to the newly listed properties for the week. Agents either went individually or formed groups to inspect these properties, crucial for them to gain familiarity and insight to later present these listings to potential buyers.

Survival for a real estate firm hinged predominantly on the quantity of properties acquired from sellers. In other words, the existence and prosperity of a real estate firm were intricately tied to the number of listings it possessed.

On the flip side, sellers had a choice in entrusting their properties to agents for sale. This choice encompassed two categories: exclusive agency and general agency. Exclusive authority to sell could take the form of an auction, tender, private treaty, or a simple exclusive contract. However, contemporary trends in New Zealand's real estate sales leaned towards auctions or tenders, where the seller bore the associated marketing costs. On the other hand, some agents disliked taking on a general agency due to the lack of control over the listings they held.

After spending 13 months selling estates at Vision Realty, my confidence had grown. This newfound confidence led me to shift my focus toward the realm of commercial real estate. As I searched to identify robust firms with a strong foothold in the commercial sector, one firm emerged as a prominent player, boasting a huge market share of nearly 50% in Auckland: Bailess Realty (disguised by circumstance).

Just a few days before Christmas in 1994, I was sitting with the Chairperson of Bailess Real Estate. We were in the ASB building, on the 26th floor of 135 Albert Street in Auckland City. Eagerly I anticipated an interview that was about to take place.

As our conversation commenced, the Chairperson's first question mirrored that of anyone else's: "Why did you come to New Zealand?" In response, I explained my pursuit of a new life in a new world. This led to the next question: If I were to join Bailess, what kind of sales plans would I have in mind? I revealed my plan to introduce New Zealand properties to the Korean market through the upcoming World Real Estate Exhibition in Seoul the following year.

Without hesitation, he welcomed my proposal, and our agreement was sealed with a handshake. During those times, Bailess was actively engaged in international marketing, reaching out to places like Hong Kong, Singapore, Sydney, and Shanghai, in a concerted effort to expand its international business sector.

Upon becoming a part of the Bailess team, I promptly ignited a surge in commercial real estate sales. At the final auction held before the end of 1994, I achieved the sale of 9 out of 16 shops located along Queen Street, the main central thoroughfare in downtown Auckland.

This was a pivotal time, with buyers not only hailing from Korea but also from China and Europe. Immigrants were flocking to the city, creating a thriving market. Within just a year, I managed to facilitate the sale of 50 estates, generating a staggering $30 million in sales volume: reflecting on those days, it's evident that my passion burned bright, propelling me forward to achieve such remarkable results.

As experiences grew, the time to introduce New Zealand properties to Korea drew nearer. Finally, on 11 April 1995, I arrived in Seoul accompanied by my manager, John Chomlie(dg), and senior agent, Bruce Whilang(dg). Our bound was the 'World Real Estate Expo' held at COEX, Seoul. Our booth became a magnet for prospective customers as they flocked to us in droves. Among them were a diverse range of individuals, from those contemplating immigration to executives of large corporations.

A few days later, at the Ramada Renaissance Hotel, I took an opportunity to solemnly introduce New Zealand properties to Korea for the first time in collaboration with a local real estate consulting company based in Seoul. The key point to clarify here is that in my situation, all expenses were personal, whereas for the other two individuals, the company covered their expenses.

Following this event, inquiries from all corners of Korea poured in: notable entities such as Pohang Steel, Sejong Academy group, Hankook Paper, and various private groups-initiated negotiations, often involving on-site visits. Negotiations spanned nearly half a year, yet unfortunately, none of them achieved successful transactions.

Throughout the negotiations, I was acutely aware of the formidable obstacle posed by the absence of mutual trust between the parties involved in the transaction. It became abundantly clear, as is often the case in business dealings, that real estate transactions, particularly those involving substantial financial stakes, were inherently obstacles to finalizing without a foundation of trust.

As I pen down these reflections in my memoir, I want to extend my heartfelt gratitude to Kim Dongchan, a sole businessman who devoted six months of hard work alongside me, despite the ultimate result of our collaboration not bearing fruit. In 2023, I came to learn that he had permanently returned to Korea with his family.

Just as Julius Caesar's political history weaved a cyclical tapestry of exchanges between progress and setbacks, strong support from citizens, and indifference from them, my own life journey has been propelled forward through the rhythmic oscillation of triumphs and failures.

A spark of rejuvenation ignited within me when I met a young businessman, Kim Suheun, with an interest in apartment projects. Our paths serendipitously converged at his tile shop, an encounter that led us through both favorable and challenging phases.

The wave of immigration that characterized the early 1990s served as a catalyst for a thriving apartment business that persisted into the late '90s. During each property section opening, a plethora of new Auckland apartment developments emerged, with a particular focus on city-core apartments. This trend was remarkably propelled by the increasing approvals of overseas student visas, resulting in many properties being sold off the plans.

Amid these circumstances, a series of questions arose: Where were these developments located? Were they experiencing robust sales? Who comprised their buyer demographic? As the landscape of apartment development continued to evolve, these inquiries would shape my ongoing engagement in the field.

On 13 December 1995, Director Kim ventured into the realm of apartment development by purchasing land and embarking on a new business venture. However, being entirely inexperienced in the field of apartment development, he found himself reliant on the assistance of Bailess' staff for various aspects of the project: ranging from design and permitting to financing, sales, and marketing.

As the marketing agent, I too lacked prior experience in this realm. Recognizing our weaknesses as developers' experiences, the Bailess team took the reins of the entire project, assuming control over project management, design, and financing.

The result of our collaborative effort was the creation of the grandiose Tower Hill Apartment, situated at 1 Emily Place. This complex, built in 1998, occupied a highly desirable location near of Auckland's Britomart, surrounded by key attractions such as train and bus stations, the waterfront, the ferry terminal, Queen Street, and Auckland University, all within easy walking distance.

Naturally, in order to thrive in society, Director Kim recognized the necessity of learning from those who possessed the field expertise he lacked. Yet, from the outset of the project, the approach taken by the Bailess staff towards us felt distinctively different manner. It appeared as though they were intent on utilizing Director Kim's business for their own financial terms.

If they overstepped this boundary and exploited Director Kim excessively, it was tantamount to crossing a line. Instead of mentoring and guiding newcomers like a parent helping a child take their first steps, the prevailing sentiment in society seemed to be one of flexing its muscles over Director Kim and me.

In New Zealand, venturing into an apartment project typically entails the necessity of preselling approximately 70% of the units off the plan. This benchmark is crucial, as it ensures the acquisition of full project funding from a bank, serving as a prerequisite that must be met. Director Kim and I were resolute in our endeavors to meet this threshold, dedicating ourselves wholeheartedly to the task. Our relentless efforts eventually bore fruit as we nearly reached the 70% presale milestone.

Buoyed by this achievement, we proceeded to apply for a project loan from the bank, a crucial step to secure the financial backing required to bring our apartment project to fruition. Unfortunately, our applications were met with repeated rejections. The primary rationale for the refusals stemmed from the perception that Kim and I, as newcomers to the construction industry in New Zealand, lacked the requisite construction experience deemed essential by the banks.

This obstacle highlighted a critical challenge faced by newcomers, particularly those from another country, trying to establish themselves in a foreign business landscape. Despite our vital accomplishments in reaching the presale benchmark and the undeniable potential of the apartment project, the banking institutions' hesitance due to our perceived lack of industry experience posed a formidable roadblock. This experience underscored the complexities inherent in breaking into new industries and markets, even in the face of tangible achievements.

Therefore, Director Kim had to hand over the project to another local developer because it was difficult to obtain financing backing from the bank. The negotiation process for handing over the project was also not so easy. Since human has been selfish animal, therefore would like to hang onto the choices that were in their favor even a little bit.

In the end, Director Kim took over some portion of the apartments, and now my commission negotiation began. Of course, I was prepared to accept some reduction, but I didn't expect it to be cut so drastically. It was originally $500,000, but they offered me only $200,000. They also had warned me, stating that if I had not accepted their offer immediately, I should be prepared to cover lawyer fees for 2 or 3 years after filing a lawsuit, which would leave me financially drained.

Thinking the current $200,000 was still better than being broke, I accepted the offer, because at the time I had already left Bailess and was running my own company, Impressions from September 1997, so I needed money to operate it. At that time, the words of a Bayless worker who was negotiating commissions with me had struck in my head like a dagger; "A large shark bites a target, causing it to bleed, and other sharks in the vicinity rush in and bite together, and the victim disappears in an instant."

This time, unlike the previous project, it was another one started by three friends from Pohang Steel, with ample funds in the form of a partnership. Also, at this time, I had become somewhat of an expert based on my own experience of failing the previous projects: Argent Hall apartment; the name of the project was decided because a motel called "Argent Hall" stood on 2 Eden Crescent. It was moved to another place, and an apartment was built in 1997. It was made up of ten floors and 107 apartment units in total.

Fortunately, not only did the three partners have ample funds, but the presale also went smoothly. As a result, I was able to receive sales commissions normally. Since the residents had settled in, an unexpected incident emerged. An accountant whom I introduced to the developer had been overseeing the building's body corporation and tragically passed away due to a sudden heart attack. His untimely death brought about significant changes in the body corporation and building operation.

Before his passing, Tony had granted my request and appointed Impression, a company I founded in 1997, as the building manager. Consequently, the body corporation was transferred to a new entity known as TBA, while Impression continued its role as the building manager. As Tony disappeared, an intrigue began to unfold to remove me from Impression company.

So, let's discuss why I decided to establish my own company. As mentioned earlier, I accurately anticipated a surge in New Zealand's real estate market due to the influx of people in the late 1990s. Given these circumstances, I had predicted that residential properties in Ak would soon transition into the rental and resale market following the completion of apartment projects. This foresight drove me to launch my own real estate firm, aiming to capitalize on these upcoming opportunities.

Thus, at 111 Wellesley Street in Auckland's CBD, Impression Real Estate was born, a venture I had strictly prepared alongside my hard worker, Chang Seungpo. Even before anything else, I widely delved into the process of naming the company. Concealing my true purpose,

I sought input from friends on a suitable name, dedicating substantial time to this endeavor as I initiated advertising efforts in the newspaper.

This marked the inception of a new chapter in my journey, one that held promise and possibility in the dynamic realm of real estate. Then, one day, the phrase *'first impression'* caught my attention in a paper. At that moment, the memory of my initial reception at the office where I had first interviewed resurfaced. Without a moment's hesitation, the name became clear: Impression Real Estate.

Truly, the concept of a "first impression" resonated with me. The decision was rooted in the belief that a business's success hinged on the ability to leave a positive mark on customers. After all, it takes merely 7 seconds to establish an impression, prompting the well-known notion that first impressions hold utmost importance: echoed in the English adage, "First Impressions Count."

The date was on 30 August 1997. An article titled "The First Korean Starts a Real Estate Company" emerged in a Korean newspaper. This triggered an unexpected phone call from the Bailess Manager, who discreetly requested I gather my belongings and quietly vacate the premises. I was well aware of who had conveyed this message, given that there was just one individual in the company fluent in Korean.

This situation aligned with a Korean proverb: "When a cousin buys real estate, his stomach hurts." This agent had pursued me previously when I moved from Vision Real Estate to Bailess a few years prior. Yet, I refrained from blaming him, understanding that such developments would inevitably surface with time.

Soon after complying with John's request to collect my belongings, I was en route to the motorway to meet a guest when a car in the adjacent lane abruptly cut in front of me without signaling. I swerved to avoid a collision, inadvertently losing control of my vehicle and colliding a couple of times with the median block.

It happened in an instant, but in my mind, time seemed to slow. At that crucial moment, the thought crossed my mind: "If I cross this median, I will die." A young following driver witnessed the accident, and I pursued the car that had caused the incident, accompanied by the witness in his car.

When the witness and I returned to the scene, police officers were already investigating. Meanwhile, a couple of Koreans passing by had spread rumors to newspapers and even informed my wife that I had died in the accident. Upon calling home after the police inquiry, my wife anxiously asked where I was. Vague rumors were circulating among the people that I had been involved in a car crash and had died. To lighten the mood, I jokingly assured her that I had just taken a trip to "hell."

Two days following the incident, on 5 September 1997, Impression Real Estate celebrated a modest inauguration ceremony at Wellesley Street in Auckland CBD. The event welcomed both clients and Korean residents. It was a moment of pride, as I had accomplished my dream of establishing my own real estate firm within just 4 years. However, this feeling of achievement would turn out to be fleeting.

After six months of operating the business, as existing properties we had listed began selling one by one, and the available listings dwindled, noticeable shifts from agents occurred. No efforts were made to secure new listings, and agents began to depart one after another. Only two agents remained: the manager I had initially met at the Torbay office of Vision Realty and another lady he had brought along. It didn't take long to understand why they had chosen to stay.

In an attempt to cut down operational expenses, I made a decision to shut down the downtown office and relocate to the North Shore. I identified a suitable two-story house on Forrest Hill Road, where the garage could be converted into an office. Upstairs, my family lived, while downstairs, the office was set up. At the same time, I assigned the lady agent to manage the recently completed Argent Hall project, where residents and tenants were moving in.

The North Shore Office was intended to be under the management of the aforementioned manager, yet he frequently made trips to the city to be with the female agent. My demanding schedule, focused on securing new listings, left me with minimal time to personally supervise their activities. Eventually, my wife brought to my attention that their relationship seemed inappropriate although I initially didn't take it seriously.

At a certain point, their relationships became increasingly noticeable to me. One day I unexpectedly arrived at the apartment and found their faces flushed and their expressions uneasy. They quickly explained that they had been inspecting a room upstairs, but their demeanor betrayed the truth.

It was evident that they had been engaged in an affair within that room. This incident marked a turning point, as it became clear that they were now inseparable, consistently at each other's side wherever they went. Later on, after I had handed over the company's operations to them, I made a startling discovery: they had been residing in an apartment provided for the building manager; furthermore, they were renting out an additional room to generate extra income, all of which I had no awareness of.

As I shouldered the responsibility of covering the manager's wage, office rent, advertising expenses, and other operational costs of the company, my focus remained fixed on acquiring real estate properties. In the meantime, these two individuals appeared to be living a comfortable life, seemingly unconcerned about revealing their earnings. Their leisurely lifestyle, made possible by their financial gains, inadvertently placed me in a challenging position.

This scenario highlighted the intricate dynamics at play within the business, as well as the moral and ethical dilemmas that can arise when entrusted with managerial responsibilities. The revelation of their actions showcased the contrast between their indulgent approach and my commitment to the financial stability and growth of the company.

During the process of transferring the company to them, a shocking revelation emerged when I examined the ownership structure of the company. From the very start of Impression Company, the manager I had hired held a 51% ownership stake, while I owned just 49%, and this ownership was registered through an accountant they designated. It became clear that I had been operating as more of a figurehead from the very beginning.

In many ways, this situation was a result of my poor supervision of the company, as I had placed excessive trust in the manager. I fully realized that I am solely responsible for my life, regardless of whether others exploited me for their own profit, leading to my prosperity or misfortune. While they might face moral condemnation from others, it appeared that these criticisms did not significantly impact them if they chose to ignore them.

Thus, without remorse, both of them, after seizing control of the company and handing it to a hired director, embarked on a life of leisure characterized by daily horse riding and golfing in the countryside. From the perspective of a female agent, she had achieved her personal dream of acquiring my company, along with the manager who had divorced his wife.

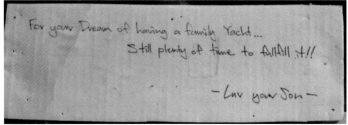

On my birthday, my elder son gifted me a cardboard with the words "Your dream is still on," serving as a source of motivation, still stands at my desk.

During this hard period, I even took on weekend shifts as a taxi driver. During the hours when the open homes were conducted, I would remove my driver's uniform, stow it in the trunk, and greet customers who visited the properties. On weekends, my elder son would drop me off at the car owner's house at dawn, and in the evenings, he would pick me up.

Upon returning home in the evenings, during mealtime, I would retreat to the bathroom to hide my tears from my children, waiting until I had composed myself before rejoining them. Occasionally, the family car my wife used to transport the children to school would be repossessed due to our inability to meet the monthly payments. Despite financial difficulties, I refrained from selling the car to shield my family from further hardship and persevered.

On my birthday, my elder son gifted me a cardboard with the words "Your dream is still on," serving as a source of motivation, and it remains on my desk to this day.

Looking back now, while the timing of my decision to establish the company and my predictions about the real estate market proved accurate, the primary cause of my own company's failure was my lack of proper people management. Unfortunately, luck was not on my side, either on account of IMF happened. Furthermore, I hadn't fully embraced the words encapsulated in the saying, "When in Rome, do as the Romans do," which emphasizes adapting to the customs and behavior of the people in a certain place or situation.

After the challenges I faced in running the firm, I found myself turning to redirect my efforts towards achieving my dream by working for an established real estate firm. Of various options available, I made a deliberate choice to join Barfoot & Thompson, my decision driven by several compelling factors.

At its core, Barfoot & Thompson stood out as the outstanding real estate firm solely operating within Auckland. With a storied history spanning over a century, the firm's reputation and legacy were deeply ingrained in the city's real estate landscape. Notably, it distinguished itself from the family model by directly managing around 75 branches and maintaining a substantial network of nearly 2,500 agents.

This characteristic structure and size lent the firm an undeniable authority and presence within the Auckland real estate scene. Joining Barfoot & Thompson offered me the opportunity to leverage this extensive network and tap into the accumulated knowledge and experience of the agents, positioning myself to achieve my aspiration within the real estate industry.

The choice to align myself with Barfoot & Thompson marked a strategic step towards realizing my dreams in an environment that combined the benefits of a historic legacy, a well-established network, and a sizeable team of professionals dedicated to the real estate field.

Reflecting on my journeys in the New Zealand real estate industry, which included approximately one year at Vision Realty in the North

Shore until November 1994, followed by two and a half years at Bailess in Auckland Downtown CBD, and three years of challenges at my venture, Impression, I came to a realization.

Being a minority from a foreign country, navigating this landscape made me realize that aligning myself with the established interests as the mainstream of this society was the most practical and feasible option. So, I had an interview with the head director of Barfoot & Thompson on 9 August 2000, and the following day marked the beginning of my tenure at the City Branch, located at 18 Commerce Street in downtown Auckland.

Coinciding with my arrival, the previously stagnant real estate market experienced a revival, and I enthusiastically embraced this resurgence. As a result, I built a team by hiring several salespersons as assistants, creating a multi-ethnic group composed of five agents: two Chinese agents, a Korean agent, my eldest son, and myself.

During this market upswing, there was also a surge in activity among developers. Luckily, I had the opportunity to actively engage in selling conversion apartments located near my office. These projects were part of a project by Manson Construction, a well-known company with strong financial support. Additionally, a close New Zealand friend of mine, Steve Clark, served as the sales manager for this project.

Within a few two months of embarking on this sales venture, I successfully sold half of the project, totaling 80 units. In the meantime, my team diligently focused on selling other properties. Remarkably, within six months of joining Barfoot & Thompson, I secured a place within the top 30 of 2500 agents in the whole company. This record continued as I ranked 27th in 2002; ascended to the top 11th in 2003; maintained a position within the top 30 in 2004, and subsequently held a spot within the top 1% every year.

While my annual total revenue amounted to $700,000 at the time, this sum was significantly impacted by marketing expenditures and assistant wages. Nevertheless, the success of a real estate agent pivoted on how these earnings were invested.

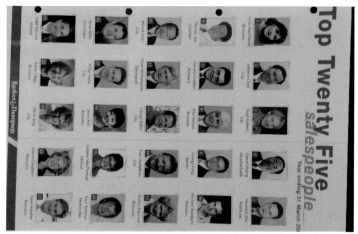

Since I joined Barfoot & Thompson, I achieved the top 11th ranking of the whole company in 2003 then maintained a position within the top 30 in 2004, and subsequently held a spot within the top 1% every year.

Five years after becoming a part of this cherished firm, one day in 2005, I was approached by a reporter from a local Korean magazine for an interview. Despite initially declining their offers several times, I eventually agreed to the interview. The purpose of the interview was to highlight Koreans who had successfully integrated into New Zealand society. During the meeting with the reporter, when asked about my family's status in the country, I replied, "While my family hasn't fully settled down yet, we plan to establish our roots here soon."

Shin Hanok, a dedicated professional at Barfoot & Thompson, humbly says that despite spending 13 years in New Zealand since arriving in April 1993 as a first-generation immigrant, he has not yet fully planted his roots, but is resolute about doing so in the future. With a notable track record of fulfillment in business, his response is marked by modesty and a steadfast commitment to his journey.

Shin finds the real estate industry to be well-suited for him and a source of great enjoyment. While there are notable differences between the real estate laws and systems of Korea and New Zealand, both countries share the common factor of dealing with people. Drawing upon a diverse array of experiences built up in Korea, he finds that these experiences have significantly swiveled his performance as a broker.

In the present, as a resurgence in the real estate market unfolds, Shin is particularly interested in the resale of apartments that were previously sold by Korea Development Company.

Since 2000, he has consistently achieved a place within the top 1% of Barfoot & Thompson's entire company each year, a feat that can be attributed to the steady support of his dependable clientele. Shin is characterized by a personality that embraces challenges and demonstrates an eagerness to explore new horizons. He attributes his current standing to his diligent preparation and unwavering effort in all that he undertakes.

While he acknowledges encountering significant challenges during the period when he was running his venture, Impression, he persevered through the crisis by adopting the mindset of diligent work and comprehensive preparation, viewing realtor as his true calling. Undoubtedly full of confidence, Shin affirms his commitment to consistently giving his best as a broker. He underscores that he will continue to strive each day until the moment he firmly establishes his roots in this land.

Thirteen years had elapsed since that news, in Dec of 2018, I found myself strolling through Albert Park on the University of Auckland campus after lunch. My cell phone rang, its ringing resounding through the air. Amid the few words we had exchanged, I immediately could recognize who was on the other end of the line. It was a voice from my junior colleague from my days at KEPCO.

Seated in a downtown Auckland restaurant, we couldn't contain our laughter as we reminisced about events that had unfolded some 30 years ago. My junior colleague had moved on from KEPCO as well and was now serving as a professor at Amada University of Science and Technology in Ethiopia. That year, when I visited Korea, he posted my story on Facebook, chronicling it under the title "Big History that makes old trees tremble.":

In our lives, there are individuals we yearn to reconnect with. Every organization harbors its own hub of admiration, a place where the network can be cultivated easily, and where quick information exchange and a vast network coalesce. I pondered over the reasons, the hows, and the whats that could lead one to venture forth.

And so, I ventured into the General Planning Department, finding myself surrounded by a multitude of truly exceptional individuals. I wondered when I would evolve into such a person. But he vanished suddenly, leaving behind only anecdotes about him.

I was on vacation at the time. While I was in Auckland, his memory crossed my mind, and I reached out to him. However, tracking him down proved elusive. Our conversation during our meeting was less about our shared past and more about our current lives, amid the flickering memories of three decades ago.

Observing the age of 80 etched on his face, he remarked that he had lessened his workload and developed a fervor for his studies. Taking me along on his thought journey, he directed my attention to the roots of a centuries-old tree before us. "Look there," he said, "at the history that's written in those roots."

As he recounted his tale, I discovered numerous parallels with my own interests – encompassing vast domains such as the wonder of existence, life, materiality, history, and being. His narrative was that of an intrepid voyager who traverses the world, all the while delving into its history.

When asked about his motivation for arriving at his current point, his response was whimsical: he had arrived aimlessly because the sky was adorned with a brilliant shade of blue.

When we gaze upon the sky, its hue appears as blue. This visual perception isn't due to the inherent color of the sky itself, but rather a result of the way light wavelengths are projected to our eyes. In 1871, England's Lord Rayleigh unveiled the phenomenon known as Rayleigh scattering. As sunlight traverses the atmosphere, shorter wavelengths, like blue light, tend to scatter more, causing the sky to take on a blue tint. Given that the scattering rate for blue light (with a wavelength around 400 nm) is roughly 6 times higher than that of red light (around 640 nm), blue light finds its way easily to our eyes. This same principle can be applied to comprehend why the sky displays hues of red during sunrise and sunset. As sunlight's path through the atmosphere becomes lengthier, blue light is dispersed and diminished, allowing the longer wavelength red and orange light to reach us directly, thereby entering our eyes through the atmospheric layer.

The natural world doesn't always perfectly align with our perceptions and the observed phenomena. It's worth pondering; isn't it more productive for us, as Korean expatriates living in a foreign land, to extend support and collaboration to each other rather than engaging in betrayed actions that use others for personal gains, or even criticize them?

Four years into my tenure at Barfoot & Thompson, an unfortunate lawsuit case unfolded, wherein my commission was unjustly taken away through collusion between local mainstream entities and some of our expatriates. Following the guidance of a fellow agent in the office, I initiated a claim for reimbursement in the High Court. This incident transpired as following chronological order, but some of the parties' names involved remained anonymous for various reasons:

In the middle of 2003, I took on the task of finding suitable properties in concert with DJ's continuous instructions. I physically introduced a vacant land of approximately 2,010 square meters used for parking at 20 Shortland St, Auckland CBD, to DJ, specifically to the local president Mr. Seo, and assistant Park.

In mid-March 2004, I presented the same property once again to the purchaser, Mr. Seo. In response to his request, I conducted thorough research and provided him with all the relevant information.

Upon receiving my information, Mr. Seo attempted to purchase the land for $12 million through me, but the vendor was not willing to sell at that price.

By mid-July 2004, I informed Mr. Seo that the property was officially on the market at around $15 million.

On 20 July 2004, I accompanied the purchaser representatives, including Mr. Seo, Mr. Park, and a site manager, to the property to measure the actual land size and to discuss a potential offer.

On 26 July 2004, I met with Chairman Mr. Huh, Mr. Seo, and Mr. Park at Sky City Hotel. At this meeting, an offer of $12 million was signed by Chairman Mr. Huh and myself, and I subsequently presented this offer to Mr. Cotley of the vendor.

On 27 July 2004, I contacted Mr. Cotley to inquire about the offer's progress. He indicated that he needed to discuss the offer with his directors and promised to provide an update later.

After not hearing back, I reached out to Mr. Cotley again on 29 July 2004, and he informed me that the vendor's counter-offer was $15 million, with a 10% deposit and a settlement date in late December 2004.

I promptly informed Mr. Seo about this counteroffer. Subsequently, on 2 August 2004, Chairman Mr. Huh made a counter-offer at $13 million, and Mr. Cotley changed the price to $14,250,000 in the offer without initializing the change.

On 3 August 2004, Mr. Huh increased the offer to $13.5 million, and Mr. Cotley indicated that the offer was getting close to an agreement.

I informed Mr. Cotley that I would be traveling overseas to address a family matter, and my son, Stephen Shin, would be taking over my role starting the next day. Mr. Cotley acknowledged this arrangement.

On 5 August 2004, Mr. Seo contacted Stephen Shin for updates. The next day, 6 August 2004, Stephen Shin contacted Mr. Cotley and requested that all communication be conducted through him. Mr. Cotley agreed to this request and mentioned that their solicitor had prepared a new agreement for the sale and purchase documentation. At the same time, Stephen Shin collected the existing agreement, which had various offer and counter-offer initials, and handed it over to Mr. Huh, DJ Chairman.

On 12 August 2004, Stephen Shin obtained a fresh new agreement from Mr. Broon, who acted as the vendor's solicitor. After verifying the contents with his branch manager, Mr. Smith, Stephen Shin confirmed the sale price at $13.75 million, with Barfoot & Thompson as the agency inserted in the agreement.

Throughout this negotiation process, Mr. Huh and Mr. Seo exchanged offers and conditions, and translation of relevant documents was provided as needed. However, the situation suddenly took a different turn as the departure date of Chairman Mr. Huh on 27 August 2004, approached.

Starting on 24 August 2004, XYZ, a lawyer working for DJ, became involved in the matter. Leveraging his connections, including his wife and the chairman's *wife, XYZ initiated actions that ultimately led to the existing agreement being removed from Stephen Shin. This was done on the pretext of incorrect contract wording. Simultaneously, XYZ received a new contract from Mr. Broon, the vendor's lawyer.*

On 27 August 2004, shortly before Chairman Mr. Huh's departure, XYZ managed to secure the chairman's signature for $13.75 million. They presented this transaction as if the company's commercial manager Mr. LH had sold the property. Subsequently, XYZ was suspected to have obtained something from Mr. LH under the table, based on this falsified transaction.

Based on the provided information, it appears that I, as a real estate agent, should have been entitled to receive the commission. I introduced the purchaser to the subject property, carried out significant dealings, and was the effective cause of the sale between the vendor and the purchaser.

This aligns with the criteria mentioned in the company manual (section 3(c)(v)), which presumably defines the requirements for entitlement to commission. My actions as an agent directly contributed to the successful negotiation and eventual sale of the property:

"To Qualify for Selling Branch Commission:
All salespeople (including the promotion salesperson) must physically inspect the property with a purchaser or meet the purchaser on-site when access is not available or relevant (faxes, emails, phone calls, and drive-buys don't count even with dealers on the property) except when a purchaser bids at auction or tender and does not inspect with any Barfoot & Thompson salesperson, in which case the listing salesperson receives the selling share..."

In reviewing the events, one can't help but wonder who truly deserved the commission in this situation. As I reflect on the details, it becomes apparent that my claim to the commission is firmly grounded in both literal and legal terms.

According to the company's manual, I fulfilled the necessary criteria for the selling commission: physically I introduced the potential purchaser to the property on-site, initiated the offer process, and continued to manage the negotiations until the deal was finalized.

However, a perplexing twist emerges. Instead of myself, an unrelated third party named Mr. LH who had never met with DJ and was not involved in the transaction received the full commission. This scenario raises an important question: why did this transpire? The answer appears to lie within the realm of socio-cultural dynamics and financial gamesmanship that can overshadow strict legal considerations. In essence, the context and social backdrop might have influenced decisions related to financial gain even before the legal aspects came into play.

The property's seller was a well-established Australian company, holding a considerable influence in the local business landscape. Complicating matters further, the lawyer representing the purchaser exerted significant power over DJ by leveraging personal connections through his spouse and the chairman's wife, who both hailed from the same Korean locality.

Adding to the complexity, key figures within DJ's ranks, including the local president, secretary, and site manager responsible for the buyer's role, hesitated to stand as witnesses, possibly due to apprehensions regarding the chairman's authority. Even within my own professional circles, my office manager refused to step forward as a witness, seemingly under the influence of higher-ups.

Considering these factors, another option of summoning them by force was contemplated, although it ultimately didn't align with the overall circumstances. On top of these, the insurance company responsible for settling the commission, should my claim be upheld, was known to be cagey in such matters, introducing another layer of complexity.

As the lawsuit progressed, it became evident that the longer the battle dragged on, the greater the financial burden on me. At the same time, the intricate web of social and personal factors involved in this situation began to take a toll.

Faced with these complex considerations, my counsel recommend-ed mediation as an alternative to pursue the lawsuit further. This decision was informed by a pragmatic evaluation of the costs, time, and intricacies of these situations.

Ultimately, my experience stands as a testament to the complex nature of real-world situations. Legal battles are not solely shaped by the laws; they can also be influenced by interpersonal relationships, societal norms, cultural elements, and even other factors.

This underscores the intricate interplay between legal justice and broader sociocultural dynamics, emphasizing the challenges inherent in navigating such intricate scenarios. On 18 October 2005, I received a pivotal letter from my legal counsel. He ultimately advised me that pursuing a compromise settlement could prove to be a more beneficial course of action compared to bearing potential costs and uncertainties associated with a trial:

Strengths of Your Case
Your case has several strong merits that can work in your favor. The chronological sequence of events outlined in the statement of claim presents a compelling narrative that underscores the significant effort and time you and your son dedicated to the matter. The fact that you personally introduced the property to the purchaser and were actively involved in the process of facilitating the sale establishes a strong argument that you were the effective cause of the sale.

The repeated instructions from Mr. Huh to pursue the sale and the correspondence with Mr. Cotley, who engaged with you as the purchaser's agent, further support your position. Your company will have to acknowledge that you played a crucial role at the request of the purchaser's chairman.

Your credibility is bolstered by the likelihood that your evidence will be accepted by the Judge as accurate and reliable. The presence of documentary evidence substantiating many aspects of your claims adds weight to your case. Importantly, your branch manager's potential testimony, if subpoenaed, could provide additional support. The manager's correspondence with the company director indicates his belief that you deserve at least 50% of the commission, which he may need to acknowledge in court.

Moreover, there is a chance, albeit risky, of challenging the authenticity of certain documents, such as the July 13, 2004 letter from the seller to LH and the alleged August 10, 2004 offer that LH obtained signatures for. Demonstrating inconsistencies or falsehoods in LH's case could significantly undermine his credibility, especially given the vagueness and lack of conviction in his existing "evidence."

The Potential for Settlement

Engaging in a public trial on these matters may not be desirable for your company, particularly considering the potential involvement of your branch manager as a witness. A public dispute of this nature could have negative implications for your company's reputation in the marketplace and its overall relationship with the purchaser. These factors make it likely that your company would prefer to avoid a trial and may be more open to exploring a settlement.

In summary, your case has strong merits, including a well-documented chronology of events, your active involvement in the sale process, and the potential for supporting witnesses and evidence. Considering the risks associated with a trial and the potential impact on your company's reputation, a settlement could be a pragmatic approach to resolving the matter.

Challenges in Your Case

There are a number of quite significant difficulties and I think it is important to set these out at this stage so that you can consider whether to try hard to achieve a settlement as opposed to going to trial. If your preference is to proceed to trial, it is important that you do so with full knowledge of potential risks. Almost every case in the court involves significant risks (which is the great majority of them settled before trial) and almost every litigant has to carry out difficult cost versus benefit assessments. This risk applies to your company as well, but as a plaintiff, you have the onus of proof.

The first difficulty is that LH was allegedly running two separate campaigns, one is by you and another is by himself, Mr. Huh did not want his Auckland staff to know he was doing so. Although the Judge may find much of LH's material provided to the director is vague and unsatisfactory.

The second significant difficulty is the fact that Mr. Cotley, a representative of the vendor, will support Mr. LH's evidence.

The third difficulty is Mr. XYZ. He too will give strong evidence supporting Mr. LH as the principal operating real estate agent in the transaction. Mr. XYZ's personal hostility towards you is well known. We may or may not be able to use that to reduce his credibility but evidence from the purchaser's own solicitor, he has written corroboration of his case by the vendor and purchaser's solicitor.

The fourth difficulty is the lack of active cooperation and support from Mr. Huh, Seo, and Park. In a situation where a sales agent needs to establish that he was able to effectively cause the sale, the most powerful evidence to support that assertion would normally come from the purchaser. The buyer's representatives are the best people to confirm all of the steps taken by you and the fact that you were the operating sales agent and the person who effectively brought about the sale. While it is possible that you will obtain the evidence of Mr. Seo and Park under subpoena. More importantly, there is a major area of uncertainty about What they will say under cross-examination. The buyer's representatives may not be sufficiently strong or clear to provide unequivocal support for your case.

A further difficulty with your case is that you did not obtain a signed listing agreement from the vendor (this is the same as Mr. LH). Also, another negative aspect of the case is the fact that Mr. LH and Mr. XYZ are criticizing your professional competence in relation to selling large commercial property (I learned better and huge knowledge from another firm).

You are dealing primarily with the company's insurers. They have deep pockets and will take a hard-nosed approach to the case. They won't pay money easily. Some of the aspects of the case that are of concern to you may not be given much weight by the Judge. The Judge will view the matter in a strict commercial light.

While you may well be correct that there has been impropriety between Mr. LH, Mr. Cotley, and Mr. XYZ, the Judge is unlikely to attach any weight to this unless it can be proved to a high degree of reliability. In practice, your only real opportunity to expose the real motivation of XYZ, LH, and Cotley is under cross-examination at trial. It is risky to assess the outcome of a case on the basis of cross-examination. As experienced and shrewd professional operators, those persons are likely to hold their ground well in the witness box.

Recommendations
However, it is important that you understand the risks involved in proceeding to trial. This is not where success can be guaranteed. If the Judge is confronted with a strong unified body of evidence between Cotley, XYZ, and LH, he may find that you have not made out a case for any of the commissions. In my view, the costs versus the risks make exploring settlement a sensible option. I believe you are better to have a commission settlement rather than to face the costs and uncertainties of trial and the possibility of not succeeding and having to pay your company's costs.

Following his advice, I engaged in further discussions with my counsel, considering the costs, risks, and the likely outcomes of the settlement conference. Recognizing that the insurance company might not offer a substantial settlement and the challenges of facing opposing parties with carefully constructed evidence, I decided to proceed with the settlement conference. This conference was held on 28 April 2006, nearly two years after the completion of the deal.

On the day of the settlement conference, all the parties involved, including plaintiff parties (me and my counsel), defendant parties, and insurance party, convened under the jurisdiction of a High Court Judge. At the beginning of the conference, the Judge directed a question to our company's director about how I would be treated if I, as the plaintiff, were to lose the case. The director's response indicated that he would retain my status as an agent due to my dedication and commitment to the work.

As the conference unfolded, LH's evidence came under scrutiny. His statements lacked consistency with regard to timing and details, leading to admonishment from the Judge. During the cross-examination conducted by my counsel, he struggled to provide coherent answers, leading the Judge to question the accuracy of his observations and truthfulness.

In the afternoon session, LH was conspicuously absent from the witness stand. The defendant's lawyer offered a vague explanation, attributing LH's absence to personal matters. This development raised suspicions about the circumstances of his departure from both the company and the courtroom.

After nearly two years of legal proceedings, the discussions of the amount of lost commission resulted in multiple rounds of offers and counter-offers exchanged between my counsel and the defendant's lawyer. While the final settlement amounts fell short of my desired sum, I took pride in not yielding to their tactics.

Throughout this process, I retained all the documents exchanged over those years, storing them in two boxes beneath my desk to substantiate the validity of my position as the plaintiff.

Meanwhile, during the initial commission lawsuit, in an attempt to conceal their misconduct, the chairman of DJ replaced the existing director, Mr. Seo, with a new one, Mr. Sohn. I felt sympathy for Mr. Seo for standing by my side.

Drawing from a soccer analogy akin to G. Hiddink's advice of finding joy in the game even during challenging times, I devised a strategy to unveil DJ and their lawyer's misdeeds by utilizing another approach.

I immediately approached the newly coming director and presented the other opportunity to jointly sell another development property. To execute this strategy, I collaborated with other commercial agents from DZT International, a tactic aimed at disproving Mr. XYZ's prior criticism of my perceived inability to sell large commercial properties.

My hidden purpose in approaching them was to find out how Mr. XYZ would orchestrate at this time the deal on behalf of DJ. The sequence of events in introducing the subject property to the new director, unfolded as follows (Some of the parties' names involved remained anonymous for various reasons.):

This vacant land, approximately 5,225 square meters in size, was also utilized for parking purposes at 85-89 Greys Avenue in Auckland Downtown. The events related to this property transpired as follows:

On August 5, 2005, I received an instruction from the newly appointed director to identify land suitable for future development, with the aim of showcasing the chairman's robust ideas for development.

In collaboration with Mr. Mckenna from DZT, I conducted research and gathered relevant information, and presented it to DJ between August 10 and 16, 2005.

By 19 August 2005, I had introduced several potential sites, including 85 Greys Ave, to the current director, the new director (Mr. Sohn), and other managers from DJ. They expressed interest in the property.

On 23 August 2005, Mr. Sohn requested that I draft an offer for $11.7 million. Subsequently, a meeting was arranged at the office of their lawyer, Mr. XYZ, to discuss the offer before its official signing.

During the meeting, attended by myself, Chris from DZT, the current director (Seo), the new director (Sohn), and other representatives from DJ, Mr. XYZ unexpectedly invited Mr. Nieuwkup, the first mortgagee and vendor, to join the gathering. This move was made to construct a convoluted deal.

As the meeting commenced, Mr. XYZ made a startling statement, suggesting that the property had already been sold for $15 million. He questioned why Chris and I were attempting to sell the property to DJ at a lower price.

Mr. Nieuwkup then elaborated on the details, claiming that a contract had been formed at $15 million, with an escape clause tied to a valuation of $18 *million. This clause, according to Mr. Nieuwkup, was unreliable due to the property's failed auction attempt where it didn't garner any interest even at a starting bid of $12 million.*

Mr. Nieuwkup's intent was to achieve $15 million due to two mortgages on the property: a $13 million mortgage with Harbour Group and a $2 million mortgage with Bridgeland, totaling $15 million.

Despite repeated requests from DJ, DZT, and myself during the meeting, both Mr. Nieuwkup and Mr. XYZ declined to provide evidence supporting their claims.

On August 24, 2005, Colin from DZT and I managed to secure an offer for $11.7 million, which was signed by Mr. Sohn. Negotiations were then initiated with the second mortgagee (who we were representing).

On 2 September 2005, we escalated negotiations directly with the first mortgagee, Mr. Nieuwkup, offering $13.5 million. In response, they counter-offered at $15.5 million.

Amidst these negotiations, DJ's chairman arrived in Auckland with his wife to make a decision. However, in a last-minute twist, the involvement of Mr. XYZ's wife and the chairman's wife complicated matters. Both women skillfully manipulated the situation, ultimately resulting in an agreement being reached at $15.05 million, signed by Mr. Huh through Mr. XYZ, their company's lawyer.

I couldn't help but wonder if there was a conflict of interest between the personal actions of the lawyer and their role as representatives for DJ in these property deals. The husband-and-wife duo appeared to have employed a similar approach for this deal as they had done for the first property at 20 Shortland Street.

I speculated about the selling agent used for this deal, perhaps LH Huker or another unknown agent. Receiving news of this deal from DJ employees, I took prompt action by sending letters to my office manager and company director to assert our rightful claim for commission. I learned that the DZT International Director had also proposed a joint commission claim to our director.

But this was ultimately dismissed due to various considerations by our director. The calculated commission amount for this sale was substantial, surpassing the first, but I had no authority to decide and thus had to let it go.

What particularly caught my attention was a series of seven emails I had received from someone who identified themselves as 'Justice Sky.' The sender seemed to be in Korea temporarily, using a false identity to communicate with me. Interestingly, they used the name 'Han' to address me, as if they didn't know me well. While they claimed their intention was to help me, I didn't heed their advice. I had a vague inkling of who they might be, but I dismissed them after secretly saving the emails.

After the DJ chairman's departure on 15 Sep 2005, I proactively wrote a letter to the new director of DJ, urging him to address the issues that had transpired and seek resolution. Unluckily, I received no response at all. These experiences taught me a valuable lesson: self-awareness can lead to a deeper understanding of others.

It was a surprising turn of events to witness the chairman who had caused me so much trouble resurfacing on YouTube in Korea in March 2020. He became embroiled in a king-labor case in Korea, shedding light on his questionable conduct.

After acquiring both properties, the chairman's relationship with his wife deteriorated, leading to the sale of the acquired sites without any development. The employees who had once flattered him had all departed, and even the lawyer who had manipulated the situations had long gone. Reflecting on these things, I couldn't help but ponder whether our present lives are shaped by our past actions. The twists and turns of life often reveal the consequences of our decisions made years ago: Karma will tell us the truth.

VII

Affection and Regret

VII
Affection and Regret

"Life's Reflections"

Life's endless flow, unceasing,
A fleeting journey with no pausing,
A vanishing tale once it's told.
Youth's brilliance dimmed by passing years,
Friends' voices lost to time's deafening hum,
Lingering in slumber within memories past.
Faces I yearned to behold, fading silently.
A whisper of sorrow,
Twilight's embrace drew near.
I've pressed onward until the last,
The final act now dawning.
Escaping the tempest of survival,
Passion's fire now cooled,
What is life but a canvas for me?
Mine alone to navigate, to bear.
A breath left for dreams,
Cherish kin and kindred souls,
A meeting brief, a dance with fate.
Let sickness and tears evade,
Live fully until the end's embrace.

In this chapter I'd like to narrate my heartful affections and regrets: every moment spent with you is a treasure I hold close to my heart, woven with laughter, shared dreams, and the consolation of your unwearying presence. Your kindness and understanding have touched my soul in ways words can't fully express, and I am forever grateful for the love we share.

Also, I recall the weight of regret rests heavily upon my shoulders as I reflect on the choices and paths I've taken, realizing that some of them led me away from the moments and connections I held dear. If only I could have rewinded the time, I would embrace those opportunities more fully, savoring every fleeting second and ensuring that no chance for happiness slipped through my fingers.

Friendships could give us a chance to enrich our lives. Also, it could provide us with an unknown sauce to our well-being, but it's not easy to adequately keep friendships. It's important to understand the value of social connection in our lives; and what we should do to develop and nurture lasting friendships.

Friends could help us celebrate good times, support bad times, prevent loneliness, and give us company. They can also increase our sense of belonging to sociality, or they can boost our happiness; they can reduce our stress.

Friendship is an interpersonal relationship of reciprocal affection between two people. It is a stronger form of interpersonal ties than acquaintances such as a classmate, neighbor, or colleague in the office. It is sometimes restricted to a small number of very deep relationships; other cases are composed of many friends.

Although there are many forms of friendship, some of which may vary from place to place, certain characteristics are present in many such bonds. Such features include choosing to be with one another, enjoying time spent together, and being able to engage in a positive and supportive role with one another.

Many of us find it hard to develop new friends and keep up with existing friends. Friends may take a back seat to other priorities, such as work or caring for children or aging parents. We may have grown apart due to changes in our lives or interests. Or maybe we've moved to a new community and haven't yet found a way to meet people. Developing good friends and nurturing them, takes our investment.

In any social relationship between two parties, such as friends, families, relatives, or partners, the measure of affection given and taken, could be seldom exactly equal. One side always cared more or less than the other. In my case, I have received more than I have given them. I haven't had enough resources to give someone: born small figure, poverty, small pocket; whatever adversity confronts me, the only thing I can do is be ready to go through it with them.

One day afternoon, while having lunch at a restaurant in downtown Auckland, I overheard the conversation of two young friends sitting next to me. Listening to their chats, I had an opportunity to once again

136

retrieve the meaning of friendship; what is a true friend they said to each other:

Friend A: Are you sure I am your true friend?

Friend B: Of course. But why are you suddenly asking about that? Who else would consider you a true friend without me?

Friend A: Oh, well. I did it because I wanted to know whether you sincerely knew my difficulties and could help me when I am in trouble. However, a red light came on for the business I'm doing now.

Friend B: When you're sick, how can I say I'm your friend if I can't share the pain with you? When you need me, I'm confident to come by at any time, so don't worry, continue the business you've been doing, don't lose courage, and do your best. I'll help you. So, won't you help me too when I need it?

Friend A: Thank you, my friend. I am proud to have a friend like you. I'm lucky too. Let's raise our glasses and toast! With your words, I will continue my business to the end with courage and confidence.

Listening to the dialogue of two young friends during lunch at a restaurant, I couldn't help but reflect on the meaning of genuine friendships. Their conversation stirred memory and contemplation about the significance of having a true friend by one's side.

Looking back, I've come to recognize that had I been really fortunate enough to have a friend like the one they were describing during my journey at Impression Real Estate, I might never have faltered in the face of challenges, but rather confronted them with an unyielding fortitude. This retrospection has opened my eyes to the sincere worth of a true friend: one who can offer solace, lighten burdens, and stand by me during times of illness and adversity.

Our journey is lifelong and so often requires companionship. However, forging and maintaining deep and useful friendships is no easy task. It dawned on me that before seeking such companionship, I must first be willing to reciprocate as a good friend. To be a true friend,

I must take the initiative to approach others and be prepared to offer more than I expect in return.

Acknowledging our inherent selfishness as humans, I recognized the need to counteract this by actively contributing to friendships. On top of these, it's crucial to cultivate relationships with friends who uplift and support us even in our absence. In a world fueled by unstoppable competition, the power of unseen goodwill can work wonders.

Genuine friendships are a treasure. They require effort and sincerity from both sides. The conversation with my young friends prompted me to reflect on the essence of friendships and the qualities that make such connections invaluable in the tapestry of life. It reminded me of the importance of genuinely caring about one another to establish a foundation of trust. This mutual trust extends to steady support, even when faced with gossip or attempts to sow discord.

Ultimately, maintaining lasting friendships requires busy effort and periodic nourishment. It's akin to tending to a garden, where we must ensure our relationships receive the attention they deserve to flourish.

As I reflect on my past friendships, I consider the roles I've played in each of them. I recognize that I've been both a source of positivity and occasional shortcomings. My approach is to offer unconditional love and equality to everyone I encounter. This outlook transcends cultural and racial boundaries, embodying a sense of cosmopolitanism that distinctions between black and white fade into insignificance.

♥

During my early years in primary school, there was a young girl who lived in a neighboring village along the route to and from school. Despite being a couple of years younger than me, we were classmates.

As the youngest among my siblings, I often yearned for a younger sister who would call me "Oppa" which meant older brother in Korean. She happily addressed me as Oppa and would tag along whenever I walked by. Our bond was strong, and I would frequently visit her home on my way to and from school. Her family members embraced me as one of their own. They treated me like family, and I felt a deep sense of connection with them.

On the morning of January 12, 2021, I awoke from a dream that transported me back to my primary school days, over six decades ago. This was a recurring theme in my Dreamline reflections:

As I entered her house, I spotted her sitting in the yard, doing some activity. My heart swelled with happiness at the sight of her. I came to her with the intention of giving her a warm embrace, but she seemed a little unsure. In a tender gesture, she beckoned to her child who was standing nearby, calling out, "Cheulguya!" Her child obediently came and stood between us.

With a curious innocence, the child inquired, "Are you my mom's friend?" This question seemed to create a barrier between us, causing a pause in our interaction. It was only after this moment that she finally addressed me as "Oppa," the endearing term that had characterized our relationship in the past. And then, abruptly, I woke up from the dream, leaving the lingering emotions of the past behind.

During my visit to Busan to see family and friends in July 2022, we organized a reunion that brought us all together. Meeting with some of our old classmates from primary school, we certainly decided to share a meal at a local restaurant. The passage of time was evident on her face wrinkles had etched their lines, her eyes seemed to have lost their former sparkle, and her voice quivered.

As I observed these changes, a sense of unease gripped me; it was a stark realization that the youthful beauty I had once known had faded. Nevertheless, my affection for her as a dear sister remained unchanged. Positioned *fourth from the left in the third row, below photo taken in February 1965* while graduating.

Shin Kija shared my age. Growing up in our village, our life paths were intertwined, and she began school alongside me, entering later due to circumstances. From the very first day, she naturally assumed the role of my closest friend and partner: *standing fourth from the right in the second row*.

Whenever interactions with girls became complicated, she was there, offering her assistance right in the middle. Whether it was during my time as class monitor, guiding our classmates, or when she sensed my interest in a girl, she would discreetly intervene.

After our time in primary school, when I moved on to middle school in Busan, she too made the journey to our city, brought by my elder sister-in-law. Given a job, she visited our home in Busan frequently. Reflecting on those days, I realized she had always been a companion and, sometimes, a rival in various aspects of my life.

Graduation photo of Woongok primary school, February 1965, I was standing 5th from right, end row

Much of her appearance had retained the features from our primary school days, though her voice trembled as she spoke. Witnessing this, I couldn't help but inwardly admit the inevitability of time's passage. I sighed quietly within myself, approving that no one can triumph over the march of years: a sentiment I carefully hid.

The very next day, we set off on another journey together with the intention of attending the primary school reunion held in another city. The class reunion brought a mix of emotions, including the somber news that Ahn Younghee (*second from the right in the second row*), who was often spotted by her runny nose, had already passed away. I remembered her as someone with large, somewhat timid eyes, and she embodied a shy and introverted nature. The news of her demise touched a chord within me, and tears welled up in my eyes.

On that particular day, I found myself immersed in memories of Ahn Sunnam, who lived in a different village. She had once taken on pivotal roles in a school play during the autumn festival in our first year. As we diligently rehearsed for it, our connection deepened over the span of a couple of weeks. The intimacy that developed between us sparked envy among a few of the other girls in our class.

On reflection about the past, I found myself seated side by side during the reunion photo (*5th from the left, in the 3rd row*). Her trademark bobbed hair, just as charming as it was six decades ago, still adorned her. Despite my reluctance to hear some of the stories she recounted in the car, her magnetic presence remained undiminished. Even now, as I pen down this narrative from my room, I frequently find myself engaged in phone talks with her, bridging the distance between us in Korea.

♥

Upon completing my attendance at the rural primary school in February 1965, I relocated to Busan. Slowly but surely, the connections with my former classmates began to fade away, as the technological advances of today were not available back then. Contacts primarily relied on letters and pen pals, offering limited means of maintaining our ties. With the passage of time and the move to a different city, I inevitably grew apart from my childhood friends. I forged new connections and intimacy as I navigated the challenges of adolescence.

My vibrant time in Busan marked the transition into adolescence—
a distinct phase of life where I began to explore my personal desires.
This period was characterized by rapid physical growth and profound
psychological change, signifying the transition from child to boyhood
and the journey towards adulthood.

Entering middle school marked a new chapter in my life, and the
first classmate I encountered in the night class was Lee Wunchan, of
many boys, a tall and good-looking lad. Before I met him, I didn't
perceive myself as a small figure; but it was only by meeting him that
I began to have an inferiority complex about my height.

On weekends, I often visited his home village and noticed girls from
the neighborhood lining up behind him, seemingly overlooking me.
Given his charm, it wasn't surprising; he possessed quite a tallness and
handsome face that made him quite appealing to those girls.

We explored Dongbaek Island and Haeundae Beach, girls would trail
along, engaging in innocent talks about naïve love. Sometimes, we
would pause to let them wait outside while we dove underwater to
gather crabs, oysters, scallops, and mussels. We shared our catches
without bothering to wash them first. Diving beneath the water
without goggles, we could easily gather the seaweeds, often not
needing to breathe for 2 or 3 minutes.

During these moments, I noticed that Lee Wunchan seemed a bit
bothered by the attention of his numerous local girlfriends. To ease his
discomfort, I introduced him to my primary school sister, Shin Wedool,
who held me in high regard like a brother as mentioned earlier.

Later on, I discovered that they exchanged pen-pal letters and dated
for a significant period. Unfortunately, due to my demanding business
schedule, I lost track of their news. I could have inquired about it
during our Busan reunion last year, but I refrained from doing so out
of concern for causing offense.

A few years ago, I received an unexpected phone call from Kim
Doosu, a classmate with whom I had shared my journey from the first

142

to third grade in middle school. Surprisingly, he revealed that he had considered me a competitor throughout our time together.

He had embarked on a military career and managed to contact me through a friend residing in New Zealand after a gap of 58 years since our graduation. Presently, we have established a bi-monthly tradition of checking in on each other's well-being and health over the phone.

Whenever we stumble upon good music, quotes, or intriguing YouTube videos on social media, we readily share them without hesitation. During one of our recent conversations, I informed him of my upcoming visit to Korea, and we made a pact to meet in New Zealand next year if the weather permits.

I am unable to forget the indelible impression left by the first teacher I encountered when I entered the middle school night class, clad in the uniform and hat my older brother bestowed upon me after primary school. It almost seems as if destiny conspired to bring teacher Gu Taebong and me together. On the very first day of school, without seeking anyone's counsel, he appointed me as a class monitor. Perhaps an unspoken connection formed between us from the moment our eyes met.

My cherished teacher Gu Taebong continued thereafter to guide me through the night class from 1st to 2nd grade. In the 3rd grade, he elevated me to the daytime class, affording me the opportunity to enter Busan High School. He also orchestrated opportunities for me to work as a private tutor, whenever I sought a part-time job, he was always willing to connect me with tutoring gigs. I harbored a deep desire to express my gratitude for his persistent support.

Several years ago, I visited the school with a heartfelt intention of expressing my gratitude to him. However, upon my arrival, I was met with the unfortunate news that the school had closed its doors due to dwindling enrollment. Regrettably, my mission remained unfulfilled, and I left with a sense of unaccomplished purpose. I often find myself pondering whether he continues to lead a healthy and vibrant life.

♥

On the first day of high school, on 4 March 1969, I was placed in Class Five under the guidance of Teacher Kim Dongchan. It was here that I first met Ha Sangjo (*6th from the right, end row, far earlier photo*). Our friendships endured until my departure for New Zealand in 1993. Ha Sangjo and I shared the common experience of being raised by a single mom.

The only distinction was that he was an only child, which could lead one to perceive him as a tenacious and perhaps even stubborn individual. It was evident that this slight stubbornness in his demeanor stemmed from his rational confidence. He possessed a personality that strongly

opposed injustice and resisted any form of inequality.

Upon return to the sophomore in March 1996, I wholeheartedly dedicated myself to preparing for the civil servant exam. However, my efforts were abruptly halted when I met an unexpected dental issue: it left me with no choice but to abandon the exam. It was during this challenging period that Ha Sangjo came to my aid.

After my immigration to New Zealand, he quietly retreated from my life, leaving without a word, as he began his teaching journey at a university. During our time residing in a boarding house near the university, he and I would engage in lengthy discussions about life and philosophy during the evenings. We found comfort in each other's company, and during challenging moments, we would unwind by sharing Korean wine at a local restaurant.

It pains me that I can no longer catch a glimpse of his radiant face, adorned with a smile that revealed his gleaming white teeth. He was renowned for dedicating his entire life to educating future generations, persistently pursuing grassroots economics without ever losing his tireless passion for learning. It's truly disheartening that he had to let go of his aspirations before realizing his ultimate dream: imparting to future generations the profound truth of the relentless tenacity of dandelion roots as they persist against the ground.

Among my high school classmates, I had a friend who made the ultimate sacrifice for the cause of Korean democracy. Kim Beunggon tragically lost his life at the young age of 37, dedicating himself to the pursuit of democratic growth in Korea. Once he entered Seoul University in 1971, he immediately was involved in student activities opposing the oppressive Park Chunghee regime, leading to his repeated arrests.

The following year, he was apprehended as a leader of the Min Youth Demonstration and faced a death sentence. Facing imprisonment and death sentences multiple times while fervently fighting against the regimes of both Park Chunghee and Chun Doohwan, he finally vanished like morning dew.

During my tenure at Saehan Motors, I found solace and connection with him in Busan. It was during this period that he reached out to me. We would often meet at a Japanese restaurant in Busan, discussing the injustices of the current regime and sharing our thoughts while raising our glasses in mutual comfort.

Even as we spoke, it was evident that his body still bore the scars of the beatings he had endured in prison. However, his voice resonated strongly, piercing through the air with unwavering determination. Our conversation left me feeling a deep sense of reflection, realizing how often I had focused on the mundane aspects of daily life.

In his presence, I couldn't help but recognize the stark contrast between his selfless dedication to a greater cause and my own preoccupations. It's imperative that we honor and appreciate individuals like him for their immense sacrifices, as their actions have paved the way for us to enjoy safety and freedom on this earth today.

In December 1976, a pivotal moment unfolded during my train journey to Busan alongside a high school senior named Sagong Sul. We had on the day completed the 19th test, the second round of the civil servant exam in Seoul. As our conversation flowed and drinks were shared, time appeared to vanish unnoticed.

Our dialogue traversed a diverse array of subjects, encompassing the global landscape, livelihoods, democracy, injustice, government policies, student protests, etc. After a substantial amount of time had passed, my senior suggested that we drop the formalities of seniority and address each other using regular terms, despite him being a senior and me being a couple of years older.

However, I firmly declined his proposal, asserting that this shift could not occur. Even though I was born a few years ahead of him, I believed that the existing system of respect between seniors and juniors within a school would remain unchanged.

Subsequently, the senior took breaks from his studies, returning to school intermittently. He actively participated in student protests against the Chun Doohwan regime and often experienced cycles of imprisonment. During this period, he sustained a back injury from a prison beating, and he passed away some time ago. Fortunately, his contributions to the 5.18 Democratization Movement were recognized, and he was laid to rest at the Gwangju National Democratic Cemetery on 12 October 2011.

♥

It was the day of the first ceremony I attended at Busan National University. I packed my back early in the morning leaving my tutoring house and arrived at the campus. On that day, I encountered Yeo Sangbum in my class. At first sight, he introduced himself as hailing from Hadong, close to Namhae Province in Gyeongsangnamdo.

From that initial encounter, our relationship quickly deepened, with our first impression leaving a strong impact. As my freshman came to an end, I had to fulfill my army service. During this time, he made a promise to personally watch over my girl until my return after three years of service.

When I visited campus during a vacation midway through, I learned that I couldn't meet her. He tearfully apologized for not being able to uphold his promise. I reassured him that there was no need for apologies and felt more sorry for him than anything else. Don't worry, Sangbeum, it wasn't your fault. That's just the way life goes.

After discharging from military service, I encountered Sangbeum again, and this time he was grappling with mental illness. He shared that he couldn't enter his sister's house in Busan due to a fear that his brother-in-law might harm him. I accompanied him to his sister's house on several occasions.

Since settling in New Zealand, I've been continuously searching for him, but I've yet to receive any news of his whereabouts. Sangbeum, if you come across this message, please reach out to me as soon as possible. I would love to share the twists and turns of my life since we parted ways.

As a sophomore returning to school in March 1976, I held immense respect for three professors who had guided me throughout my five years of university and postgraduate school: Professor Lee Wanyoung, Professor Kim Hakryo, and Professor Jeong Kwonsub were instrumental in shaping both academic and personal experiences.

Professor Kim was the son of a distinguished figure who had previously served as a president of the same university, hailing from a prestigious educational lineage. He not only accurately assessed my academic abilities but also didn't hesitate to reprimand me if he noticed any shortcomings. He played a pivotal role in helping me secure a scholarship and even officiated at my wedding. His wisdom and humility inspired me to respect Professor Lee Wanyoung, despite his own significant accomplishments, showcasing his virtues.

Professor Lee, renowned for his role in crafting civil exam papers, was exceptionally helpful in preparing me for the exam. He praised me consistently for my achievement in front of other students, regardless of my whereabouts. Even though due to timing constraints, he couldn't officiate at my wedding, which was truly regrettable.

Among the three professors, Dr. Jeong Kwonsub held a prominent position as the dean of the Law School. I interacted with him the most during those five years, as I served as the leader of the law school reading room. He had a keen interest in the reading room's affairs, often summoning me to his office to discuss its status. At one point, he introduced me to a female assistant working under him. Unfortunately,

147

I wasn't accepted by her parents due to my shortness. Interestingly, it seemed that Dr. Jeong hadn't even considered my height as a factor.

These three professors played pivotal roles in shaping my academic journey and instilling valuable life lessons, and I will always hold them in high regard.

Friendship manifests in diverse forms as we navigate social life post-graduation. While these bonds may vary based on location, they often share defining characteristics. These features can unexpectedly enrich our lives, serving as a source of well-being.

In the Talmud, there is wisdom to be found regarding the landscape of friendships and the dynamics it entails. Whether it is reflecting on the bonds between three friends or searching into the teachings that emphasize the significance of human connection, these insights offer valuable guidance on the art of building and maintain- ing important relationships:

One day a man receives an intimidating summons from a king, compelling him to appear before the monarch. Fearing this situation, the man decides to reach out to his friends for assistance. He has three friends with different levels of closeness to him.

The first friend, the closest of the three, disappoints the man by refusing his request without offering any explanation. This showcases that even close friends might not always be reliable or willing to help, which can be disheartening.

The second friend, who is also close but not as intimate as the first, agrees to accompany the man, albeit only up to the door of the palace. This response portrays a willingness to provide support, albeit with limitations.

Lastly, the third friend, who is not as close to the man, happily agrees to accompany him and even expresses his intention to speak well of him to the king. This unexpected response highlights how sometimes, those whom we least expect can offer sincere assistance and unexpected acts of kindness.

Ultimately, this story underscores the unpredictable nature of friendships and the varying degrees of support that friends may offer in different circumstances. It serves as a reminder while close friends might not always be dependable, others might pleasantly surprise us with their real willingness to help.

Throughout our lives, we encounter a multitude of individuals in various contexts, including our homes, schools, workplaces, military service, hobbies, and religious communities. Many of these initial meetings occur by chance, but over time, chance encounters can develop into useful relationships and even fate if nurtured.

To transform a chance encounter into a lasting friendship, it's essential to uncover commonalities that can serve as the foundation of deeper connection. Identifying shared interests, values, or experiences provides a basis for engaging in conversations that can bring two people closer. True closeness often requires time and the willingness to engage in meaningful dialogue.

Often, friendships can remain uneventful during calm and routine periods of life, but it's during challenging times that the strength of these bonds truly shines. Through difficult experiences, friendships are put to the test, allowing us to both recognize and appreciate the invaluable support that true friends provide. In this way, enduring friendships are forged through shared experiences, understanding, and mutual support.

♥

As graduation approached, I found myself deeply concerned about my future career path. While I had a strong desire to continue my studies and prepare for exams, financial constraints made it difficult. The thought of giving up on education was disheartening, so I decided to find a way to earn money during the day while pursuing studies at night. I applied for a job at Saehan Motor, a car sales company, in the central office located in Busan.

On the first day, I met a superstar who would profoundly impact my outlook on my life: sales manager, Park Taeho. Observing his headship

149

over the team, I was immediately struck by his kind and admirable personality. In every aspect of his interactions with subordinates, his management and perspective left a lasting impression on me. I was determined to learn from him, to emulate the way he approached life. This influence went beyond the workplace. I married my wife soon after joining the company, and we even became next-door neighbors. Furthermore, I made a decision to convert to Catholicism, a faith I hadn't previously considered, largely inspired by his beliefs.

Since shifting to New Zealand nearly 30 years ago, I haven't had many opportunities to see him. However, during a short visit to Korea just before the last year, I was able to reunite with him. Despite his physical appearance remaining largely unchanged, I noticed a slight shift in his mindset. This reminded me that time can bring about internal transformations that are not always visible externally. During this visit, I also reconnected with some of our mutual friends from that time, including Joo Chelsu, Ko Sihwan, and Hyeon Huseong.

♥

Since arriving here in New Zealand, one of my closest friends Steve Clark and I shared the bond of having navigated through challenging times around the same period in our lives. Sadly, he departed from this world not too long ago, leaving a void that I deeply feel. Whenever I attended events organized by him with his local friends, he proudly introduced me as his "Korean brother," highlighting our firm relations.

Our initial meeting occurred at the office of a property development firm where he held the position of sales manager. It was during a project involving the conversion of a flour mill factory into apartments and commercial parking, located near our office. This collaboration provided me with the opportunity to handle the sale of these projects. Through this mutual undertaking, we crossed paths frequently hand in hand, gradually forging a stronger and closer bond.

Our friendships faced challenges in their early stages due to the differences in our cultural backgrounds, shaped by where and how we had grown up and lived. Despite these initial barriers, both of us have weathered our fair share of hardships allowing us to connect on a profound level. This shared fashionable compassion and empathy formed a bridge between our different social upbringings.

From then on, our interactions became more frequent, involving heart-to-heart conversations, shared meals, and lighthearted banter. Tragically, he recently passed away due to natural causes, leaving behind his cherished daughters and grandchildren. At this moment, my words seem inadequate; it's a time of quiet reflection and honoring his memory.

I have also a couple of other Kiwi friends, whose names are kept anonymous for privacy reasons. They once held prominent positions in significant companies. These individuals stood out as leaders of some of the largest companies in New Zealand during a certain period.

The first one I'd like to mention is Dave Hartfield. His journey began as a plumber before he carved into the world of business. He initially found big success by converting an old office building into flats in downtown Auckland, a path that other developers have also taken.

As Auckland experienced an influx of migrants, his focus shifted towards earnestly constructing apartments, becoming a notable success story in the realm of property development. Our initial encounter can be traced back to my involvement in selling off-plan units for the Tower Hill Project in 1997. Due to financial constraints, the pre-selling phase under developer Kim Suhyun came to an end. He had no choice but to transfer the project to him, who was then actively engaged in a property project. This turn of events, while marked by project sales challenges, paradoxically led to the emergence of our close friendship.

Notably, Dave had achieved a substantial record by doing expansive Princes Wharf Apartments, strategically located along the Auckland waterfront. Selling these high-end units at a favorable moment resulted in significant financial gains. But this tale also encompasses a mix of triumphs and misfortunes that eventually intertwine. As a result, his fortunes took a turn, leading to bankruptcy and challenging times.

However, little did anyone foresee that this success would pave the way for his descent into a downward spiral. He succumbed to gaming, relationships, and junkies, ultimately culminating in the declaration of his bankruptcy.

During the early stages of the Princes Wharf project, Dave earnestly requested that he would take my elder son under his wing to provide him with hands-on experiences in construction industry. I was most delighted to accept, and Stephen gained valuable insights through this association.

Our mutual relationships developed in different ways. A few years ago, Dave acquired our clifftop house overlooking the water, a property that my family had previously lived in. He now shares this residence with his family.

Occasionally, when he faces financial stress, he reaches out to my eldest son for urgent help. Hearing this, I find myself expressing my disapproval and questioning why the substantial profits from his previous business endeavors weren't managed more prudently, just as I faced challenges with the mismanagement of Impression.

This pattern is not exclusive to Dave alone; in fact, it seems to be a recurring theme among many successful businessmen I've met here. A common trajectory emerges: after achieving business success, a course of events unfolds that involves entanglements with casinos, partner relationships, and doping, ultimately culminating in financial challenges over time.

Nevertheless, there's a remarkable exception in the case of Anton Butt, a well-known property developer. I find it intriguing to engage in a comparative analysis while contemplating my interaction with these two individuals. Both encountered insolvency for similar reasons, especially their inability to fulfill debt obligations. However, a conspicuous divergence becomes apparent in how they have confronted this testing phase. This contrast prompts us to further explore this phenomenon.

Dave, unfortunately, has not well managed to rebound from the aftermath of his insolvency, enduring ongoing financial difficulties.

Conversely, Anton has showcased his resilience by actively pursuing new business ventures.

While an individual's competence undoubtedly plays a pivotal role in these outcomes, I am inclined to believe that the social background to which they belong has also significantly influenced their respective trajectories.

Dave originated from Western European blood, while Anton is an integral part of the Jewish community. Upon even closer scrutiny, it becomes evident that Anton's capacity to weather the storm and forge ahead with new business endeavors may be attributed to a confluence of factors, including his own sagacity and determination.

In contrast, Dave's struggles could be influenced by a combination of diverse factors, encompassing personal choices, societal norms, and the availability of support systems. His experience, stemming from a different cultural backdrop, might have intersected with broader social dynamics in a manner that imposed greater hurdles to recovery.

This comparison underscores the intricate interplay between an individual's intrinsic qualities, cultural milieu, and external factors.

Anton's journey commenced when he was a university student as my family settled in New Zealand. He stepped into a well-seasoned and accomplished businessman. His upbringing in a Jewish family, often cast in the limelight of newspapers, profoundly contributed to shaping him as an astute property developer. His capacity to grasp intricate details and concepts was genuinely extraordinary.

Nevertheless, in our casual conversation on the street, his demeanor remained one of unwavering respect, a testament to his commendable character. There was a wealth of wisdom to be gleaned from him. Noteworthy is Anton's intrinsic generosity, particularly evident in his interactions with business partners. His exchanges were permeated with warmth and respect, a true reflection of his compassionate nature.

Our initial encounter occurred during my early days at Bailess real estate firm, with my connection in selling the Apartment project he had launched. At the first time, skeptics doubted the project's potential for success, yet he persevered and triumphed. It was a 38-story, sophisticated hotel and residential mixed units.

Despite financial setbacks, he remained undeterred in moving head. He astutely noted that financial difficulties, while they often stemmed from external circumstances, did not alter his intrinsic humanity.

Indeed, Dave Hartfield himself acknowledged that Anton's financial deals were astutely crafted endeavors. Many people found it dare to comprehend the intricacies of these transactions. But Anton displayed an unwavering willingness to take substantial risks. His remarkable ability and resourcefulness equipped him to navigate any setbacks he encountered.

He stood out as someone who possessed the capability to overcome challenges and difficulties. His presence and contribution were greatly valued in New Zealand, and he was seen as a valuable asset to the country.

Ryong Kevin holds a distinct and significant place in my memories as I reflect upon the Korean community in New Zealand. In my real estate career, I have been given the privilege to meet and forge connections with various individuals, with some of these encounters evolving into professional partnerships, and on certain occasions, blossoming into profound personal friendships. Among these individuals, Kevin stands out: he had once taken on the role of president within the Auckland Korean Association.

Our initial encounter took place at a motel in Pannell, Auckland. At that juncture, he was in the process of preparing a residence for his family in New Zealand. After perusing various housing options, he settled on one particular house. When it came time to place an offer due to a shortage in the down payment, he hesitated. Observing this, I proposed the idea of personally covering the deposit on his behalf, allowing him to reimburse me later.

It seemed that my gesture established a sense of trust and fellowship between us, as he continued to involve me in his real estate dealings thereafter. He exhibited immense dedication when he served as the president of the Auckland Korean Association. He invested a considerable effort, even utilizing his personal funds, for the acquisition of the office.

Sadly, his dream of fully realizing this endeavor was never achieved, as he passed away in solitude on 12 July 2022, at his farmhouse in Hamilton during a brief visit I made to Korea.

Fortunately, I had the opportunity to see him before departing for Korea and had the privilege of gifting him my book. Following my return to NZ, I endeavored to maintain contact with his cherished son, albeit with some difficulty. I await the day when he reaches out to me, and I hope that Kevin found contentment in his life while he was among us. May he rest in peace!

Another significant figure is Elder Kwak Joongsong, with whom we consistently stayed in touch and convened to share our respective paths. Our gatherings have transformed into a routine occurrence, happening almost once a month. Almost every four days, Elder Kwak sends me a lengthy excerpt from the Bible, regardless of whether I read it or not. He also serves as an exceptional life mentor to me.

Interestingly, I was not even aware that we both worked for the same company until we crossed paths in New Zealand about 30 years ago. Given that KEPCO had around 45,000 employees at that time, it's certainly understandable that we remained unfamiliar with each other, given our positions in different departments.

My first meeting with the elder was when his family arrived and purchased the initial home. interestingly, their current home marks the third one they have owned. I also facilitated the sale of a house for my eldest daughter after she got married, which became the fourth deal with the elder's family.

The house where the elder's family resides now had an unfortunate leak due to the fault of the previous owner and builder. The elder took a legal suit against him and after nearly three years of litigation, it emerged victorious. However, he didn't receive a single penny in damages from his win and ended up shouldering the costs.

Observing this arduous trial from the sidelines, I found that the elder's religion played a pivotal role in persevering through such challenges. While I provided encouragement and advice to the best of my abilities, I must admit it felt inadequate.

Subsequently, when I sold a house to the elder's eldest daughter, I contributed the entire commission towards the elder's legal expenses. Yet, I recently found myself facing a sincere complaint from the elder: he voiced my disbelief in God. Ironically, despite my lack of faith, the elder extended an invitation for me to be buried next to him in the same cemetery, implying a possible way for me to enter heaven. It's a perplexing gesture, offering me a ticket to heaven despite skepticism.

This week, on the 2nd of May 2023, we finally managed to go fishing on Waiheke Island after a prolonged delay. During the boat ride to the island, we engaged in conversations regarding the translation of a book the elder recently published in Korean into English; and also, discussions about maintaining good health.

The elder took care of all the preparations for fishing, and I was simply to accompany him on the excursion. Even though our fishing expedition wasn't particularly successful, we decided to give it another shot after releasing a few undersized fish back into the sea.

On August 21, 2023, I met with the elder at Commercial Bay in Auckland Downtown. Our conversation covered a wide range of topics, including something that required translation into English. I provided explanations, showing him how to translate using ChatGPT.

Several years ago, I found myself wandering around the University of Auckland campus after a quiet lunch alone. Lost in contemplative thoughts, I observed the expression of passing students, the resilient tree roots that had stood for centuries, and the statues that stood with stoic expressions. At that moment, a phone call interrupted musing. It was a call from a junior colleague, Dr. Ma Samsun, who had been with KEPCO and was currently a professor at Amada University of Science and Technology in Ethiopia.

Meeting at Albert Park on the university campus, we engaged in conversations spanning life, history, time and space, friendship, astrophysics, and more; almost as if we were picking up threads from the past. The interaction was so engaging that I invited him and his wife to my home the following week. We were joined by another friend, Kim Taeheon, a former flight attendant with New Zealand Airlines, and his wife. All together, we shared even more stories over a meal.

The following year, during my visit to Korea to meet friends and family, he managed to take a break from Ethiopia and we met in Seoul. Our conversations picked up where they left off, accompanied by a small drink.

Furthermore, in publishing my first book, "Will Humanity Last Forever?" in Korean and I sought Testimonials, he promptly sent an endorsement via email from Ethiopia. I look forward to spending more time with him once his contract with Amada University in Ethiopia concludes.

Throughout my 13-year tenure at KEPCO, a steadfast and profound friendships emerged: one that endured during and after my time there. This bond was forged with Manager Lee Kiyoung, my connection that grew stronger with each passing day.

Our initial contacts took place at the New Project Department in headquarters in KEPCO in March 1986, and from that point on, our interactions extended far beyond the confines of work matters. Be it personal or professional, we remained in constant communication.

During my time at the Seoul headquarters, which coincided with the rapid escalation of housing prices in anticipation of the 1988 Seoul Olympics, the concept of a residential construction consortium gained traction among workers. It was a collective effort aimed at addressing the soaring housing costs. In collaboration with him who was also part of my department, we endeavored to undertake this venture diligently. Unfortunately, our efforts to secure suitable land for this endeavor were met with obstacles, ultimately leading to its abandonment.

Little did I know that our dream I couldn't realize at the time could persist and evolve until my journey to New Zealand. Reflecting on the role of a true friend, an ideal guidepost emerges: a genuine friend doesn't merely tell you what you want to hear; they communicate what you need to hear. Dispensing candid advice to friends requires a healthy dose of humility and compassion.

Admittedly, you might not always grasp what exactly they require to hear, especially if geographical distance or sporadic communication hinders such understanding. But in the instances when I sought the counsel of good friends, I always took the initiative to reach out to them proactively, rather than waiting for them to initiate contact.

This discipline, I believe, holds the key to nurturing enduring relationships with friends over time: it's a secret source, so to speak, for maintaining strong and lasting connections. Even in the present, he continues to fulfill the same supportive role, just as he did when I was departing.

As years passed, my younger son, who returned from Germany, expressed his desire to pursue soccer at Yonsei University. As this journey unfolded, he sought admission through the university's foreigner recruitment program, and during this process, Kiyoung proved to be indispensable. He willingly undertook the arduous task of translating all of his English records into Korean and ensuring their notarization.

When I took the initiative to achieve autonomy for the computer business domain separated from KEPCO, my friend Kiyoung and I joined forces once again. Our collaboration facilitated the seamless efforts in this endeavor, resulting in the establishment of a subsidiary firm by us. Since my family and I embarked on an immigration journey to New Zealand, there lingered a genuine worry for my friend, who remained behind.

In deep reflection, it becomes apparent that our connections are guided by the threads of karma woven across lifetimes. If I had fulfilled a supportive role for him in a previous existence, perhaps this lifetime would have been an opportunity for him to reciprocate.

Just a few days ago, a long-distance phone call brought news that his youngest son, who seemed like a newborn just yesterday, is now of age for military service. During this conversation, we made a solemn pact: to be lifelong friends who serve as beacons in the vast, tempestuous sea of life, as depicted in the song sung by Yoon Hanggi. This pledge embodies the essence of friendships, a commitment that endures until our final moments.

♥

The moment we enter the world and our first cries echo, we commence our journey of forming relationships with our family. This connection becomes an inescapable fate, binding us to a tapestry of kinship. Regardless of the size or composition of our families, each member plays an indispensable role in shaping our lives.

Many studies underscore that the greatest sauce of life satisfaction revolves around spending time with those we cherish and who hold us in their hearts. Among those I share the most time with, it is you, my family, who hold a special place. Families stand as a wellspring of confidence and a source of solace. They stand as resolute pillars of strength, offering support that never falters, fortifying us to become better versions of ourselves.

In truth, the role of my wife is to support the education of our children, assist in my aspirations, and avoid attempting to dominate me. Talmud aptly advises, "Love your wife as you love yourself, and cherish her eternally! God treasures the tears she sheds when you cause her pain." Such sentiments celebrate the presence of my wife.

My introduction to my wife Morana occurred in 1979, marking 45 years of shared history. Since then, I've learned that she values her privacy and avoids the limelight: an aspect I am respectful of. Thus, instead of revealing our extensively shared experiences, I will touch upon her role as an essential seasoning, to dispel any notion of me as a solitary figure without a spouse.

Above all else, I am profoundly grateful to my wife for giving birth to our healthy progenies and nurturing them with care. While our lineage will not end here, I hope that future generations will flourish and imprint their mark on human history.

Naturally prone to fearing the night and struggling with restful sleep, my wife's apprehension has inadvertently cemented our bond. Even now, she waits for me while I'm away, refusing to slumber alone. As I depart her, I'm going to purposely assure her leaving my words, "Honey, I'll be back soon," affirming my definite return.

However, a lingering question persists in my head. Since 2004, when our younger son embarked on his journey to Germany to pursue

159

his soccer career, I have been astonished by how she was able to guide him, despite her insomnia condition, while acting as a guardian during his two-year stay there. This was a necessary condition for her stay to be allowed, as she pursued full-time German studies.

While I might not fully grasp it, I believe she navigated this serious challenging situation with a contemplation similar to Shakespeare's famous question: whether it is nobler in her mind to endure the challenges and uncertainties that life presents or actively to confront and overcome them.

❤❤

In this intricate world, attaining perfection proves to be a daunting endeavor. No matter how earnestly we strive, perfection remains elusive. Love, while profound, can lead to unintended outcomes; parents' excessive love may inadvertently harm their children, and the reverse can be true. A failure to prioritize health during youth can cast shadows on the path to a contented old age. I grapple with regrets, lamenting that I couldn't craft my life exactly as I wished. The unresolved conflict with a dear friend still brings tears to my eyes.

Gazing back over my 75 years, a pang of regret tugs at my heart. Let's glance at a few chapters: *failing to uphold a promise to my mother forged in childhood; faltering at the second round of the civil exam; parting ways with a college sweetheart without confessing an affection; the missteps in raising my two sons weigh heavily on my conscience.*

In my infancy, my father passed, leaving me bereft of meaningful growth. My mother with the aid of two in-house servants, shouldered her burden of caring for my grandparents while tending to our family. An inheritance of ample fortune, bequeathed by our forebears, scattered away due to my father's gambling, leaving Mom to navigate trying times to provide for us.

As night came, I came to reach an age where I comprehended the mom's lamentation. She poured her heart out, sharing the adversities she had weathered. She yearned to chronicle her struggles across myriad volumes had she her literacy, an unfulfilled aspiration that weighed on me. Comforting her, I repeatedly vowed to care for her at the moment, treating her to savory delicacies. Alas, my promises lay unfulfilled, even though I ventured to New Zealand with hopes of redemption.

During my preparation for the civil service exam, while working as a housekeeper even in her eighties, she sacrificially provided financial support to me. A poignant pang lingers as I can no longer grasp her gentle hand. My heartful bond with my mother remains unbreakable and priceless: an enduring relationship steeped in love and devotion. She bestowed life upon me, nurtured me with affection, guided me through my first life lessons, and stood as my guardian through all emotional tempests.

Before my migration to New Zealand, I bid farewell to my mother, who resided with my eldest brother in Busan, alluding her to an overseas business venture. Several years later, her earthly journey ended. Upon my visit to Korea, only her portrait rested in the ancestral shrine. Before her passing, a message lay beneath her pillow, a motivation that resonates: "Hanoka, Keep your head up!" I strived to honor her words, guided by her memory that occasionally graces my dreams.

Mother! A newfound promise stirs within me: I shall give life to your untold story. On the morning of April 26, 2021, at 6:26 AM, my eyes opened to a memory: a scene of you and me gathering cups from a market corner, a cherished moment from childhood.

I recalled the shopkeeper I first met on the first day of university, engaged in conversation with another customer nearby, meticulously counting cups one by one. Though you are no longer with me, I believe you sensed my deep longing to reconnect with that girl. In the realm of my dreams, you orchestrated a serendipitous encounter between us. Moments of reflection often generate the splendor of the past, helping us bridge the gap between the present and those who remain dear to us, yet are no longer by our side.

♥♥

In the spring of 1889, an Irish poet Yates, at first sight, fell deeply in love with Maud Gonne, a 23-year-old Irish independence advocate. Their differing beliefs created an impassable division: he was an Anglo-Irish Protestant, while she was a passionate advocate for Irish nationalism. This marked the beginning of what Yates would later admit was "The troubling of my life," partly due to his hesitance to join in her nationalist activism.

A couple of years later, Yates proposed marriage to Gonne on more than three occasions, each time met with rejection. Finally, in 1903, Gonne wedded an Irish nationalist major, John MacBride. Yates was ruined by Gonne's marriage, heartbroken to have lost his beloved to another man. Yates expressed his disdain for MacBride in both letters and poetry. Additionally, Gonne's conversion to Catholicism before marriage had added up his disillusionment.

Though Gonne's marriage to MacBride was tumultuous, Yates took some satisfaction in it. After the birth of their first son in 1904, she and MacBride agreed to end their marriage. Yates' friendship with Gonne also dissolved in 1908. Before I narrate my adore story, the reason for putting Yates' tale extensively in front of you lies in its similarity to my own unrequited love. Just as Yates faced a love that wasn't reciprocated, Maud Gonne refused to walk the golden or silvery path laid out before her, making it a daunting task for Yates to twist her otherwise.

As I settled into bed last night, I held onto a fervent wish to catch a fleeting glimpse of my beloved girl, even if only in the realm of dreams. Miraculously, my wish was granted on the morning of 26 April 2021, at the stroke of 6:00 in the morning.

She appeared before me in a dream, reminiscent of a shopkeeper selling cups at a familiar market corner in my hometown, orchestrated by a serendipitous chance led by my mother. This rendezvous mirrored the emotions shared between Yates and Gonne, an affair that unfolded five decades ago on 5 March 1972, during my first day at university.

In hindsight, why did I not confess my affection before embarking on my army service? Naivety had cast me as a fool, acquainted only with

162

the fervor of love. Was my affection left unreciprocated? Then, in a subsequent dream, she reappeared before me, embodying the spirit of a new generation:

As I boarded a train, she joined me in an awkward exchange of glances before taking a seat. Beside me sat an unfamiliar Western woman, engrossed in conversation. After a while, my beloved girl interjected herself between us, settling beside me. But within minutes, she moved again, choosing a seat a few spaces to the left, closer to the front.

Just before she sat down, she turned back, her eyes meeting mine as if she wanted to convey something. This was a departure from the past, revealing a new incarnation of herself.

Adorned with lovely makeup and dressed in a two-piece outfit—quite unlike the trousers she used to wear—she radiated a sense of transformation. In that fleeting moment, I discerned a subtle expression on her face. It seemed as though she wished to announce to the train guests that she was indeed my lover.

The initial instance of her appearing in my dream was early on 21 December 2020. In this dream, she visited my hometown and joined me in our room to enjoy a sauna with her son. I suspect that this emergence into my dreamscape was triggered by my ongoing work on my memoir, gradually pulling her into the tapestry of my virtual reality. Since then, she has frequently made her presence known in my dreams.

At around 6:45 am on 13 June 2021, my dreamscape was graced once again by her presence. This time, she took on the guise of a student, venturing to New Zealand, my current abode, to engage in a brief period of study. It seems that the boundaries between reality and dreamland blur as she continues to weave herself into the fabric of my thoughts:

On my journey back from the language academy where she was diligently studying English, our paths crossed. I shared with her the news about her classmate's sister, who also attended the same academy.

It seemed that her sister had successfully reached her goal and was making her way back to Korea.

In response, she shared with me a heartfelt sentiment: that she herself was yet to achieve her own aspirations. Her words struck a chord within me. She conveyed that the moments we spent together were a source of joy for her, the only bright spot in her days. The thought of losing her left me grappling with the daunting prospect of loneliness.

Bearing the weight of this emotional exchange, I was awake from the dream, my heart still echoing with her plea to stay. As I reflect on my past, one thing I've come to realize is that perhaps it would have been more fruitful to share my future comings and aspirations rather than dwelling on regrets.

♥♥

One of the pivotal moments in my life that I often reflect upon is my failure in the civil servant exam. This failure, along with the painful toothache anecdote that occurred in my second year at university, left an enduring impact on me.

During my preparation within two months, I managed smoothly to pass the initial round held in May 1976, alongside a fellow student from our school. As I tackled the second round of exams, I felt a surge of confidence. I had performed well in school practice tests and had even secured a place in a scholarship competition for all law students. The wave of self-assurance was riding high.

Finally, on 17 December 1976, the 19th essay test for it took place in Seoul. I tackled the questions on civil law, criminal law, public administration, and economics with fervor, relieved that the finance-related questions matched my diligent studies. With a strong confidence, I submitted it, hopeful that my diligent efforts would finally bear fruit.

However, when the list of successful candidates was published in the newspaper, my name was nowhere to be found. It's a harsh blow to my expectations and confidence. I reached out to the newspaper to double-check, and my suspicions were confirmed: I hadn't made the cut.

Regardless of the outcome, I should maintain my mental equilibrium myself. I acknowledged the commonality of facing setbacks and dissatisfaction, and that this exam result did not define my worth or my accumulated knowledge. Rather than dwelling on the past, I turned my focus to what I could have achieved had I succeeded in the exam. I would rather envision myself dedicating my energy to the education system in Korea.

During that period, Korea possessed abundant human resources despite the scarcity of natural resources. I held the belief that by cultivating the potential of its people, Korea could have risen to the ranks of a globally recognized nation. Education plays a vital role in shaping the position of a country's future.

Given Korea's geographical circumstance of being bordered by the sea on three sides, it was clear that leverage of this unique position would be essential for its advance. I have assumed the potential for Korea to thrive among advanced nations, making the most of its geopolitical advantage.

Pondering my potential role in reshaping the Korean education system, I couldn't help but confront some of the deeply ingrained issues that had plagued it for years. The education landscape in Korea was laden with trials that needed a fresh perspective and epoch-making plan.

First and foremost, the prevailing mindset dictated that every student should secure a place in university, often setting the stage for their parents' life aspirations. The coveted SKY universities: Seoul National University, Korea University, and Yonsei University stood as symbols of success. This pursuit of academic achievement came at a high cost, with parents sacrificing their own lives to support their children's educational pursuits. Falling short of these expectations could lead to feelings of failure and intense societal pressure.

Additionally, a striking educational inequality existed within the system. Around 68% of students turned to cram schools, private tutoring institutions supplemented regular classes. These schools were accessible primarily to families with financial means, further widening the gap between affluent and less privileged students. This unequal access to education could perpetuate disparities and hinder upward mobility for those who couldn't afford such opportunities.

Therefore, Korea's education placed highly excessive emphasis on uniformity, with the ultimate goal being high scores for university admission. This overemphasis on standardized testing stifled creativity and diversity, even qualities vital for success in today's world. Parents were pushed to invest substantial resources into preparing their children for the intense competition, often extending their working years just to meet these demands.

Given these pressing challenges of Korean education, I envisioned a series of steps I might have taken to address these issues had I passed the previous exam. Imagining a scenario where I secured a position in the Ministry of Education Planning Team, I formulated potential strategies for reform:

Expert Advisory Group: to reevaluate the strengths and weaknesses of Korean education, I would assemble a group of education experts. Their insights and analyses would lay the foundation for meaningful change.
Educational Manifesto: drawing inspiration from historical charters, like the National Education Charter, I would recommend the creation of a long-term educational manifesto. This document would provide a steady vision for the next century, immune to shifting political winds.
Universal Exploration: recognizing the transition from a terrestrial to a cosmic perspective, I would advocate for preparing Korea to play a role in universal exploration and development.
Global Leadership: I would stress the importance of leveraging human resources to propel Korea into a leadership position on the global stage. Healing divisions and polarization within the nation would be essential to achieving this goal.
Environmental Sustainability: given the alarming state of our planet, I would emphasize the urgency of creating a sustainable environment. Addressing waste, resource depletion, radiation, and water scarcity

would be pivotal. So, the implementation of an ESG program was recommended for all schools.

Family-Centric Education: acknowledging the family's central role in education, I would encourage a shift towards incorporating education into family life. The family dinner table would serve as a nucleus for discussions, fostering learning and bonding.

Long-Term Vision: shaping education with a long-term vision that focuses on the needs of future generations can guide policy decisions. Avoiding short-term fixes and embracing changes that will stand the test of time is crucial.

In these proposed steps, I envisioned that the Korean education system would become more balanced, inclusive, forward-looking, and focused on holistic development. Though these ideas were not implemented in reality, they stand as a testament to the potential for change and progress in the realm of education. Fixing education inequality deeply rooted in all society requires a multiple-faceted approach that addresses both the structure of it and the implementation of it. While the challenges are complex, the solutions can be summarized as follows:

Holistic Assessment: reducing the overemphasis on standardized tests like Suneung is a critical matter. The educational system should shift towards a more holistic assessment that recognizes a wide range of skills, including creativity, critical thinking, communication, and emotional intelligence. This approach would help identify diverse talents and encourage students to pursue various paths beyond the confines of traditional exams.

Broader Definition of Merit: Instead of solely relying on university prestige as a measure of success, the education system should recognize accomplishments beyond academic performance. Encouraging achievements in arts, sports, social service, and innovation can level the playing field and promote a broader understanding of merit.

Equal Opportunity: ensuring access to quality education for all socioeconomic backgrounds is essential. This could involve huge investments in public schools, providing scholarships and resources to underprivileged students, and offering supplementary education support to those who need it the most.

Teacher's Training: teachers should be equipped with the tools and training to address diverse learning needs. Additionally, offering incentives to educators who choose to work in underserved areas can ensure that even disadvantaged students receive high-quality education.

Diversified Career: encouraging students to explore various career paths above the traditional definition of success can alleviate the pressure associated with university admission. Developing skills in vocational education, creativity, entrepreneurship, and innovative industries can broaden the definition of success to be more inclusive.

Parental Involvement: promoting a broader understanding of education among parents can lead to healthier expectations and reduced pressure on students. Parents can be educated about the importance of holistic development and encouraged to support their children's diverse talents.

Public-Private Partnerships: collaboration between the government, private sector, and civil society can create initiatives that bridge educational gaps. Corporate partnerships, scholarships, and mentorship programs can yield to more equitable education system.

As I reflect on my experiences as a parent, it's clear that parenting comes with challenges and growth. Acknowledging past mistakes and seeking to create a better future is a testament to my willingness to evolve. Education is an ongoing journey, not just for students but for parents and society as a whole. Just as I have learned and grown through reflection and change, it also can undergo transformation to ensure a brighter and more equitable future for all.

I have two sons: an older one, Stephen (in Korean Chorok, means green), and a younger one, Leo (in Korean, Puronsol, means blue). Because their original names were a bit difficult to pronounce, we changed them once we shifted to New Zealand. Although neither of them is tall, they were born with the athletic genes in my family: older son excels in basketball, while younger one has a talent for soccer.

When it comes to being successful parents in raising our children, I wonder what they think of me. It's often said that the ideal image of parents is to hear from our children, who would become parents themselves in the future, that they've become respectable parents.

Finding the right balance between being overly strict with my older son and excessively lenient with my younger one has proven to be a challenge, much like it is for many parents. Earning the respect of my children is something I've found to be a difficult task.

Raising children well is an irreplaceable desire of parents and a duty given to us by nature. It's also the privilege of children to seek love and attention from parents. The combination of these factors contributes to cordial home education. Education, in itself, is an eternal task that transcends time and national borders. However, it's a highly diverse business influenced by different races, religions, income, social engrave, family settings, individuals, and the country we belong to.

Nevertheless, one constant factor remains: both the subject and the object of education are human beings. We're destined to end our lives as imperfect beings, and education plays a pivotal role in our journey towards becoming more complete individuals.

In our home, we have a cat that was left behind by the previous owner. She's adorned with colorful patterns and exudes a sense of curiosity. Similar to this cat's curiosity-driven life, we humans explore every nook and cranny to complete our big picture. Learning is integral to our growth; without it, we wouldn't be able to mature and become well-rounded members of society.

Honestly, during the time when I was actively working for a power company in Korea, I often neglected my parental duties and immersed myself in my own world. I spent nights drinking with my friends and rarely came home before dawn. On weekends, I slept merely to shake off fatigue. I did not have the time to properly look at my children's faces or spend quality moments with them. Looking back, I realize that

I wasn't the successful parent I aspired to be; rather, my actions were something I felt ashamed of.

One memory that stands out is when I took my older son to catch locusts in a rice field near our house before my younger son was born. I assumed he would be excited about catching locusts, but his reaction was quite the opposite:

He couldn't only catch the locusts in his hands, but he also couldn't even get close to them. I started scolding him by slapping him with my hands all at once. What would a boy do if he couldn't catch a single locust with his hand?

He had a delicate personality from birth; little did I know whether he was such a child that he couldn't touch such a small creature. A respectful parent, in that situation, would have been able to evaluate his traits and not try to scold him for what he was curious about and how he could do it himself.

I instructed him to catch them without giving much thought to his emotional needs. I should have allowed him to make his own decisions, as long as they remained within societal norms. I should have guided him gently on how things could be done better, using a patient and supportive approach.

Children should be aware that they can always seek help from their parents. Spending quality time with them and participating in compassionate activities together is important.

Fortunately, when we got home, his mother scolded me and hugged him, which comforted him much less harm. Humans naturally learn from their parents how to navigate society and survive. I wonder why I couldn't show my children how to handle that matter; perhaps it's because I didn't learn it from my father.

As Stephen grew up, he began to display his talents in various fields, often with a certain time gap. He started showing interest in sports, music, and car racing. Even when we moved to New Zealand, he was passionate about the violin, although his interest waned when I stopped paying as much attention to it. Then, his interest shifted to painting.

His approach to painting was unique when drawing a person, he would start with their feet and finish up with their head. There's an unfinished painting from that time hanging in our living room, which might be mistaken for a finished piece. The portfolio works he had created in high school even became models for the paintings of his juniors at the same school for a while.

Regrettably, I failed to show my steady interest and consideration for his talent deserved. If I could turn back time, I would provide him with ardent support.

Stephen was selected as a Player of the Year in 1999, at Rosminis College School.

His passion and interest in basketball, however, continued burning endlessly to this day. His basketball journey commenced when our family moved to New Zealand and purchased a house in Greenhithe a year later. He started waking up early in the mornings, sometimes being late for school, to spend time with friends playing basketball on the court in front of the garage.

171

Entering high school, he was once chosen to represent the North Shore region and participated in various national basketball tournaments. Of course, he held the title of the school's basketball captain.

John Stockton, a point guard for the NBA's Utah Jazz team, was his idol during that time. Despite not being particularly tall, Stephen possessed exceptional ball-handling skills and a wide field of vision. His dream at the time was to enter the American basketball world after completing high school. Regrettably, his mom and I overlooked his aspirations and failed to truly listen to him.

However, he hasn't spoken about it since he often sits in his office and watches basketball games on YouTube whenever he finds the time. I can't help but wonder what could have happened if I had listened to him instead of dismissing his dreams. Perhaps, he could have achieved his aspirations.

On the other hand, younger Leo has grown into a gregarious child. From the moment he began talking, it seemed he never stopped. When I took him out on his bike in the morning, he engaged in endless conversations with the neighbors, often returning home late. He even became friends with the apartment security guard, sharing meals and chatting throughout the day. This social nature continued when we moved to Greenhithe village in New Zealand when he was of preschool age.

Despite not knowing a single word of English, he effortlessly made friends with all the neighbors, regardless of age, time, or background, turning the entire Greenhithe Village into his playground. His true nature came to light after he enrolled in primary school. He excelled in various school sports, from the 100-meter sprint to long-distance marathons, setting records that remained unbeatable.

Later on, he transitioned to soccer and was swiftly chosen as a youth delegate for the northern region. At this point, I was fully invested in supporting his soccer journey, even going to great lengths to fulfill his requests. I would buy new soccer boots for him without any hesitation, even if he had received a pair just the day before. I was always ready to fulfill any of his wishes, sometimes staying up all night to ensure his comfort.

While his mother and older brother expressed their concerns that my excessive support could potentially spoil him, I still remained unwavering in my support for him.

In 2002, he followed in his brother's footsteps and enrolled at Rosmini High School, a Catholic institution, where he also joined the school's football team. During this period, he played a pivotal role in leading the second division of the high school to a championship victory. His exceptional performance on the field earned him the coveted title of Most Valuable Player, ultimately resulting in Rosmini High School's promotion to the first division.

Upon hearing this remarkable news, Glenfield Club coach and Leo's youth team coach, Gib Beattie, recommended Leo as a potential talent to Westlake Principal. Acknowledging the reputation of Westlake for its strong high school soccer team, the principals of both schools mutually agreed to facilitate his transfer to Westlake Boys School in accordance with his agreement.

Leo transferred to that school on January 27, 2004. During his time there, he and his brother also underwent a trial with a German club. After returning for a brief period of around 4 months, Leo achieved an astonishing feat by scoring 15 goals in 12 games in the school soccer tournament, earning him the title of top scorer. He eventually departed for Germany in August of the same year.

Also, just a week before departing for his soccer endeavors abroad, he triumphed over all 300 young competitors from across New Zealand at the Nike-sponsored Pana KO circular race. He emerged as the inaugural first Pana KO champion, leaving an indelible mark with his passionate pursuit of victory.

The following records, brief extracts from the 12 games, documented by the school reporter on a weekly basis, have gradually faded from the memories of me, our family, friends, and even his teammates. However, my soul insists on preserving these valuable memories within the pages of this book:

8th May 2004 (Sat), *Westlake won 3-0 against Avondale: on a day perfect for football, Westlake was given the honor of being the first team to play against newly promoted Avondale College. The field was in good condition, if not a little too short and the game started at the designated time for the season, 12 pm. The deadlock was broken in the 9th minute. Wilson delivered a corner into the box and a well-timed run saw another debutant; Shin Leo head the ball into the roof of the net. Westlake continued to dominate possession and at this stage were playing some attractive football.*

At 23-minute Shin scored his second goal, firing home after Pilay had crossed from the left. There was one scare for the visitors, a back pass being miscued by goalkeeper McMurtrie, but the Avondale forward was unable to take advantage of his opportunity and his shot sliced wide. After the second, Pilay, Van Rooyen, and Wilson all had a chance to extend the lead, but it was not until the 83rd minute that the game was but beyond the home side. Shin gathered the ball 30 yards from goal, outstripped the defender with pace, and finished with aplomb past the faultless keeper for his hat-trick.

15th May 2004 (Sat), *Westlake won 2-1 against MAGS: the second half was only 8 minutes old when the deciding goal was scored. It was last weeker's hattrick Shin Leo, who did the damage. He turned the defender inside out before hitting an early shot with his left foot from 22 yards. Berry was obviously taken by surprise and the ball rocketed low, inside the keeper's near post. Berry then went on to take center stage, twice making fine saves to deflect shots from Shin and then Plauman over the bar.*

5th June 2004 (Sat), *Westlake drew at 1-1 against Auckland Grammar: It was a match that drew people's attention because both teams had maintained an undefeated record. After 27 minutes the deadlock was broken. It was a goal all of Shin Leo making. He won possession, ran at the defense, and finished strongly across the despairing dive of Kenealy.... Shin had a couple of half chances to extend the home side's lead but it was....*

174

19th June 2004 (Sat), *Westlake won 6-1 against St Peters: Westlake started positively but it was not until the 24th minute Shin Leo with a goal, lashing in a right-footed shot from full 30 yards. In a carbon copy situation only 7 minutes later, Shin fired narrowly wide. On either side of these incidents, Henrik Plaumann had been denied by a full-length dive from the keeper.... Shin made it 3-0 with a neat finish before Sheldon Pilay stole the show......*

23rd June 2004 (Wed), *Westlake won 3-0 against Tauranga Boys: further goals were added in the next 10 minutes. Firstly, McQueen got on the end of a Shin Leo crossed and another was Shin himself who added the third after breaking through from the halfway line.*

26th June 2004 (Sat), *Westlake won at 3-0 against Avondale: Westlake continued to dominate and in the 83rd minute Shin Leo found himself unmarked and was able to steer home a Nick Gibbon cross at the second attempt. Like London buses, after a long wait, another one immediately came along. This time it was Rhode again scoring from the far post after a great ball from Van Rooyen.*

6th July 2004 (Tue), *Westlake drew 1-1 against Rangitoto: following the disappointment of Saturday's draw with King's game on 24 June, Westlake quickly had an opportunity to put things right. This is a catch-up game, the previous game having been abandoned, following Cameron McCarthy swallowing his tongue. The game was played on the narrow lower field at Rangitoto with the rain incessantly pouring down. During the early exchanges, there were no real actions of any note as the midfield dominated. Shin hit the side netting....*

The game was wrapped up with the last kick of the game and it was fitting that it was Shin Leo, playing his last game for Westlake, who scored. A Van Rooyen shot was parred by the keeper and it fell to Shin, who made no mistake for his 15th goal in 12 games. Leo now moves to Germany to pursue a potential career in the game with Herta Berlin. The coaching staff would like to thank Leo for all his efforts, and he leaves with the best wishes of all at Westlake.

At the age of 14, on August 14th, 2004, he set out on a journey to Germany with his mother, brimming with aspirations for his future. During his high school years, luck certainly favored him, but his undeniable skill and talent also held great significance.

As he played for the Berlin youth club *Hertha 03 Zehlendorf* for around two years, he achieved remarkable records. He played a substantial role in his team's triumph in the U17 Bundesliga Northern Germany Championship and secured victory in the Pokal U17 Coca-Cola Cup Championship in Berlin.

Played	Won	Lost	Drawn	For	Against
12	9	0	3	35	7

Team Statistics

	League			Cup/Exchange		
	Appearances	Sub	Goals	Appearances	Sub	Goals
McMurtrie	10	0	0	2	0	0
Evans	10	0	0	1	1	0
Shin	10	0	14	2	0	1
Halliday	2	5	0	0	0	0
King	0	5	0	0	0	0
Norris	0	0	0	0	0	0
McQueen	2	5	0	1	1	1
Ujdur	1	0	0	2	0	0
Feneridis	1	1	0	0	0	0
Choi	1	3	0	0	0	0
Fleming	0	1	0	0	0	0
Own Goals			1			

Leo struck 15 goals in 12 games, before leaving for Germany. Most of the goals for his Westlake High School were from his toes.

He particularly shone during the Coca-Cola Cup final, and this outstanding performance led to an offer from another Berlin club, SV Tasmania, to play in the Berlin U19 regional league until 2006.

Nonetheless, the substantial support I had offered, which was perceived as advantageous, gradually began to have its downsides. Despite his promising start, he eventually confronted difficulties while abroad, such as grappling with loneliness, experiencing discrimination against minorities, and feeling homesick for his friends and family in New Zealand. As a result, he made the decision to return home in 2006, before his contract with the club had expired, unable to withstand these pressures.

Reflecting on this journey, I find myself contemplating what I did right and where I fell short as a father. For those who might read my story, I'd like to offer a few words: balancing strictness and leniency as a parent is truly challenging. However, I've come to realize that the key to finding this balance lies in providing warmth and unconditional love for children. If I embraced my children with love, they would be more likely to understand and follow my guidance, and that love could endure and flourish throughout their lives.

2004-2005, Shin Leo was played for Northern Under 17 Bundesliga, by Hertha 03 Zehlendorf Team.

Shin Leo was selected for New Zealand Youth Team Representatives at 13 years old.
When he was back in New Zealand, he was selected as National U20 Youth Squad.

Also in 2006, Leo played for SV Tasmania Gropiusstadt, under 19 Bundesliga Northern,
In Germany.

VIII

Plan for Enriched Ageing

VIII
Plan for Enriched Ageing

Am I truly prepared to face death? It's difficult to provide an answer. The concept of the plan for ageing gained increasing importance as the average life expectancy continues to rise: due to advancements in medical technology, bioscience, improved nutrition, reduced infant mortality rates, and enhanced healthcare attributes to it. This shift has prompted a focus on how to lead a healthy and fulfilling life in the later stages, particularly given the various factors that can impact longevity and quality of life.

Let me see dividing life into three major stages: the first being the formative years of learning; the second encompassing the working period; the final phase unfolding after retirement. The focal point of this chapter, however, resides in the blueprint for the ultimate stage of life, which often commences after retirement. This phase requires serious contemplation to ensure a rich and secure existence.

As the population of individuals surpassing the ages of 80, 90, and even 100 continues to rise, it becomes crucial to acknowledge the significance of these extended years. Yet, the emphasis must shift from mere longevity to the quality of life. To lead a fulfilling life during the latter years demands a methodical approach to maintaining physical, mental, emotional, and financial well-being.

Drawing a parallel between life and voyage is a powerful analogy. Just as a ship needs a clear destination and a well-planned route to navigate the seas successfully, our lives benefit from having a clear sense of purpose and a well-crafted plan. By setting our goals, aspirations, and maintaining a positive outlook, we can navigate the journey of aging with purpose and direction.

The ageing life plan presented in this chapter aims to guide individuals toward a well-prepared, purposeful, and fulfilling later life. It starts to acknowledge the value of quality over quantity and encourages embracing the journey with enthusiasm and intention. As a captain of our own lives, we have the power to shape our aging experience and make the most of the years ahead.

Before we have set the plan, we have to come to terms with our aging: the decline of physical powers, injury, fear of death, social remoteness, emotional dysfunction, and financial instability. These will vary in intensity and severity in different individuals of different ages. We will have to make continuous adjustments to our daily declines and ripples in our emotional and psychic lives. In later life, we may find ourselves facing new issues and attempting to overcome these issues.

The real problem that aged persons often encounter is that they don't recognize that they are getting older and experiencing a decline in society. Therefore, I propose five categories for the plan for enriched aging: ①*physical strength,* ②*brain function,* ③*financial security,* ④*social connection, and* ⑤*daily rejuvenation.*

In order to comprehensively address these facets, individuals can embrace their later years with resilience, purpose, and a deep sense of fulfillment. These domains encompass not only physical and emotional well-being but also financial stability and meaningful social flooding, embodying a holistic approach to an enriched ageing plan.

Physical Strength

Maintaining physical strength is paramount to enjoying a fulfilling and active later life. Regular exercise routines tailored to my capabilities, such as walking, swimming, or meditation can help keep my body strong and flexible. Embrace a balanced diet rich in nutrients, and prioritize hydration to support my overall well-being. Regular health check-ups and preventive screenings ensure I am in tune with my body's needs, allowing me to address any concern proactively. Nurturing my physical health contributes to a vitality that paves the way for an enriched aging experience.

As I journey through the ageing process, I have noticed occasional lapses in memory: these instances manifest as challenges in remembering the names of acquaintances met on the street or even the characters in a drama I'm engrossed in. There are moments when I misplace car keys and briefly forget my intended destination while embarking on a drive.

A recent slip in the bath resulted in a hospital visit, and despite undergoing physical therapy for almost 2 months, my injured shoulder hasn't fully healed. All these occurrences are part of the ageing process. Aging is widely recognized as a natural phenomenon stemming from the gradual accumulation of changes within the body over the course of time.

This process is influenced by genetic factors, lifestyle choices, environmental influences, and so on. The very act of aging involves the generation of limited oxygen during the breakdown of the food we consume, causing a decrease in our body's resistance to DNA damage, unsaturated fatty acids, and proteins. This leads to the aging of our body.

Interestingly, each time a cell in our body divides, the telomeres located at the ends of chromosomes become progressively shorter. Eventually, these telomeres reach a point where the cell can no longer divide and it dies. This phenomenon brings about the unwelcome guest of unavoidable aging. The question then becomes: how can we navigate this journey of aging and live a healthy old age?

The human longing for eternal life has persisted for centuries. Dating back to around 2000 B.C., Gilgamesh, the mythical King of Uruk in Mesopotamia, symbolized the quest for immortality. This aspiration has transcended time, appealing to individuals from all walks of life: rich and poor, young and old, ruler and servant. We continue to explore the idea of living longer lives, even today.

Figures like Raymond Kurzweil, a futurist and American computer scientist, have attempted to extend their lifespans through a variety of methods: taking numerous pills undergoing chemical intravenous treatments, and consuming red wine. Kurzweil even predicts a future where everyone will live indefinitely.

Yet, our modern lifestyle choices often contribute to accelerated aging and its associated health issues. From heavy reliance on cars for short distances to overeating, indulging in fast food, and leading excessively sedentary lives, we're inadvertently nurturing the conditions for early ageing and the troubling phenomenon of '*living too short and dying too long*'.

So, what steps am I personally taking to avoid the pitfalls of ageing? It all comes down to a few basic principles: eating in moderation, staying active, and keeping my mind engaged. At its core, keeping a healthy body is the outcome of expending energy. Regardless of some weight loss theories, the universally proposed way to preserve health is a simple theory: eating less and keeping moving more, while supplements may offer some benefits, however, they can't replace the fundamental importance of balanced health.

In addition to these guiding principles, I place great emphasis on routine medical checkups. Regular consultations with doctors are of essential option for early detection and effective management of any underlying health conditions that might potentially affect my overall health and bodily functions.

Brain Function

Throughout our life's journey, our brains remain central in shaping our experiences and interactions. The hippocampus, a crucial hub for memory, thrives when we engage in activities that challenge it, such as learning new skills and exploring unfamiliar subjects.

The hippocampus plays a role in transforming short-term memories into lasting ones, enabling us to store and later retrieve experiences and information. It contributes to our ability to create mental maps of our surroundings and navigate through space.

Our language skills flourish when we immerse ourselves in reading and writing, and word games, supporting the vitality of the temporal lobe. The parietal lobe, responsible for spatial recognition, benefits from creative pursuits and spatial puzzles. The occipital lobe, which handles visual processing, can be nurtured through involvement in visual arts and memory games.

Physical movement not only keeps our bodies fit but also sustains crucial blood flow to the brain, promoting cognitive appreciation. Our emotional health, overseen by the amygdala, gains from mindful practices and engaging in hobbies that bring happiness.

As our ageing progress, the prefrontal cortex's role in decision-making can be preserved through critical thinking exercises and a willingness to embrace novel experiences. By embracing activities catering to various brain functions, we embark on a journey of enriched ageing, nurturing our minds for a vibrant and fulfilling life.

Hence, maintaining a sharp and engaged brain is a key component of enriched ageing. Cultivating mental well-being involves partaking in activities that challenge cognitive abilities, like reading, writing, puzzle solving, yoga, and deep breathing exercises. These activities not only provide respite from stress but also foster emotional balance.

Prioritizing brain well-being is an integral part of a holistic approach to graceful ageing. The mind and body are intrinsically interconnected, where our daily actions are a result of the physical interactions and properties of the brain and nervous system. Every movement is driven by the electrical signals through synapses between cells in our brain.

Hence, understanding how to maintain optimal brain function in later life is essential. Proper brain function is pivotal for maintaining a high quality of life during the ageing process. Here are some strategies to promote my brain health and function in daily life:

Mental Stimulation: keep my brain active with puzzles, games, reading, listening to music, and learning new skills. Activities like crossword games, Baduk, Chess, or even learning new words can help maintain cognitive function. Engaging in regular physical activity has been improving blood flow to the brain and stimulating the growth of new brain cells.

Adequate Sleep: make quality sleep a priority, as it plays a vital role in memory consolidation and cognitive function. Aim to get 7-9 hours of rejuvenating sleep each night. Additionally, consider incorporating a 30-minute daytime nap to complement any insufficient sleep from the night.

Healthy Diet: a balanced diet rich in antioxidants, omega-3 fatty acids, and nutrients like A, B, and C vitamins support brain health. Foods like fruits, vegetables, whole grains, lean proteins, and fish can be beneficial.

Also, dehydration can impact cognitive function, so I regularly intake water throughout the day and night.

Limit Stress: modern people are under stress in various fields. Minimizing this stress as much as possible helps our mental health. So, it is recommended to calm my mind by listening to music or taking deep breaths. It is also recommended that indulge myself in everyday things that I like.

In summary, I solemnly dedicate myself to daily reading and writing, harnessing my physical and mental capabilities to the fullest extent. This commitment reflects a profound recognition of the importance of nurturing cognitive well-brain functioning for a fulfilling and enriched ageing plan.

Financial Security

Planning for financial security ensures peace of mind as I navigate the later years. Developing a comprehensive retirement strategy, including savings, investments, and budgeting, helps to maintain stability. It's important to have a clear picture of my financial needs and resources; to factor in potential healthcare expenses and unexpected situations. Consulting with financial experts and updating my plan as needed could help construct a solid foundation for achieving financial peace and independence during my ageing journey.

Being financially prepared and having a thorough understanding of the concept of financial security for the elderly is of paramount importance. Those who are well-prepared are more likely to enjoy a comfortable standard of living and reduce the likelihood of needing additional support from family or the government.

Recent studies have highlighted a concerning trend: not only are elderly individuals more likely to carry debt, but the level of debt has surged significantly over the years. This increase can be attributed to factors such as the widespread use of credit cards, rising medical expenses, and the financial support required for family members.

Debt, in its essence, isn't inherently troublesome and can indeed serve as a tool for enhancing financial well-being when utilized deftly.

185

However, the perils of excessive debt should not be underestimated. This is especially pertinent in the later stages of life, where an overwhelming debt load can render retirees financially fragile, and susceptible to unforeseen crises like a significant health emergency or the sudden loss of a spouse.

The period between ages 65 and 80 is often referred to as the 'golden years.' During this phase, individuals have typically retired, are living without dependents, and still possess the physical and cognitive abilities to pursue their interests. However, the appeal of the golden years diminishes when its financial resources are insufficient to maintain a comfortable lifestyle. Financial independence becomes a pivotal aspect of elderly life, though it's not always adequately considered or prepared for.

One of the challenges in financial planning is that there is though no one-size-fits-all savings target. The required amounts would vary for each one, and while some general guidelines exist, the concept of financial independence is broader and more nuanced. So, what exactly is the case of my financial security in retirement? It's the assurance of having sufficient passive income to cover my expenses for the remainder of my later life. For instance, if I possess a rental property, superannuation, or savings account interest that collectively sustains my lifestyle I can achieve financial security.

As of May 2023, it could be estimated that sustaining a standard lifestyle would necessitate an annual budget of approximately $75,000, translating to a weekly expense of $1,500. This raises the fundamental question: How can I generate the amount of income needed to meet this level of financial commitment?

A potential breakdown could consist of $800 from the pension per fortnight for each person ($800 per week in a couple), along with $700 from rental income or part-time work. In some cases, rental income could constitute a significant portion of the budget, covering costs of home maintenance, transportation, food, insurance, overseas travel, and entertainment. It's worth noting that a substantial portion of the budget may be allocated for an annual tour to overseas. The ultimate objective is to maintain a minimum standard of living without relying on others until the end of life.

Social Connection

Cultivating social connections is a profound source of enrichment in my life, for it is through these bonds that we share the tapestry of various individual experiences. Among friends and family, we navigate the currents of joy and sorrow, creating a treasure trove of shared moments. In order to nurture these vital connections, I recognize the importance of maintaining relationships with those who have been constants in my life while also seeking to forge new connections. Whether through community involvement or shared interests in groups, these interactions constitute the very fabric of our existence.

Nurturing injection isn't solely vital for plants, also it's equally essential for the people in their lives. Throughout our lives, we are interdependent beings, relying on others from the moment we are born first. As infants, we are heavily reliant on our mothers for care. As we grow and navigate the world, we build relationships with friends, families, colleagues, and lovers. These relationships persist until our final days, shaping our experiences and defining our existence. Given this innate interdependence, it's only fitting that we strive to live with passion and empathy alongside those who share our journey.

I recently had the privilege of hearing an extraordinary story about a man named Mr. Kim from a close friend I frequently meet in the city. Mr. Kim, now well into his 80s, has a captivating tale to tell. According to my friend, many of Mr. Kim's companions have gradually distanced from him over time due to their interactions.

During each meeting, Mr. Kim has a tendency to reminisce about his past, all the while generously insisting on covering the bill for meals. While this gesture undoubtedly stems from a place of kindness, it often results in a peculiar dynamic where the person seated across from him finds it challenging to contribute to the conversation.

This anecdote highlights the significance of balanced interactions and the art of listening. Engaging with those around us involves not only sharing our stories but also attentively embracing the narratives of others. A genuine connection blossoms when conversations are a two-way street, allowing both parties to contribute to each other. This reciprocity nurtures bonds, enriches experiences, and fosters a sense of understanding and respect.

A true friend is someone who can genuinely praise us in front of others even when we're not present. Finding such a true friend isn't always easy, but it's worth the effort. Once I find one, it's important to nourish those friendships with care and attention.

There's no one-size-fits-all solution to preserving friendships. Not every friendship is meant to last forever, even if we may wish they would. The key to maintaining a sound friendship lies in understand-ding, trust, support, and communication.

Taking an active role in managing them is absolutely crucial. I would reach out first, stay in touch regularly, make an effort to attend special events and express my heartfelt congratulations. Just as I'd provide nutrients for the plants to grow well, friendships require ongoing nurturing and care.

Rejuvenation

Integrating daily rejuvenation practices into my routine is an essential step in nurturing holistic well-being. I place a premium on ensuring I get the quality sleep I need to rejuvenate both body and mind, allowing me to awaken each day feeling refreshed and poised to embrace the challenges and opportunities ahead.

Engage in such activities that bring joy and creativity, whether it's pursuing hobbies, such as reading, gardening, or fishing. Prioritize daily moments of rejuvenation nourishes my spirit as I savor the present and anticipate the future.

Seek out cultural experiences, attend performances, visit museums, or explore new interests to stimulate my mind and keep my curiosity alive. Or have a short domestic tour with family or friends.

Once upon a time, in a rural area of Korea, a little boy named Shin Hanok was born into a humble family of farmers. As grew older, he began pondering the meaning of happiness. He made a bold decision to leave a stable job in Korea and set out to find genuine happiness in

Aotearoa, a land 10,000 km away, where white clouds drifted across the sky.

Throughout history, countless men and women have embarked on quests to uncover the purpose of life and discover happiness, yet clear answers have remained elusive. The pursuit of happiness, a timeless endeavor, might ultimately stem from a collection of simple pleasures. Alternatively, a few significant joys could pave the path to happiness. In the end, our lives may be filled with these mundane daily pleasures that bring us joy.

Knowing oneself better than anyone else allows us to treat ourselves kindly; putting ourselves first is a vital step in self-care and cultivating happiness. The joy derived from pleasing oneself is unparalleled, for no one grasps me better than I do.

I, as part of New Zealander, have mastered the art of seeking joy in simple pleasures: reading, gardening, fishing, walking, or beach outing. On top of them, I am willing to invest in enjoyable experiences like dining in the house, watching movies, or engaging in listening to music.

Human beings are inherently social creatures, driven by a need to connect with others. Looking closely at New Zealanders, I will observe their penchant for friendships and social networks, driven by a shared love for peace and equality: a fundamental national spirit.

After settling at Northcote Point, my wife and I took turns hosting our neighbors, sharing food, conversations, and building friendships. This process taught us that mutual understanding and appreciation of different cultures were vital in adapting to a multicultural society. Over time, these interactions allowed us to deeply understand our neighbors' personal lives: so that we could tell how many chopsticks were in each household.

Over time, we evolved into proud New Zealanders, relishing shared activities like golfing, fishing, and rugby. These interactions served as bridges that effortlessly guided us into embracing a compassionate understanding of the multicultural society.

Also, I would allocate much of my alone time to reading and writing. Reading not only broadens my knowledge but also brings irreplaceable joy to my life. It also serves as a preemptive measure against potential dementia. Another source of solitary pleasure is traveling. My wife and I prefer to travel back to our home country for 3 to 6 months annually to see relatives and friends.

IX

Messages to Grandchildren

IX
Messages to Grandchildren

Cicadas lead fascinating lives, spending the majority of their existence as underground nymphs before emerging during the summer for a brief month of a song. It's important to note that only the male cicadas produce these songs, and they do so with a purpose: to attract females for mating and ensure the continuation of their species. The resonant sound of their song can reach volumes of 70 to 90 dB, similar to the noise level of a blender. Some species even produce an incredibly loud song, reaching up to 120 dB, which places them among the loudest of all insect-generated sounds.

Most cicadas have relatively short life cycles, spanning less than five years. However, certain North American species display unique life cycles of either 13 or 17 years. Interestingly, cicadas tend to adhere to odd-numbered cycles such as 3, 5, 13, and 17 years, a phenomenon that aligns with Darwin's Theory of Evolution and the concept of natural selection.

Cicadas face a variety of predators in their environment, including birds, bats, squirrels, mantises, wasps, and spiders. Their uncommon emergence patterns and synchronized appearances may have evolved to help them avoid being overly preyed upon. By emerging sporadically and in massive numbers, they make themselves less predictable as prey, and their sheer abundance can satiate predators before causing significant harm to their population.

These insects employ various strategies to evade predators. Some species possess aposematic red and black coloration, serving as a warning to potential predators. Many cicadas are also masters of camouflage, helping them blend seamlessly into their surroundings. Singing males may even modulate their songs to distract potential predators or cease singing together in the presence of danger.

Following the act of mating, both male and female cicadas perish. However, the female leaves behind a legacy by laying her eggs within a slit in the bark of trees, often where she resides. In a matter of weeks, the eggs hatch into larvae that make their way underground, sometimes digging chambers near the roots of trees. Here, they sustain themselves by feeding on xylem sap for their predetermined period of 3, 5, 13, or 17 years. Eventually, these nymphs mature into adult cicadas, emerging during the summer to engage in a brief month of amorous activities before their lives come to an end.

Commencing this chapter by likening human existence to that of cicadas offers a thought-provoking and enlightening perspective, especially for my beloved grandkids. Through the analogy, I intend to underscore the cyclicality of life, the hurdles you will encounter, and the decisions you will face. Here's a refined version of the passage to convey my message effectively:

"Life's Reflection: Embracing your Unique Journey"

Imagine the lives of cicadas, those intriguing insects that spend most of their existence hidden beneath the earth, emerging only for a brief month to sing their song. Their lives, although shorter than human's, mirror a cycle that echoes the patterns of our own existence. As I explore the depths of this chapter, it's important to recognize that while your journeys differ from those of cicadas, there are remarkable similarities worth pondering.

My cherished girls, as humans, tread the path of life, day by day, surrounded by an everchanging world fraught with challenges. Just like cicadas contend with predators, disasters, and changes in their environment, you grapple with your own adversaries: whether it's a quarrel between peers, a virus pandemic, countries, resources, looming specter of nuclear threats, climate change, and tumultuous world.

We also bring new life into the world as time progresses, passing the torch to our offspring, only to eventually return to the embrace of the earth, much like the lives of cicadas. However, there's a subtle yet profound difference that sets us apart from cicadas: our inherent capacity for free will.

As humans, we possess the remarkable ability to choose our paths, make decisions, and influence the world around us. This gift of free will grant us the privilege to craft our own stories, shape our destinies, and sow the seeds of change.

Dear grandchildren! As you stand at the threshold of life, remember you are born into a world brimming with opportunities and choices. Your existence is a testament to the culmination of countless generations, an embodiment of the most privileged free will. With this gift, you hold the power to chart your course and carve your legacy upon the tapestry of time.

In the English proverb, "Where there's a will, there's a way," lies a profound truth: the resolve to achieve, the unyielding determination to overcome, can overcome any obstacle. This adage teaches you that in the face of trials, perseverance and ingenuity become your allies. It's a message that has stood the test of time, underscoring that every dream, every aspiration, and every endeavor you embark on can be realized if your will is strong enough.

As you delve into the stories that illuminate the profound wisdom of this proverb, remember that life's journey is yours to mold. The anecdotes that follow will serve as guiding lights, illustrating the indomitable spirit of the human heart and the boundless potential of the choices you make. Just as the cicadas' song echoes through the summer breeze, let the echoes of your choices reverberate through the tapestry of your life.

So, my beloved grandkids! step forward with the knowledge that you possess a unique blend of free will and destiny. Embrace the journey ahead with open arms, for it's a journey where you have the power to turn dreams into reality and navigate the twists and turns of existence.

An ordinary student who consistently achieved passing grades in exams. Despite his average academic performance, he harbored an unyielding dream of becoming a doctor. His friends ridiculed his ambition, asserting that only highly achieving students could aspire to such a profession. Although their mockery hurt him, he chose to accept their criticism with grace and resilience.

As time elapsed, the years rolled on, yet his determination to become a doctor remained unwavering. His conviction remained steadfast despite the doubts cast by those around him. One day, while watching a TV show, he was struck by a teacher's statement: "Where there is a will, there is a way." This proverb resonated deeply with him, as it encapsulated his own life's journey.

On that day, the young man had an epiphany moment. He realized that he possessed the willpower to fulfill his dream of becoming a doctor, but he needed to amplify his efforts and exhibit more assertiveness. With renewed vigor, he plunged into his studies, dedicating his days and nights to his goal. He pursued his medical aspirations with an unwavering focus, treating it as his sole ambition without any fallback plan.

Through relentless dedication and steadfast resolve, his hard work eventually bore fruit, and he achieved his lifelong dream of becoming a doctor. This story beautifully illustrates the adage, "Where there is a will, there is a way," highlighting the remarkable potential that determination and unwavering dedication hold in turning aspirations into reality.

Approaching the threshold of puberty, my two grandkids engaged in heartfelt conversations with their grandma. Their discussions covered various topics, ranging from the art of time management and the pleasures of culinary exploration to the allure of travel, the challenges of school life, and even the complexities of relationships, with no subject deemed too influential or too significant for their heartfelt exchanges.

As Grandma listened attentively, she assumed the role of a steadfast support system, sharing her wisdom, personal experiences, and thoughtful perspectives. The bond between them deepened through these conversations while creating a secured haven where guidance and understanding flowed seamlessly: These interactions held a volume of significance that surpassed mere verbal exchanges; their dialogues are destined to flourish as the grandkids traverse their own paths, fortified by the invaluable insights they have gleaned from their loving and wise grandma:

Grandkids: Grandma, if you were reborn next time, would you marry Grandpa again?
Grandma: No, I don't think so.
Grandkids: Why not?

Grandma: While we have lived together, he has disappointed me over money. When a husband has a good pocket of fortune, his wife has such a strong confidence in her life.

Grandkids: Grandma, we are getting into the age of dating our boyfriends, who would you advise us to choose our boyfriends with good money or a good-looking boy without it?

Grandma: Needless to say, the first. You know what: a man having a big pocket is always full of energy, and tries to comfort his wife by giving her more chances to enjoy. Additionally, when you have the opportunity to visit them, take into account their positive relationships with their parents and siblings in the family.

Grandkids: Understandable! Grandma. Today, listening to your advice, we could make up our minds about whom to choose. Thank you, Grandma, for your advice!

As people reach certain ages, they begin to broaden their horizons and look beyond their surroundings. However, many individuals continue to live their lives day by day, focused on fulfilling their desires: John finds joy in playing golf; Olivia engages in anonymous chats with boys around her; Jolly indulges in a lavish lifestyle and luxury fashionable items like Louis Vuitton.

The underlying connection that enables them to engage in these pursuits revolves around money. However, money doesn't materialize out of thin air; it requires effort and deliberate action on how to obtain and spend. Let's set aside the philosophical perspective for now and return to the practical role of money. For many, money serves as a source of security and a means to achieve personal goals and dreams. It can cover basic needs like food, housing, and healthcare while also providing for luxuries such as vacations and high-end cars.

Others view money as a means to attain power, status, recognition, and respect within society. Certainly, money itself plays a vital role in your life. It's important to note that there are numerous elements essential to your well-being, and these can vary from person to person.

My goal is to teach my beloved grandchildren how to earn and manage money in a practical manner, offering them guidance as they navigate their futures.

Reflecting on my childhood, I was raised in a rural area by a single mother. I never aspired to become a scientist or company director, I credit my accomplishments to the education and support provided by my own family. Nevertheless, I can't help but wonder if I could have become a different person with a bit more motivation and encouraged by others during that time.

Now, it's my return: it's my responsibility to establish our family legacy for my cherished grandchildren, who are on the brink of entering the real world, guided by the enduring warm affection left behind by my mother and grandfather, Shin Chigap. To achieve this, I embarked on a journey of searching for moral virtues that could serve as valuable lessons for you.

I dedicated years to curating a comprehensive list of moral virtues designed to empower my cherished girls to cultivate these qualities, ultimately guiding them toward a life of contentment and happiness. I delved into various books, "The Autobiography" written by B. Franklin, "Letter to His Son" by Philip Chesterfield, "The Secrets of Happy Families" by Bruce Feiler, insights from the Talmud, and even my own experiences.

Besides, I further explored texts like "How a Woman Spends Her Twenties Without Regret" by Hidenori Sakurai, and "Top 10 Things to Do in Your 20s" curated by Samsung executives and employees; along with many books and essays.

Through these undertakings, I've come to realize that the principles parents should impart to their children remain unchanged even in the present day, much like they did centuries ago. Those stand as a testament to the enduring resilience of humanity and its ongoing prosperity on this planet.

When I was young, I grappled with shyness that hindered me from stepping in front of others. My pursuit of overcoming this challenge led me to a technique from a book on 'mind control'. I stood in front of a mirror, looking at myself squarely with a smile, and repeatedly affirming, "Shin Hanok, you can overcome this shyness, can't you?" I continued by myself this exercise until my confidence grew. Today, I'm confidently able to face others without trembling, as my shyness has long since dissipated.

Benjamin, for example, crafted a plan of 13 virtues at the age of 20, in 1726. He dedicated himself to practicing these virtues in some form every day for the entirety of his life. While some of the virtues he chose may seem outdated by today's standards, they still hold enduring significance in various aspects of life.

I am pleased for you to follow the practices in this way: take on one of 15 items at a time, then after mastering that, and then shift to another through until 15 virtues. Also, I recommend you accept this practice to implement each virtue. Of course, if you guys have a better way, I won't stop you from doing that way.

However, I advise you to prepare a small notebook, to allocate a page for each of the virtues. On each page, create seven columns, one for each day of the week, and label each column with a letter representing the day. Divide these columns into 15 lines, marking each line with the letter of one virtue (as you see next page). You can use a small '**X**' to indicate every fault you commit in relation to the respective virtue.

Dedicate one week of strict attention to each virtue in succession. For example, in the first week, your primary focus is on avoiding the slightest offense against "Money," while leaving the other virtues to their turns. Each evening, mark the faults of the day with an 'X' or an '**O**' if you had no faults that week. If you have no 'X' marks in the first week, consider the habit of that virtue strengthened and its opposite weakened, allowing you to extend your extra attention to the next virtue in the following week. Continue this pattern until you complete a course of 15 weeks, and aim to go through many courses a year.

In addition to the notebook, I strongly recommend you prepare a whiteboard to supplementarily record your progress in practicing these. Because a visible reminder of your successes and areas for improvement can be highly beneficial.

Form of the Pages

		M	T	W	T	F	S	S
MONEY								
Save & Wisely Invest								
MONEY		O	✗					
TIME				✗				
HEALTH				O				
FAMILY								
FRIENDS						✔		
COMPASSION							✔	
TRUST								
MODERATION								
DEMEANOR								
COMMUNICATION								
HISTORY STUDY								
DILIGENCE								
ADAPTATION								
APPRECIATION								
REJUBINATION							✔	

It's also important to note that while you don't live entirely under these virtues and acknowledge falling short of them many times, you believe that the attempts to practice them made you a better person, contributing notably to your success and happiness. This is why I

devoted more pages to this plan in my autobiography stating a hope that my cherished grandchildren follow this way and
reap the benefits.

In addition to my own words, the moral virtues I wish to impart to you here have been gathered from my knowledge, experiences, the wisdom of ancestors, and the quotes of great men I've encountered throughout my 75 years of whole life. There are many more virtues to be found if you open your eyes to seek them, but it's challenging to list them all in my book.

But if you faithfully practice the virtues summarized here, you will find it easier to overcome others in due course. Here is my selection of virtues, not listed in any specific order, only considering that you are girls: ①*Money,* ②*Time,* ③*Health,* ④*Family,* ⑤*Friends,* ⑥*Compassion,* ⑦*Trust,* ⑧*Moderation,* ⑨*Demeanor,* ⑩*Communication,* ⑪*History Study,* ⑫*Diligence,* ⑬*Adaptation,* ⑭*Appreciation,* ⑮*Rejuvenation*

Money

When I was born and raised in the countryside, the use of money was limited, and we didn't really know how to spend it. Consequently, most parents didn't provide their children with pocket money, and some didn't even consider the idea of what was necessary for children.

On moving to Busan, I gradually grasped the influential role of money as it became more integrated into daily life. However, coming from the environment of my brother's household, I found it difficult to muster the courage to request an allowance when the need for money arose frequently. Reflecting on my upbringing in the countryside with experiences of scarcity and deprivation, I have had a longstanding aspiration to instill in my beloved grandkids the value of money.

For many people, money serves as a source of security and a means to achieve their goals and aspirations. More crucially, it's necessary for covering basic necessities like food, housing, clothing, healthcare, and even simple pleasures like music and travel. The list of necessities is exhaustive. On the other hand, some view money as a tool to gain power, status, and respect within society. In reality, we can't go a day, let alone an hour, without the influence of money.

In this context, the term "money" encompasses wealth, assets, real estate, and even modern concepts like cryptocurrencies. However, for us living in the present day, money primarily represents a convenient medium that facilitates our lives. To add to it, virtual currencies like Bitcoin are being developed even now. I do not intend to provide an extensive lecture on money, but rather to underscore its importance and share insights that can guide my beloved children throughout their lives.

Throughout extended history, debates have raged about whether money can buy happiness or not. While money cannot directly replace happiness, it certainly amplifies it. For instance, when John lacks the funds to purchase the Mercedes-Benz he desires, his happiness is curtailed. In contrast, Peter who has some disposable income, can go on the trip he's been longing for. The varying levels of happiness reveal the influence of money in our lives.

Educating children about financial responsibility is a universally confronting task. A survey asked thousands of people about their arguments with their spouses; the top reasons for women were children, housework, and money, while men cited women, money, and leisure. Money still remains an issue that both sides agree to disagree on.

In 2016, a significant political upheaval in South Korea involving Choi Sunsil, a woman who used her influence to manipulate President Park and led to her impeachment, highlighted the skewed perceptions around money. So, it's of utmost importance for me to prioritize the discussion of the power of money as the first topic when we talk about moral virtues.

Money wields immense influence. With a certain amount of money, lives can be saved in hospitals, support can be extended to those in need, and educational pursuits can be pursued. On the flip side, the lack of money can create hurdles, even in attending school due to the inability to cover transportation or other expenses.

This principle extends to everyday situations as well, including preparing gifts and cards for your friends' birthdays or hosting your own birthday celebration. Especially in your era of technology-driven

201

culture and entertainment, money's influence is magnified. Yet, it's essential to remember that money is a means to an end, not the ultimate goal.

Therefore, focusing on how to earn money and use it wisely is a key thing. Two distinguished figures and your dad highlight how people can acquire financial wisdom and skills through various paths and experiences.

Bill Gates, co-founding the software giant Microsoft, had learned from his parents underscore the importance of early financial lessons. His learning from them the value of saving and rational spending at a young age could lay a solid foundation for his successful business journey.

On the other hand, a business magnate, investor, and philanthropist, Warren Buffett's approach to earning and managing money through his endeavors provides a life example to everyone.

As my cherished girls are well aware, your father's involvement in real estate ventures, under me, during his university years proved the practical application of financial concepts. His hands-on experience likely has offered him a unique perspective on how money works. Back then, your dad and grandpa had created and distributed a money-making guidebook to our customers.

The satisfaction of hearing that people are using and benefiting from our guidebook is immensely gratifying. The principles in the pamphlet we created are simple and basic investment techniques: ① *Save seed money for investment by cutting unnecessary expenses,* ② *Leverage the bank's advantages for investment: a crucial benefit of real estate is not needing to fund the entire investment,* ③ *Invest in well-known areas,* ④ *Hold onto properties rather than selling immediately,* ⑤ *Purchase during market down-turns and wait for the right moment to sell. This patience and diligence can lead to wealth.*

Thus, I conclude the discussion on money in the first of the fifteen Virtues, I would like to draw a well-known adage "Don't boast about having a lot, and don't be sad about not having enough" which remains relevant. If you find yourself lacking something, it's essential to take responsibility for addressing that lack on your own.

Time

It is widely accepted that time is a universal resource, distributed equally to anyone. Each day, we wake up with the same 24 hours to allocate as we see fit. Regardless of our background – whether rich or poor, black or white, male or female, famous or unknown – everyone is granted the same amount of time. But, the significance and utility of the time we experience can vary greatly.

Consider an hour in the life of different people; for me, it might hold a distinct value compared to the way Elon Musk, with his remarkable ability to generate value, might perceive it. Similarly, residing in a developed country with abundant amenities can enable one to derive more satisfaction from the time compared to someone in an underdeveloped nation.

My cherished girls, you've reached an age where contemplating time is of great importance. Regardless of who you are, your lifespan is finite. The present may appear endless, but it's a regrettable truth that the days you spend will never be recovered. Younger generations would often assume they have an abundance of time ahead, leading them to potentially squander it. However, as history has shown, even great fortunes inherited from ancestors can vanish over time. Once gone, these treasures are exceedingly difficult to reclaim.

A curious aspect of time is that it eludes our direct perception. This intangibility makes it easy to overlook its perpetual presence. This oversight is especially common among young individuals engaged in bustling lives, where time can inadvertently slip through their fingers. Rather than dissecting the mechanics of time, I wish to emphasize the importance of utilizing it wisely.

I implore you to recognize that 'the invaluable time of youth' is a resource that cannot be restored. This sentiment cannot be stressed enough. It is said that how you spend today significantly shapes your tomorrow.

Allow me to share a practical tip to make the most of your time: imagine having a 12 o'clock appointment with a friend, and they don't arrive on time. In this scenario, having a light book on hand can be a clever solution. A book that doesn't demand intense concentration is ideal for such instances.

In our modern age, the boundary between study and leisure can be blurred. The ubiquity of the internet allows for both learning and entertainment anywhere, with the responsibility of managing this access falling squarely on your shoulders.

Here's another time-saving notion I'd like to propose. When your father spends time in the bathroom, often for 20 minutes or more, that interval could be utilized for reading. Carrying a book can transform these moments into productive reading sessions, accumulating a huge number of hours over a year.

Furthermore, you can maximize time by engaging in light reading or completing homework while traveling by bus or train. However, it's important to remember that humans aren't meant to solely study. Adequate rest and recreation are crucial for efficient work tomorrow. View play as a restorative pause that enhances productivity. Therefore, those who adeptly manage and control their time are poised to face the future with contentment.

Health

No one in this world can achieve great feats without considering their health. Alexander the Great, the renowned king of the ancient Greek kingdom of Macedon, ascended the throne at the age of 20 and led a far-reaching military campaign across Western Asia and Egypt.

By the age of 30, he had established one of the largest empires in history, spanning from Greece to northwestern India. Regarded as an unparalleled military commander, he remained undefeated in battles. However, on 10 June 323 BC, at a mere 32 years old, his life came to a close in Babylon due to a fever exacerbated by wine consumption.

My dear Girls, remember that health should neither be taken for granted nor unduly worried about. Even the illustrious Alexander the Great, as mentioned herewith, succumbed to a seemingly minor ailment despite his youthful age, abruptly ending his dreams and ambitions. This serves as a reminder that health, no matter how much we emphasize its significance, is not invincible.

In my eyes, it appears that my beloved princesses are fortunately blessed with reasonably good health. Your interest in running and swimming or badminton is indeed reassuring. Good health not only holds intrinsic value but also bestows you with the confidence necessary to face life's challenges. Consider how essential it is to possess sound health when participating in competitions alongside your peers. Today's world is brimming with busy schedules and hidden health issues that can unexpectedly diminish your quality of life.

I share my concern regarding certain behaviors that can have negative impacts on health and well-being, especially among young individuals. Staying up late engaging in recreational activity, drinking, smoking, and relying on instant dining options and fast food can indeed pose risks to both physical and mental health.

Promoting a balanced lifestyle that includes regular exercise, a well-rounded diet, sufficient sleep, and healthy recreational activities is essential for maintaining good health and preventing future health problems. In most cases, good health is not innate; it's an outcome of dedicated effort. Allow me to share the health rules I've learned and embraced. In the pursuit of success and fulfillment, prioritizing your health is a foundation that will stand you in good stead for the journey ahead:

Firstly: adopt a balanced diet and engage in regular exercise. While these principles generally apply to everyone seeking good health, considering your age and impending growth, the emphasis on quantity may not be immediate. Lessening intake as you progress through the latter part of adolescence remains a sound approach, validated by Longevity Village's health orders.
Secondly: allocate ample time for rest. Strive for app. 8 hours of sleep each day, as adequate rest acts as a catalyst for productive days ahead.
Thirdly: cultivate friendships and engage in meaningful talks to alleviate the stresses of daily life. Whenever possible, travel is a wonderful opportunity, although curiosity-driven smoking has to be avoided. It's worth noting that I have never smoked cigarettes throughout my life.

205

Fourthly: guard against overeating and opt for multigrain rice. Consume warm tea and fruits for dessert. Lastly, consider incorporating supplements such as vitamins A, C, and D into your routine.

Family

I hope that Yoorina's exploration of our family traditions through the homework assigned by Kadima School proves to be an enriching experience. Although Grandpa lent a helping hand by sharing my knowledge and experiences acquired over the years, it would have been wonderful if you could uncover more on your own. While our family may not boast a grand tradition, we have inherited valuable customs from our ancestors that I hope you can take pride in.

During my childhood, my family had a mission notably displayed at our main bedroom door: "Family is All." This simple phrase held profound meaning for each family member and resonated like a harmonious melody.

As time goes on, the significance of home remains constant and unwavering. Let me capture the essence of what home truly means: family harmony forms the bedrock upon which everything else is built. Ideally, the home should be a space for both learning and restoration, a place where one can find solace and rejuvenation.

However, contemporary times have witnessed a shift in the concept of family. Traditional family structures have given way to nuclear families living in separate homes, and even divorced families sharing a residence. Some children are raised by two mothers, while others may not have their parents at all. The notion of what constitutes a family is rapidly evolving, rendering the imposition of existing family traditions less relevant.

Nonetheless, despite these changes, a home remains a haven of safety and a sanctuary for each family member. While it's true that love and peace flourish within these walls, it's equally true that disagreements and conflicts are natural occurrences between parents and children, and among siblings.

Research indicates that only one in eight such disputes conclude with reconciliation or compromise. From my perspective, occasional conflicts between you guys are, while not frequent, a part of growing up and not a cause for undue concern. Yet, from your parents' point, these may appear less trivial, possibly suggesting family discord to outsiders. In the event of such conflicts, I strongly recommend that one of you shift the atmosphere by taking a brief break, stepping outside to get fresh air, or engaging in solitary reading. Afterward, when emotions have settled, offer apologies to each other.

Rest assured, by following this process, any anger or resentment will likely diminish naturally. Remember that family quarrels rarely have a prolonged impact; in the worst-case scenario, they fade within a few days, or even within minutes.

In today's fast-paced world, every family member has their own busy schedule. Fathers may be engrossed in business to provide, mothers managing the household, and children balancing school, extracurricular activities, and playtime. Amidst this, a question arises: is the tradition of family dinners still relevant?

Recent years have witnessed a surge in the importance of family dinners, with Hollywood stars and prominent individuals advocating for regular family gatherings around the dining table. Former US President Obama frequently mentioned his nightly dinners with his daughter in the White House; a tradition followed by President George W. Bush.

Research indicates that children who partake in family dinners are less likely to engage in risky behaviors such as substance abuse and are more likely to possess larger vocabularies, better manners, healthier diets, and adaptability to society. Interestingly, family mealtime seems to exert a more profound influence than time spent studying, attending institutions, or participating in sports.

Once again, my cherished grandchildren and family are everything; I cannot emphasize this enough.

Friends

Yoorina and Yoojina, there's no doubt that friendships are among life's most precious treasures. A friend you choose to hold close is akin to a mirror that reflects your true identity. Have you missed your old friends from Kadima School since you moved to Glendowie School? There's a saying that holds true in such cases: old friends become better with time. This thought stems from my concern, and I hope that you will continue to cherish your existing friends from Kadima and maintain those connections.

At the same time, it's crucial to establish new friends at your new school, forging friendships with new companions. This will expand your social circle and enhance your life through novel interactions. The number of genuine and lasting friendships you nurtured throughout your life will contribute significantly to your bright future. To achieve this, always remember to care for your friends, nourishing your relationships to keep them vibrant and mutual.

Allow me to offer a recommendation about making friends as you venture into this new chapter of your lives: embrace a gradual approach, in line with the old English proverb "softly, softly, catch monkey." This means that with patience and perseverance, you'll eventually achieve your goals. Building real friendships requires a steady pace; mutual trust is a cornerstone that takes time to develop.

When selecting friends, consider making companions as better than you. Surrounding yourself with such friends will encourage personal growth, as you'll naturally aspire to their level. Conversely, associating with people below your own standard might lead to your own disgrace.

This concept aligns with the saying "Birds of a feather flock together." Strive to associate with individuals who elevate you, as it benefits your personal growth. Similarly, avoid a company that may lead you astray, epitomized by the Spanish saying: "Tell me whom you live with, and I will tell you who you are."

A vital aspect of maintaining lasting friendships is to refrain from financial transactions among friends. Imagine a situation where a friend borrows money and struggles to repay it. Such circumstances could strain your friendship, potentially leading to its breakdown. It's crucial to manage your friendships before cracks appear, nurturing them through the stages of growth and connection.

Distinguish between friends and acquaintances; the latter is often referred to as company. An acquaintance is someone you know but not on an intimate level. A casual friend, on the other hand, is someone you share a more profound emotional bond with, someone you'd meet one-on-one. Ultimately, your aim should be to cultivate true friendships and to do so, you must learn how to maintain them sincerely and enduringly.

Speaking from the context of today's divided world, well-preserved friendships serve as catalysts to heal estrangement, polarization, and division. In a society marked by bitter divisions, nurturing positive relationships can prevent anger and isolation. Amidst the culture war that seems to pit opposing factions against each other, well-nurtured friendships stand as a beacon of unity and understanding.

As the crisis of personal isolation and cultural division deepens, the need for close connections grows stronger. With the rise of social networks, people are spending less time with those of differing opinions, exacerbating the sense of estrangement. In this context, well-maintained friendships provide solace and connection beyond hyper-interactions.

If you find a genuine friend, seize the opportunity and show the virtue of initiating contact. Regularly reaching out and caring for these connections will help sustain your friendships over time.

Lastly, a note on dating: remember, everyone has their own pride. Men are often hesitant to reveal their weaknesses and imperfections. Personally, I've lived my whole life with an inferiority complex about my short stature. Criticizing someone's intellect, appearance, or his background could provoke deeper resentment than candid honesty. To avoid making an implacable enemy, it's best to refrain from addressing their shortcomings.

As you embark on your journey into the real world, Grandpa's wish is for you guys to encounter countless brilliant friends and lead joyful, fulfilling lives. Good luck!

Compassion

Compassion is a beautiful quality that means caring about how other people feel. It's like when you see a sad friend, and you want to help them feel better. Think of it as a warm, fuzzy blanket for your heart, keeping it cozy with love and kindness: embrace love for parents, friends, grandparents, nephew Millie, pets Winston and Mimi, and anyone else who holds a special place in your heart.

Dear beloved girls, love comes in many forms. It can be the joy you feel when you savor your favorite meal, the deep bond between a mother and her child, or the warmth you share with your friends. Love isn't just about attraction; it's also about kindness, compassion, and empathy towards others.

Our world is evolving into a more diverse place, with people from various backgrounds coming together. For instance, consider New Zealand, where recent Census data from June 2023 shows a population of approximately 5.22 million. Among this diverse population, 60% identify with European ethnicity, while Māori make up 16.5%, Asians 15.3%, Pacific Islanders 7%, and others contribute 1.5%. It's an incredible mix of cultures and backgrounds that defines New Zealand as a truly multicultural society.

In this diverse world, compassion is like a bridge that connects people from different walks of life. It helps us understand and empathize with others, even if they have different cultures or beliefs. Embracing cultural diversity and inclusivity is essential, as it reduces inequality and fosters collaboration in our communities.

Navigating this diversity might seem challenging, but the rewards are profound. To thrive in a multicultural society, you must approach people with compassion, empathy, and an open mind. It means understanding others deeply and appreciating the richness of social diversity.

Imagine you see someone hurt; compassion is that feeling that makes you want to make them feel better. It's about spreading love and kindness in the world. Picture a world where everyone cares for each other - that's the power of compassion! Even small acts of kindness, like sharing your toys with a friend who has none, can make a big difference.

To succeed in this kind of multicultural society, it's crucial to be competent in understanding and respecting different cultural perspectives and beliefs. People from various backgrounds may need to approach situations differently, and it's essential to appreciate these differences.

So, my dear girls, remember that compassion is like a magic hug that makes the world a better place. The more you show compassion, the more love you spread, and the happier the world becomes. Picture a world where everyone cares for each other; that's the power of compassion! Remember, even small acts of kindness can make a big difference, and that's what compassion is all about: compassion is when you share your toys with a friend who doesn't have any to play with.

Trust

My beloved princesses, do you think life is meant to be enjoyed with Grandpa? You might say "yes," and I feel the same way. However, life is more than just enjoyment; it delves into the realm of destiny, a philosophical concept that tells us each person's life is an inescapable fate. We are born into this world with a destiny we cannot reject. Despite this daunting truth, we must believe in the continuity of existence, an unavoidable aspect of our lives.

Trust is a challenging thing to place in anyone other than ourselves. Yet, trust is the cornerstone of a functioning society; without it, a society would crumble instantly. Thus, trust plays a vital role in our lives, enabling us to function collectively.

Have you ever found yourself in a situation where people lacked trust in each other? If so, you understand the challenges and toll this situation can take. A team without trust is not a team; it's merely a group of individuals attempting to collaborate but often achieving inadequate results. Likewise, have you ever thought about families that lack trust? Everyone is hostile towards each other, and the family is likely to fall apart.

However, in an environment of trust, each member of the team becomes stronger, as they are part of an effective, harmonious group. When people trust one another, the group can reach significant goals. So, as a leader, how can you foster the trust needed for your team to flourish?

Trust is defined as "reliance on the character, ability, strength, or truth of someone or something." Ponder this definition. Trust signifies the willingness to depend on someone else to make the right decisions. It's a belief in their integrity and capabilities to the point where you are willing to take risks, even at your own expense.

Trust is indispensable in a productive team as it creates a sense of safety. When team members feel safe among each other, they are more likely to share openly, take calculated risks, and reveal vulnerabilities. In the absence of trust, innovation, collaboration, creative thinking, and productivity suffer, as individuals focus on safeguarding their interests rather than pursuing collective goals.

Cultivating trust holds equal significance within a family setting. We all aspire for our families to be robust and harmonious. Achieving this goal demands that your family unit operates as a cohesive team, necessitating effort akin to any other team endeavor. To shape your family into a unified entity, the foundation of trust must be laid, and explicit expectations established. Through trust, family members place faith in each other's words and have confidence in the fulfillment of promises.

Trust is a fragile element; once broken, its restoration becomes a challenging task. Furthermore, trust serves as the cornerstone of robust relationships. If you don't impart to someone the significance of trust and the methods to nurture it, they will encounter hurdles in establishing substantial connections with you.

Therefore, my cherished girls, incorporate the notion of trust into your life journey: it stands as a vital component for cultivating thriving relationships and fostering your personal growth.

Moderation

My dear girls, the concept of moderation can be summarized as the process of eliminating or lessening extremes. It's a virtue that extends across various aspects of human behavior, from eating to education. The idea of moderation dates back to ancient Greece, where it was seen as a guiding principle for a balanced life. The temple of Apollo at Delphi famously bore the inscription, 'Nothing in excess,' emphasizing the importance of avoiding extremes.

Moderation encompasses the notion of not indulging excessively in anything. For example, someone practicing moderation in their diet aims to include all food groups while limiting the intake of items that might have negative effects on their health.

In Chinese Confucian philosophy, moderation is considered a high virtue. Confucius emphasized the principle of "Zhongyong," which translates to moderation in one's words and deeds. This principle suggests that everything has its limits, and maintaining moderation, neither exceeding nor falling short of those limits, is essential for balanced living.

In today's world, with the increasing prevalence of technology and algorithmic decision-making, maintaining the virtue of moderation without being overwhelmed by them has become a challenge. It's essential for you to adopt a mindset of moderation, utilizing effective and appropriate methods through diligent review processes.

Allow me to draw an analogy to the role of a conductor in a musical performance. A conductor directs an orchestra or choir, interpreting the musical score and guiding performers through gestures, tempo, and phrasing. He assures each musician's contribution is harmonious and aligned with the overall performance. Similarly, moderation involves staying within a set range and avoiding extremes, just as a conductor guides musicians to create harmonious music.

Remember, my cherished girls, that moderation is not just about what you eat or consume, but also about how you manage life. Don't overindulge simply because there's an abundance of something. The principle of moderation extends to various aspects of life, including managing desires, and burdens, and seeking happiness.

Imagine you have a favorite dessert, like ice cream. You love ice cream, and it's so delicious that you want to eat it every day. But you know that eating too much ice cream every day wouldn't be good for your health. So, you decide to enjoy ice cream as a special treat, like on weekends or after doing something special, instead of having it every day. This way, you get to enjoy your favorite dessert, but you also make sure to eat other healthy foods like fruits and vegetables to keep your body strong and healthy.

In a world filled with desires and challenges, living in accordance with the moral virtue of moderation can be a practical philosophy to lead a good life. By embracing moderation, you can find balance, contentment, and freedom amidst the complexities of modern life.

Demeanor

My beloved princesses, the concept of demeanor is a reflection of a person's outward behavior, encompassing their actions, speech, experience, body language, and dressing. It's how you present yourself to the world, and it plays a significant role in your interactions with others and your overall life. Let's delve into the significance of maintaining a positive demeanor in various situations.

To uphold a good demeanor in life requires ongoing self-discipline. It's the foundation upon which you can build improvements. A person with a nice demeanor is comfortable in any company, displaying care and integrity. This individual is often sought after for important tasks due to their positive character.

Both of you, my dear princesses, have shown a shy, friendlier, and warmer demeanor. These qualities have a gentle effect on your friends. Remember to maintain this demeanor even in challenging situations when delivering bad news. It reflects your character and shows that you care about the feelings of others.

Francis Bacon, once an English philosopher and artist, emphasized the importance of a graceful and pleasing demeanor. He highlighted aspects such as well-dressing, refraining from vulgar behaviors, clear expression of one's opinions, active listening, and maintaining a warm smile. These qualities obviously contribute to a positive image and lasting impressions on others.

The art of living is intricately connected to relationships with someone. In a world filled with diverse individuals, flexibility is also essential to navigate interactions without conflict. Just like reeds that bend without breaking in the wind, you should adapt and be open-minded.

Paying close attention to your appearance, particularly by dressing neatly rather than lavishly, is crucial. Your appearance can convey respect, self-esteem, and attention to detail. In many cultures, neat clothing carries symbolic value, and presenting yourself well speaks to your demeanor.

Interacting with various people allows you to learn from their experiences and broaden your perspectives. Active listening and expressing yourself thoughtfully are vital in conversations. The ability to handle small things skillfully prepares you for bigger challenges in the future.

To live a successful life, strive to show a positive side to everyone you meet. This requires personal effort and daily practice of keeping a positive mindset. Remember that endless effort and practice can shape your demeanor and interactions positively.

Now, let's explore a parable about inheritance. In this story, an elder Jewish man leaves a will for his son, and the son has to choose between his father's possessions or inheriting the faithful slave. The son's choice to the faithful slave carries profound meaning, and I encourage both of you to discuss and interpret the parable, as Jews are known for their wisdom.

Lastly, fairness is not about equal outcomes, but rather about equal opportunities. It means that everyone in a group has the chance to benefit, even though the results might not be identical. Understanding this principle can guide your interactions and decisions as you navigate through life.

Communication

My cherished princesses, communication is a fundamental aspect of human life. From the moment we are born, we begin to communicate through cries and expressions. As we grow, it becomes an essential tool to express ourselves, share ideas, and make decisions. The ability to communicate effectively through speech is a valuable skill that can shape our personal and professional success.

A competent speaker often possesses strong communication skills that extend beyond simple dialogue. Successful businessmen are adept at various forms of communication, including texting, emailing, speaking, verbal conversations, body language, and facial expressions. Communication, in all its forms, is an integral part of our daily lives and impacts various aspects of decision-making and negotiation.

Negotiation is a key element of our lives, whether we're deciding bedtime for kids or discussing a salary increase with a boss. The challenges we face during negotiations often stem from our own attitudes and perspectives. It's crucial to shift our focus and consider the other party's viewpoint. Empathy and understanding are crucial in successful negotiations.

I have been a bit concerned that our two princesses may not be inclined to actively stand out in front of others. But don't worry too much. You can overcome this through sufficient practice in advance.

Becoming a skilled communicator requires dedication and practice. To start, set a goal to become a talented speaker who excels in various social contexts. Hone your speaking skills in everyday conversations and work on acquiring an accurate, dignified, and genuine speech style. Reading books about speech written by orators, both classic and modern, can provide valuable insights into effective communication techniques.

When you're reading with the intention of improving your dialogue skills, pay attention to style, word choice, and expression. Develop your unique speaking style and practice it before conversations. If you don't prepare beforehand, reflect on the conversation afterward to improve your speaking skills.

Just as a skilled shoemaker learns how to fit shoes to individual feet, a good communicator learns how to effectively deal with various perspectives. Learning effective communication is a lifelong journey, and by honing this skill, you'll become a confident and persuasive speaker.

History Study

My beloved princesses, the importance of waking up early each morning cannot be emphasized enough. It grants you a precious hour or two of uninterrupted time for reading, or studying before the distractions of the day take over. This practice not only enhances your personal growth in knowledge but also helps you find your roots

In the early morning, history studying is a powerful way to gain insights into the world. History helps you understand the societies and nations in which we live, guiding our lives and fostering critical thinking. It gives us a sense of identity and direction, enabling us to learn from both the successes and mistakes of our ancestors.

Remember that a nation without knowledge of its history has had no future. For instance, consider the history of Kadima School, rooted in Jews. Understanding the value of studying the history of different cultures enrich your perspectives and foster pride in your heritage.

I often reference the history of different countries to illustrate my points because history is a universal teacher. Jews have faced challenges and persecution in many countries, yet they've emerged as influential contributors to the global economy and technology. This underscores the importance of studying history.

When reading history books, it's helpful to have maps, data books, biographies of important figures, and historical references. This information will assist you in comprehending historical contexts and connecting events.

The essence of history lies in the fact that we stand on the shoulders of those who came before us. Our democracy, peace, and happiness are the outcomes of their struggles. Understanding the past is vital to appreciating the progress we've made.

Now, let's take a brief overview of our own history. Our roots trace back to 2333 B.C. with the establishment of the first Kingdom of the Korean Peninsula. Throughout various kingdoms and dynasties, our nation has faced challenges and achieved significant milestones, even enduring periods of Japanese rule and old Chinese dynasties.

Understanding our history helps us appreciate our current circumstances and the sacrifices made for our well-being.

While studying history is crucial, it's equally important to study in conjunction with other areas of subjects, math, bioscience, chemistry, mechanics, and AI technologies. Regardless of age, lifelong learning is a continuous journey and joy through study to the end.

My dear princesses, as you grow, remember the ancient sayings about learning: "If you don't study hard when you're young, you'll regret it when you're old." As you see, Grandpa, too, keeps continuing to learn and read. The pursuit of knowledge is driven by the desire to expand your horizons. Learning habits, which I recommend to you, should be short and focused, with about 30-minute study sessions followed by short breaks.

But consistency is key, and habitual learning is a more effective way. Minimize distractions during studying and consider it an opportunity to acquire amazing knowledge. Embrace the delight of learning, for knowledge, serves as the key to unlocking a realm of endless prospects.

Diligence

My dear princesses, the virtue of diligence is a powerful force that drives progress and development in your lives. Diligence is marked by carefulness, persistent effort, and a strong work ethic. It's the belief that work in itself, holds value and contributes to personal growth and the better of society. Diligence is a means to an end and not the end itself, therefore it is an ongoing journey without a finite conclusion.

The wisdom of Benjamin Franklin, a renowned figure in American history, shines through his advocacy for diligence. The virtue of 'Industry' in his book emphasizes the efficient use of time and engaging in useful activities, aligning closely with the concept of diligence.

Also, Thomas Edison, a prolific inventor, epitomized the idea that success is primarily built on persistent effort. His quote regarding diligence, "Genius is 1% inspiration and 99% perspiration," highlights the role of hard work in realizing one's potential. Our human brain, similar to a tool, requires continuous development and utilization to remain effective.

Much like Lamarck's 'use and defuse theory', exemplified, by the giraffe's neck stretching, that human brains develop when actively used, but can deteriorate more rapidly when neglected, it implies that acquired physical characteristics can be passed down to offspring based on the parent organism's use or disuse during its lifetime. Your abilities and capacities are honed through consistent effort and dedication over time.

That's why my beloved girls go to school every day in the morning to learn something from school. Schools and teachers serve as providing you a vessel for acquiring wisdom and knowledge that you will harness as adults.

However, complacencies many of you may perceive can impede progress, underscore the importance of individual effort in sustaining and enhancing the civilization we presently enjoy. Countless scientists, inventors, and even scholars tirelessly work to advance human knowledge. Their contributions have shaped the world's development.

Bear in mind that your potential knows no bounds, and the possibilities ahead of you are infinite. Only your diligence contributes to the progress of humanity, much as the great people have done throughout history. Once again, it's crucial to understand that the principle of "use and disuse," is exemplified by the stretching of a giraffe's neck.

In a world that often lauds genius, acknowledging the efforts of the majority becomes paramount: those diligent and hardworking individuals who play a pivotal role in propelling society forward. Your willingness to diligence can position you to make a significant impact on the world.

As you pursue learning, personal growth, or the pursuit of growth in society, remember that diligence acts as a guiding light, leading you toward productivity and fulfillment. Whether you're walking the dog or heading to school, don't let your mind go idle. Instead, choose a topic you prefer, put in your earphones, and listen to it daily. You'll notice significant progress in that field after just a few days. This is your grandpa's way of diligence.

Adaptation

My cherished grandkids, adapting to change is an essential skill in today's ever-changing world. Just as the ancient philosopher Heraclitus noted, change is a principal aspect of existence, so you learn to navigate it effectively. As you wisely observe, there are several significant changes taking place that will shape the future of your lives, careers, and society as a whole. Here's how you can navigate some of these changes:

Technology: a rapid advancement of technology is altering the way you interact. Embrace new forms of communication, from smartphones to cutting-edge work technologies, and consider how they can be integrated into your personal and professional life.

Connection: in our hyperconnected world, it's essential to develop the ability to work with diverse cultures and environments. This will be key as traditional centers of power shift, making you connected to effective collaboration with different people and societies.

Diversity: every culture possesses its unique set of norms, values, and ways of life. It's important to understand that what could be considered appropriate or acceptable in one culture might not hold true in another. Showing respect for these differences is essential for fostering effective cross-cultural awareness.

Populism: populism often emerges in response to perceived today in every area inequality and dissatisfaction. It tends to emphasize the concerns and interests of ordinary citizens, claiming to represent their voices and champion their needs. But it's important to understand the underlying reasons behind these and engage in open discussions to address concerns effectively.

You're right, my princesses. The emergence of populism and the blurring of distinctions between different regions have indeed brought profound changes to the forefront in any corner. As societies become more interconnected and divided, it is essential for my dear girls to understand the cultural nuance and sentiment that shape your actions. Therefore, adaptation is crucial when dealing with diverse people and cultures around you.

Imagine a bustling city, where people from different cultures come together. Adaptation is at play here too, as individuals learn to navigate different customs, languages, culinary arts, and lifestyles. It's the story of an urban lifestyle, where diversity thrives through adaptation. In the realm of modern technology, adaptation takes on a whole new chapter. Consider the rapid evolution of smartphones and high technologies, with XZY generations adapting quickly to the demands of a tech-savvy world. It's a story of innovation and adaptation in the palm of your hand.

The ever-changing world of nature calls for adaptation as the key survival strategy. Take, for instance, the chameleon, a master of blending into its surroundings. Its ability to change colors is a living testament to nature's incredible power of adaptation.

My beloved grandchildren, how have you managed to adapt so effectively to the rapid changes faced you? You're intimately familiar with smartphones, laptops, and Wi-Fi, to the extent that you could probably work from the bottom of the ocean. What's your secret?

Rather than resisting change, you embrace it with open arms, always ready to welcome to seize new opportunities. Older generations mistakenly perceive younger lads as lazy, but in reality, your generation possesses a unique quality: you constantly question the status quo.

One of the significant issues for the elderly is their struggle to keep up with the latest technology. Many of them have settled into routines and may rely on younger generations to handle technological tasks for them. But the excuse of "We didn't have this in our day" is no longer acceptable in the ever-changing world.

In the late fourth century BC, a Chinese philosopher Zhuangzi stated that shifting our perspective enables us to transcend our customary way of perceiving the world and instead view it through a lens of vibrancy and creativity:

A monkey trainer distributed nuts, stating, "You receive three in the morning and four at night." The monkeys became furious. However, he adjusted and said, "Very well, you shall have four in the morning and three at night." This delighted the monkeys.

Despite receiving the same quantity of nuts, their emotions of happiness and anger fluctuated. This tale underscores how shifting perspectives can influence our perceptions and emotional responses.

Appreciation

A valuable lesson learned from happiness research is that expressing gratitude to others holds tremendous power in making the recipient feel happier: sending thank-you notes, leaving messages of appreciation, or even a small blessing from parents to children, have all been proven to enhance your happiness.

There is an ancient Korean proverb that goes, "*A single word can settle a thousand debts.*" This saying highlights the power of gratitude to alleviate accumulated negative emotions. However, many of us are often hesitant to convey our appreciation to others. We may worry that our intentions will be misinterpreted or that the recipient might feel uncomfortable.

Conversely, as human beings, we shall yearn for appreciation and recognition from others. Whether it's taking on extra tasks alongside your own, dedicating weekends to launch a project, or extending a helping hand to your classmates in their time of need, a simple acknowledgment or a heartfelt "thank you" can significantly boost our sense of fulfillment in the contributions we've made.

However, many of us hold fears regarding expressing our gratitude. We might worry that the other person will reject or misconstrue our intentions, or we might struggle to find the right words to convey our appreciation. A method that I've found effective in overcoming these fears is starting small with a simple thank-you note. Following a few guidelines can ensure that your efforts are truly heartfelt. Emails can get lost, while handwritten cards are cherished. Therefore, write your message on paper, a post-it note, or a card, and deliver it directly to the person. If you're at work, leave it on their desk or in their mailbox. If you won't see them soon, take a photo of your message and send it to them, or better yet, mail the card.

The more you offer praise for the positive actions of others, the more abundant the results you'll harvest as a potent source of happiness. From the moment humans are born, they are wired to thrive on praise. If you scold a child, they may burst into tears, but a word of praise can instantly light up their face as if no negativity had occurred. There's even a proverb that suggests praise has the power to make even a whale dance:

A boy was born in Odense, Denmark on 2 April 1805. His father runs a tailor shop and reads to his son stories like a book, 'Arabian Nights' every night. He had a dream of becoming a writer while listening to the story. But his friends and teachers at school discouraged him, "You don't have a talent to write"; but his mother always praised him for his writing skills. The boy grew up later to become a world-famous fairy tale writer: he is Hans Christian Andersen.

However, offering others praise, it's essential to tailor your approach to match the individual's personality. For instance, a shy person like my dear girls might feel embarrassed by public praise. In such cases, it's more effective to offer praise in a quiet and private manner that respects their introverted nature. Additionally, praise should be given promptly, as soon as you notice something praiseworthy. Furthermore, it's advisable to focus on praising the process rather than just the end result.

In today's world, it often appears that many people seek constant attention around the clock. However, I want to express that it's not my wish for you to become the center of such attention. Rather, I hope you will contemplate carefully the actions you could choose to undertake in the world and the areas in which you may dedicate yourselves. Your grandfather's aspiration is for you to make thoughtful decisions that positively contribute to the world around you.

Rejuvenation

My dear young ladies, homo sapiens cannot simply work or study tirelessly all day long. Sometimes, it is essential for you to take breaks and seek moments of rest. These timely pleasures serve as a touching reminder of the delicate joy that comes with embracing those points at precisely the right juncture in our lives. They symbolize the art of embracing happiness when it aligns with your working conditions. This enrichment not only enhances your well-being but also elevates the very quality of your existence.

This concept paints a vivid picture of the importance of finding delight in the present, an outlook that includes a spectrum of activities: from savoring a tranquil moment with a cup of coffee amidst a breathtaking view to devoting time with loving partners, to pursuing personal passions, and engaging in activities that ignite your inner joy – all these aspects collectively underline the significance of seizing the here and now.

This ethos of timely pleasure beckons you to honor and give precedence to those gleaming instances of happiness that punctuate your daily journey. As you thoughtfully think of this theme, you're encouraged to grasp these moments, thereby relishing the elegance of existence. It's in these fleeting instances that you achieve a balance between the responsibilities of work and the rejuvenation of leisure, nurturing a holistic sense of well-being.

Amidst the characteristics that define our humanity, lies the ability to relish what brings you joy. Imagine your dad, for instance, indulging in the exhilaration of driving a luxurious car at full speed or immersing himself in the electrifying realm of NBA basketball via YouTube. It's an undeniable truth that no one can remain tethered to the demands of work incessantly. Thus, there arises a need to pursue the activities that truly delight you, whether it's watching movies, enjoying knitting, embarking on thrilling adventures, or even indulging in the solace of reading books and crafting tales.

The essence of Daily pleasure hinges on the art of dwelling in the present moment and seizing the chances to revel in life's splendors.

It's a reminder that experiencing joy in the very now, rather than consistently postponing it for an uncertain future, is what fosters a life that's fulfilling and harmonious. Whether it's pausing amidst work to savor a steaming cup of coffee with a mesmerizing view or dedicating quality moments with loved ones, these seemingly small gestures weave together to create a tapestry of timely pleasures.

In light of this, I extend an invitation to both of you: explore and uncover what your hearts truly yearn for, whether it's the art of knitting, getting fresh air with your pets, or reading a romantic novel: the choice is yours, and it's a means to alleviate the strains of daily life. This journey of self-discovery can lead to heightened life satisfaction, bridging the gap between the rigors of hard work and the rejuvenation of personal passions.

Many of us strive for tranquility and alignment by momentarily stepping back from the demands of the world, steering clear of entanglements that often trigger discomfort. Whether it's enjoying a coffee break, watching a movie, embarking on a vacation, or attending a retreat, these are the ways in which we can reestablish equilibrium and find happiness.

And so, I pose a question to my cherished princesses: What path will you choose? The answer lies within, waiting to be embraced. For it is in pursuing what you adore that you'll discover the journey to becoming not only seekers of satisfaction but also architects of your own happiness, leading lives adorned with joy and fulfillment:

One day Newton had an appointment with a scholar for a meal. He went outside to freshen up for a while, while he immersed himself in unresolved problems. But he forgot his appointment and returned home to find that the scholar had finished eating alone and was gone. Newton continued research and research like this and could give us the essence of classical physics called "universal gravitation."

Are there any ways for my princesses? reading or sport, even playing piano, listening to music, or walking with pets? Whatever you would like to do, please do it: that's what makes you satisfier and happier; it would make you lead a happy life.

X

Where is the next Destination?

X
Where is the next Destination?

During my childhood, I shared innocent love with friends. As I grew older, I pursued a respectable career and earned a living. I became a parent and encountered both love and regrets along the way I traveled. Eventually, I passed on my wisdom to my blossoming grandchildren, imparting the virtues of life to help guide them through the challenges they'll face.

Now, I find myself at a juncture where it's fitting to reflect on my journey and eagerly anticipate what lies ahead, envisioning a graceful conclusion to this chapter of my life: how I can meet a beautiful ending.

I lived out my early years in Korea, like a mere dot, a space seemingly tucked away in the corner of our spiral galaxy; then, I embarked on a journey to New Zealand, leaving behind it. The three decades that followed seemed to pass in the blink of an eye. As I step into the latter half of my life, the anticipated duration of my remaining years remains uncertain. It's impossible to ignore the thought that the days I've already lived may outnumber those that lie ahead. At this juncture, I find myself contemplating the path of my remaining journey and asking, "What's our purpose in life, and What lies ahead?"

This universal question accompanies every individual on their life's voyage, and it's challenging to determine how many have stumbled upon a definitive answer. In a past article by a British reporter, an estimate of 117 billion people (world population of 7.8 billion x 15) is mentioned as a rough estimate of those who have pondered this question.

However, as far back as the 4th century B.C., Aristotle is believed to have provided an elusive answer. He asserted that the purpose of human life is 'the pursuit of happiness,' closely tied to our current and next destination.

Another philosopher of his time, Diogenes, rejected the trappings of civilization and opted for a life of minimal possession. Upon hearing of this, Alexander the Great visited him, and they engaged in a profound conversation.

Alexander: I am Alexander the Great.
Diogenes: I am a dog called Diogenes.
Alexander: Aren't you afraid of me? Are you a good person?
Diogenes: Yes.
Alexander: Then why should we be afraid of the good man? Then, Alexander the Great asked to tell him if he had a wish.
Diogenes: Ask not to block the only 'sunlight' in front of him. When King's subordinates came forward to say that such a rude person should be executed immediately.
Alexander: Dissuades them and says, "If I did not become King, otherwise, I would have been like him!"

Indeed, the pursuit of happiness is a complex and deeply personal journey. Alexander the Great, who held immense power and seized much of the known world, may have appeared to have everything one could desire. However, his quest likely went beyond mere power and material wealth. He might have been seeking a sense of purpose of existence, meaning, or inner contentment: elements that contribute to the broader concept of happiness.

Conversely, Diogenes deeply advocated for living with one's own universe in his heart and proposed a different path to happiness. For him, happiness wasn't tied to external possessions or societal status but rather to inner contents, simplicity, and self-sufficiency. His teaching to Greek citizens encouraged an individual to pursue finding happiness within themselves, independent of external circumstances.

The path to happiness, therefore, varies from person to person. Some may seek it through external achievements and material possessions, while others, like Diogenes, may find it through inner peace and contentment. Ultimately, the pursuit of happiness is a deeply philosophical and personal endeavor, and individuals must discover their unique path to fulfillment and well-being.

In my journey through life, I've cherished the innocent friendships of my childhood, toiled and prospered through honest work, nurtured and guided my children through the intricacies of life, and have known both love and regret intimately. As I have transitioned into the role of teaching blossoming grandkids the virtues and wisdom that will prepare them for the unpredictable paths ahead, I find myself standing at a juncture where I can reflect on my past and look forward to the beauty of the conclusion that awaits.

Since I embarked on a new chapter by immigrating to New Zealand. Three decades have whisked by in the blink of an eye, leaving me at the threshold of the latter half of my life. The wisdom captured in the adage, 'Leave nothing to say on leaving!', reminds us that at some point, death will be an inevitable part of our journey, causing us to halt all our earthly pursuits.

And now, I must embark on my final journey. Death, as defined by Wikipedia, refers to the perpetual halt of all biological functions that sustain an organism's existence. After death, the remnants of what was once a living being begin the natural process of decomposition. This inescapable phenomenon is an eventual destiny for all forms of life.

My contemplation of death began during my early years, perhaps as I stepped into primary school or even earlier. Lying in bed beside my mother, I was plagued by the fear of mortality, of fading away from the universe. It wasn't so much the concept of death itself that scared me, but rather the idea of disappearing altogether after it. The anxiety and fear grew unbearable, and I finally roused my sleeping mother, inquiring, "Mom, what is death? Do we cease to exist after we die?" She attempted to ease my concerns by likening death to sleep, akin to the slumber I was currently experiencing by her side. However, despite her words, comprehension still eluded me. I cocooned myself in the blanket, attempting to drift off, but the rest remained elusive. I eventually drifted into slumber, and upon awakening the next morning, the familiar rhythm of my daily life resumed.

A few years back, I found myself standing at my father's gravesite, accompanied by my elder sister, nephew, and my wife. The grave had rested in my hometown for over 75 years until we received news of its impending relocation due to an adjacent factory's expansion. While honoring my father, we spread food offerings, symbolizing the connection from before my birth to the present. Though I lack memories of him, his genetic legacy flows within me.

"Father, where are you now? Where did I originate? Who am I, and where is my last journey leading?" These kinds of existential queries, as elucidated by Wikipedia, were famously captured in a painting titled "Where Do We Come From? What Are We? Where Are We Going?" by French artist Paul Gauguin in 1897-98. Created during his stay in Tahiti, Gauguin's work emerged from the aftermath of his beloved daughter's passing and reflects his profound contemplation on life and its mysteries.

In more recent times, a new term 'living funeral', begun in 1990s Japan, has often featured, signifying a unique ritual where People often gather their loved ones and friends while they are still alive to arrange small-scale events that celebrate life and share final wishes. This practice, also known as a pre-funeral, provides individuals with the autonomy to hold their own farewell celebration. Family and friends have the opportunity to express their respect in person, while they reflect on their lives, and communicate their health, funeral, and legacy desires to loved ones, ensuring that their wishes are known.

The contemporary context has shifted, where rituals and religious customs have taken a backseat to individualized expressions. The practice of a living funeral is a powerful testament to an individual's autonomy over the final chapter. It enables one to bid farewell on his terms, providing a valuable opportunity for useful interaction with loved ones. Although anyone can partake in a living funeral, it is more prevalent among those approaching the end of their lives; often among the elderly or individuals facing terminal illnesses. The opportunity to orchestrate one's farewell imparts a sense of control and a measure of comfort as life's end draws near.

Consider the case of Kim Byungguk, whose funeral took place in August 2018. Diagnosed with terminal prostate cancer at the age of 85, he welcomed guests at the hospital, holding a sign reading 'My Fantastic Funeral'. Expressing that a conventional funeral held little meaning for him, he wanted to bid adieu to all his acquaintances before his passing. Attendees donned vibrant attire, shunning traditional black attire, and the gathering was marked by dance and song, commemorating his unique living farewell funeral.

In New Zealand, a survey has revealed that a significant majority of respondents, up to 87%, express a preference for cremation as the method of disposition. Interestingly, 12.1% of these individuals also express a desire to donate their remains to research institutes. Delving into the details, cremation cost is estimated couple of thousands in New Zealand dollars, while traditional burial expenses can amount to ten thousand for land and interment. Among various reasons driving the inclination towards cremation is the fact that newer generations rarely engage in visits to the graves of their ancestors.

However, instead of factoring in the cost, our couple made a decision, possibly related to burial, with great consideration for my wife, who has been afflicted with a lifelong fear of the night, making it impossible for her to sleep.

Prompted by thoughts stemming from our recent decision, I made an unplanned visit to Albany Cemetery. Alone in contemplation, I wandered the cemetery and engaged in conversations with the staff overseeing it. Amid the tranquil beauty of the surroundings, I felt a profound sense of comfort and serenity.

Upon my return to the office, I sat down at my desk and composed an epitaph, envisioning a future where I would return to this very place. "Here lies Shin Hanok, forever resting." My dear sons: Stephen and Leo, when the time comes for me to depart this world, I am going to make arrangements to be interred under my name at the Albany Memorial Park, a space I intend to purchase in due course. I may even consider erecting a tombstone well in advance. When I eventually pass away, I hope to be buried in this chosen spot with your mom.

Reflecting on the journey that led us to New Zealand in April 1993, where your mother and I rooted our lives, the choice to continue residing in this country or explore other horizons will rest with you and your children once your mother and I have departed. With the fervent hope that you will carry forward our family legacy to future generations, I have decided to reserve this cemetery plot despite opting for the burial. This symbolic gesture stems from the anticipation that you will continue to visit this site for years to come, even long after I am no longer present.

In a matter of years, I am contemplating a living funeral of my own. This gathering will involve only close family and friends who have been a part of my life's journey thus far. Following this living funeral, the actual funeral, which will be held when I truly depart this world, will be a simple affair, offering solace to the family at home before my remains are interred in the previously designated plot. I envision a departure with a simple ceremony.

I have lately been grappling with shoulder pain, undergoing acupuncture and physical therapy for the past three months. Unfortunately, the pain shows no signs of abating. As I grow older, my once robust body gradually tires, and the faces of those I encounter on the street become a haze. Friends are departing one by one. It seems that the time has come to prepare for an impending embrace of death. Also, I advise you I am scheduled to insert a pacemaker in my heart next week.

Throughout our lives, we all confront a myriad of fears: loss of lovers, unemployment, health concerns, financial instability, natural disasters, personal failures, darkness, and so on. The list is extensive and impossible to catalog in its entirety. Amidst these, the fear of loneliness of being left alone in this world may be the most profound.

For 45 years, my cherished wife has endured sleepless nights due to her fear of the night. During my active days working for the power company, before migrating to New Zealand, she remained sleepless with chronic insomnia, which defied any cure. As I indulged in nights of revelry and intoxication with office coworkers, I failed to recognize her silent struggle.

On a typical evening, our rounds of soju-infused meals commenced at a restaurant in Gangnam; and then continued across the river at a bar named 'Cobblestone' in Hwayangri, Seoul. While nursing a hangover with office coworkers, beer unexpectedly cascaded over me. Blinking in disbelief, I met my wife's eyes as she poured beer over my head, her face devoid of words before vanishing without explanation. I promptly hailed a taxi and returned home, spending the night in silence. The following day, I inquired about the incident of the previous night.

It transpired that on that evening, she had settled our children into bed early. A ringing phone interrupted the stillness, and she assumed it was me. However, the call was from a random individual engaging in phone sex antics. Unaware of how to disconnect the call, she was ensnared in an uncomfortable encounter. Despite her escalating frustration, she's compelled to confront me about the matter. Unacquainted with the bar's location, she relied on my usual post-hangover debrief to assure the locale.

Summoning a taxi, she conveyed the destination to the driver, and I narrowly escaped discovery as I ventured to another room, while my drinking companions had retired for the night. Had my escapades been revealed, it would have surely led to a tumultuous confrontation.

In 2004, she supported her younger son's soccer pursuits in Germany under guardianship, facing sleepless nights on her own. Recollecting those years of restlessness and navigating her academic commitments, she describes them as a nightmare. Even abroad, her life was far from enjoyable in the absence of my support for those two years, and she faced challenges in caring for her son alone.

During one of her shopping trips to a department store after classes, a dashing Italian gentleman tentatively came close to her with a greeting. He had been observing her from a distance, contemplating saying hello, but learning of her marital status, he opted to leave without a word. Poor fellow! If his approach had caught the attention of an unaccompanied woman, who could predict the outcome?

To explore the root causes of profound fear of the night and heightened sensitivity to minor details, a studies group at China's Sinan University conducted the research with 120 female participants. The results that they garnered from the participants were intriguing. They unveiled that the night triggered more terror than complete darkness itself. The research team orchestrated diverse experimental scenarios and exposed the participants to various settings.

234

They observed that in the situations where participants were exposed to the sounds of nature and couldn't tell between day and night, their replies remained consistent regardless of the time.

On the other hand, when participants were exposed to disturbing images and sounds, their sense of fear was far more profound at night compared to daytime, they attributed this heightened fear during the nighttime to the impact of the participants' 24-hour biorhythms.

My wife and I, both familiar with these nocturnal fears, frequently have engaged in conversations about our own mortality. Should she pass away before I do, she has decided that her remains will be buried, placed within an urn, and kept beside me in bed until my own passing, at which point she will be interred on the same day at the place I had secured.

Conversely, if I were to pass away first, I have made prior arrangement to proceed to the cemetery I selected in advance. Her wish is to relocate to a locale where human activity is relatively consistent, allowing her to hear people's voices even during the night to minimize her night fear. Subsequently, she plans to join me at the planned graveyard, a poignant testament to the bond we share and the promise we've made to each other.

The concept of death can be traced back to the inception of human existence. In the past, death was often regarded as a taboo subject, seldom discussed openly. However, recent times have witnessed a surge in people's curiosity about death, coupled with a more positive shift in their attitude toward this inevitable aspect of life.

Humans progress along the timeline of existence, moving from birth to growth, aging, and eventually death. It's a journey that we all undertake. Throughout our lives, we metabolize the sustenance we consume to derive energy, maintaining the equilibrium of the human body to sustain life. Yet, every life concludes with death. We are all part of this cyclical narrative.

But what truly is death? One can experience a natural passing while alive, or meet death in an unfortunate car accident. Some individuals choose to end their lives due to dissatisfaction or despair. The path to death varies widely. However, the trajectory leading to death is the same. Professor Shelly Kagan, renowned for his enlightening lectures at Yale University, eloquently expounds in "What is Death" that death is a physical occurrence signifying the cessation of brain function:

Upon the cessation of blood circulation within the body, the supply of oxygen is halted. As a consequence, the brain's oxygen saturation diminishes. In the absence of oxygen, cellular metabolism grinds to a halt, resulting in cellular damage and a disruption in the supply of vital amino acids and proteins. The cascade of decay commences, leading to the eventual breakdown of all cellular structures. With the eventual destruction of major organs and the cessation of brain activity, the final threshold of death is reached.

At this juncture, I find myself pondering a fundamental question: "Does the soul endure beyond our mortal existence?" This inquiry arises in the debate surrounding whether the soul should be perceived as distinct from the physical body. This division is primarily characterized by the dualist perspective, which recognizes the soul as separate from the body, and the monist viewpoint, which does not acknowledge an autonomous soul but rather perceives consciousness as a byproduct of the material body.

Monists argue that consciousness ends with the body's death, considering the soul as an outcome of the body's specialized functions. They suggest that consciousness is linked to physical processes and ends when body functions stop. I lean toward this view, as our consciousness emerges from complex cellular interactions: synaptic electrical works between cells. And it fades when these processes come to an end.

Conversely, dualists posit the existence of an immaterial entity distinct from the body: the soul. This nonphysical entity is believed to inhabit a certain realm within the body, and as death approaches, the soul is said to detach and depart to another place. Individuals often recount experiences akin to an 'out-of-body' phenomenon in support of this notion.

As of 17 November 2023, our current house is located at 65 Green Road, Auckland, New Zealand; when spring comes, cherry trees blossom on the 8-acre land.

A grave accident involving my wife nearly ended her life. On the morning of 5 April 2015, she left for church around 4:00 AM. At 4:50, my phone repeatedly rang. I picked up the phone, and from her tone, I instinctively knew something was amiss. She managed to convey to me in her weakened voice, "Honey, I had a car accident!" Racing to the scene without even properly dressing, I found the police already investigating on the spot.

In the incident, an elderly driver disregarded a red light and collided directly with my wife's vehicle, causing serious damage to its front. A mere few seconds' difference would likely have resulted in her death. He admitted his fault during the police inquiry, and her insurance claim was promptly processed. Her car was demolished to replace it. She was hospitalized for a thorough checkup, miraculously escaping any physical harm.

A few days after the accident, my wife recounted a surreal experience of traversing a long tunnel within a matter of seconds. She conveyed this experience with a sense of humor, quipping that her moment of demise had yet to arrive, punctuated by her laughter.

After my wife's car accident, there was intense debate between two groups in the church. One believed that god's intervention saved her, while the other argued that early morning praying had almost caused her death. I found myself in agreement with the latter perspective. After the incident, she followed my advice and stopped attending church.

Reflecting on my own case on the national highway in 1997, which I detailed earlier in this book, as well as the recent accident, my wife and I often jest that it's not yet our time to depart in separate car crashes. Even in the face of near-death experiences, we share jokes and laughter, as if embracing life's uncertainties.

I hold the belief that I entered this world through an extraordinary coincidence, a probability of 1 in 400 trillion. Embracing the value of happiness and life according to my free will has been my guiding principle.

As I reflect on the finite nature of life, I imagine an ending to our journey that aligns with our shared desires - departing together. However, I also recognize that this scenario is nearly impossible to achieve. When pondering the potential of serious illness, my wife and I had once contemplated Switzerland as a destination, given its acknowledgment of euthanasia. In May 2018, I learned of Dr. Goodall, Australia's oldest scientist, who chose euthanasia in Switzerland. His decision wasn't driven by the physical pain of his condition, but by the anticipation of greater unhappiness as his health declined. His choice reflected a desire for control over life and death, unaffected by external factors.

Fortunately, New Zealand adopted euthanasia on 7 November 2021, offering an alternative to our original plan. This allows us to change our end-of-life direction. Our final wishes, as already outlined in this book, will be entrusted to our children.

If we are tired of life's journey, and relying on our children or family members becomes necessary, we choose the path of natural death. However, if this isn't feasible, we contemplate euthanasia. Faced with the bleak diagnosis of a debilitating illness, if recovery becomes implausible, we won't pursue futile treatments. Instead, we would confront the disease, and if necessary, embrace euthanasia.

The story of Dr. Scott Nearing, a university professor who sought personal satisfaction in harmony with nature, resonates with my aspirations. Despite living a long life, Dr. Nearing's physical and mental faculties waned in his mid-nineties, leading him to embrace his mortality. Reflecting on his journey, I find inspiration to lead a life of purpose, even as I document my musings in these late-night writing sessions.

Life expectancy has risen remarkably due to advances in life sciences and improved nutrition. The average lifespan now exceeds 80 years, with some approaching 100. Yet, the true architects of our lifespan are our parents, through the union of sperm and egg. Our bodies, composed of approximately 60 trillion cells, perpetually divide, playing out the drama of life's cycle.

Cellular aging, driven by the gradual shortening of telomeres, marks the progression of time. Telomeres, the protective caps found at the tips of chromosomes, shrink with each cell division until they eventually stop dividing after approximately 70 cycles. Much like the aglet at the end of a shoelace, telomeres fray as time passes, ultimately leading to cellular aging and death.

The length of our telomeres, influenced by various factors, serves as a reflection of our stress levels and lifestyle choices. Stress, particularly rooted in fear and anxiety, plays a role in the shortening of telomeres. In such instances, it becomes imperative to shield telomeres by transforming the threat response into a challenge-response. This shift not only pertains to our mindset but also involves aspects like dietary choices, physical activity, and sleep patterns, all intricately tied to telomere health.

Of these factors, regular exercise has shown itself to be the most effective in preserving telomere length. Engaging in activities like walking or exercise for 4 to 5 minutes, three times a week, is recommended as a valuable practice for maintaining healthy telomeres. Our couple aspires to a life filled with joy, love, and connection, surrounded by friends and neighbors, savoring life's simple pleasures. When that unforeseen moment of death approaches us, may we greet it with serenity and bid farewell to this pale blue dot.

Acknowledgement

Acknowledgement

At last, a small man's long journey is nearing its end. The process of writing these reflections and contemplating life's challenging story has been a profoundly personal journey for me. As I approach the final pages of this memoir, my heart is brimming with sincere gratitude for the influences, experiences, and insights that have molded and enriched my perspectives.

First and foremost, in the process of crafting My Life story, I received invaluable assistance, particularly through editing support provided by ChatGPT. Also, I have made extensive use of the Collins English Thesaurus, Google translator, and modern techniques to the best of my ability.

I extend my heartfelt appreciation to all those who have so far accompanied me on this introspective path, offering their wisdom, encouragement, and understanding. A special thank you goes to my mother, who had tried to instill her intellectual genes in me, my grandparents, my immediate family, and my friends. Your steady support has made you the pillars of strength throughout the twists and turns of my life.

I am deeply indebted to the trailblazers in the realms of science, philosophy, and human exploration. Their groundbreaking ideas have ignited a spark of curiosity within me, propelling me to explore profound questions about existence. The legacies left by these pioneers, whether known or anonymous philosophers, knowledge donors, or street thinkers have profoundly resonated with my journey in the pursuit of the art of life.

To my readers, your engagement with my words is an honor beyond words. Your willingness to share in my thoughts, ponderings, and musings is a testament to the human connection that transcends time and distance.

I owe a special debt of gratitude to the dedicated individuals in the fields of medicine, science, and ethics, who tirelessly work to navigate the complexities of life and human experiences. Your contribution inspires me to continue seeking knowledge and understanding.

Lastly, I wish to acknowledge the profound mystery and beauty of life itself. This memoir is a humble attempt to capture fleeting moments, ponder existential queries, and explore the interplay of mortality and the human spirit. It is a celebration of life's impermanence, a reminder to cherish each day, and an exploration of the uncharted territories that lie within and beyond.

With heartfelt gratitude,

Shin Hanok,
A humble small man!

Our Family Genealogy
attached

靈山·寧越辛氏大同譜 首卷

辛 鏡 신경

二世 雲敏 운민

三世 永繼 영계

四世 夢森 몽삼

五世 覺繼 각계 千繼 천계 縣繼 현계 周繼 주계

六世 百鍊 백련

七世 喜 희

八世 至和 지화

九世 蔵 천 革 혁 蘊 온

上將軍公派

周繼 주계
夢森 四子
高麗明宗丙辰(一一九六)生高宗甲戌(一二一四)及第正衙上將軍設官九世公之墓設神位書于詠格祠與文宗宗廟失傳故今浦項市北一區杞溪面未峰齋設于靈增每歲行祀西使云

六世	七世	八世	九世
子舜賢 수현 進士	子克圭 극규	子就忠 취충 朝奉大夫	子之宜 지의 郎將 女陳益明 朝散大夫 子 女陳處安縣監 陳處明進 郎修縣監 女李斯道 子欣 흔 子成烈 奉大夫 女仇松立 殿直 縣令 女孔斯文 女全祐 子良起 양기 奉翊大夫 殿直 13卷 2
		子恭近 공근 朝奉大夫	
子舜尚 수상 進士 子全玘進士 孫全宗琥軍器監 全宗義軍器監 全宗實軍器監 孫女辛 革靈山府院君 女全允基 郎將 女楊至雄 郎將 女金和甫 郎將	子克純 극순	子革奇 혁기 高麗元宗庚午(一二七○)生忠烈己酉及第奉順大夫 女朴修奇 夫 女愼義 大護軍 子愼昌吉郎將 女尹熙監務	

245

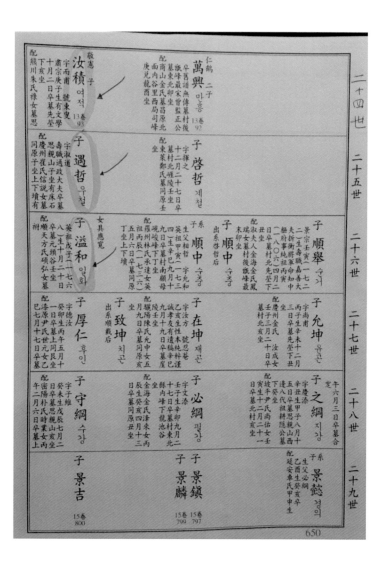

二十四世

仁鶴 二子
萬興 만흥
13卷 92
配 商山金氏墓昌原北庚坐
面內山谷里西局坐
配 面內龍谷峰酉坐
卒壬辰譜燕傳墓村後甑峰巖宋曾監正公
墓東北卯坐

敬憲 子
汝積 여적
13卷 93
字而甫 號東皐
肅宗庚子生有文學
十月二日卒墓先塋
下亥坐
配 熊川朱氏祿女墓思

二十五世

子啓哲 계철
字擇之
十二月二十七日卒
墓東村北唯陵壬坐
配 商山郭氏墓同原壬坐

子遇哲 우철
字淑通 政大夫床墓
壽職庚子生有文學
思覲山子坐有床墓
配 同慶州崔氏信說女墓石墓
原子坐上下墳有

二十六世

子順舉 순거
景宗壬寅一一七二
生壽職嘉善大夫
二月折衝將軍命知中
樞府事統祖丙寅
(一八〇六)四月二十
丑坐墓村北先塋下
配 淑夫人金海金氏胤
壬子墓村後甑峰巖坐

子順中 순중
出系啓哲后

子順中 수중
系生父英哲
字允和
四月生乙英
九祖坤辰年辛母九
墓峻陽陳氏允女英
坐上下墳丁五日辛
丁丙村林坐承建女
(一七三二)上下墳同原

二十七世

子之綱 지강
字慶添
生甲辰生山西達八代祖覲隱公亥坐
配 坡州金氏汝成女
三日卒墓先塋下丑坐
坐丙子三月二十日卒
配 慶州金氏北子坐
一丑午墓村北壬子坐

子允坤 윤곤
字尚甫一一七二
生乙亥丙午知中
折衝將軍命知中
樞府事統祖丙寅
配 淑人金海金氏
壬子墓村後甑峰巖坐

子在坤 재곤
字汝立誠成性本編妹允
乙亥縣女九祖陽陳氏允
九坤九日辛乙墓崖
月墓金氏允女五
辰五日卒墓同原亥

子致坤 치곤
出系順中后

二十八世

子之綱 지강
午六月三日卒墓合
聖午六月三日卒墓合
墓坎寅坐同北村亥坐
達八代祖覲隱公西
乙酉生癸亥卒
配 延安車氏甲申生

子必綱 필강
字文添
壬子生辛
九月二日
十四日卒墓村北
坐金氏漆未女丙
配 金海金氏龍池谷
辰癸酉卒墓同原丑坐

子守綱 수강
字子組
癸未生戊戌
七月山墓思山女
配 密陽朴氏時業女
午二月六日卒墓先瑩
亥坐

二十九世

系生父必綱
子景懿 경의

子景鎮 경진
子景麟 경린
15卷 799　797

子景吉 경길
15卷 800

二十五世	二十六世	二十七世	二十八世	二十九世

視山上壬坐
配密陽朴氏禮生女墓
降神峙乙坐

床石

二十五世

子再哲 재철
字聖三
十月三日卒墓村北

二十六世

子受和 수화
字致玉
九庄純祖壬午一七
八二二五月十一
卒墓筍峰西麓民

配晉陽姜氏萬柱女八
月二十七日卒墓降
神峙中麓亥坐

子極和 극화
字汝三
配文化柳氏萬墓失傳
女朴德成
女李東浩

子極和 극화

子泳和 영화

二十七世

上同丑坐

子成坤 성곤
字致謙
丙寅生五月一日卒
墓思視山上子坐
配玄風郭氏以畢女
二十四日卒墓村南秀峰
七月三日卒墓合窆

子厚宅 후택
字德一
戊生壬辰四月二
十日卒墓村南秀峰
配玄風郭氏

子奉儀 봉의
卒墓失傳 안동이坐
配慶州崔氏萬先業女墓
同原

子宅坤 택곤

二十八世

同良坐

子孝綱 의낭
丙戌生二月十日卒
墓上同丁坐
配達城徐氏大周女墓
同原二十八子坐

子允綱 유강
字悌
甲午生十月六日卒
壬午坐上同東
配延安車氏昌大周女墓
同原二十八子坐上
午日卒墓祔

子載綱 재강
字乃承
壬午坐甲戌二月十
四日卒墓村東
配密陽朴氏春明女壬
午日卒墓丁亥六月十四

子繼龍 계룡
三月五日卒墓失傳
配密陽朴氏萬女墓
龜尾孤岩山子坐西

子始英 시영
二月二十六日卒墓同
原東迅

二十九世

子景早
15卷 801

子景禹
15卷 802

子景淑
15卷 804

子景周
15卷 806

子景萬
15卷 806

子景伯
15卷 808

子得昌
15卷 810

子景泰
15卷 811

九綱
子 景禹 경우
13巻
651
配慶陽朴氏正輔女八月二十八日卒墓附
宇榮伯丁巳生乙亥一月十七日卒墓思親山子坐

子 達昊 달호
配慶州李氏宗林女二月二十申生辛丑二月二十
宇文讚丁未生丁未六月十日坐墓思親山艮

女李聖城 星山人 子萬益
女周宰八 尚州人 子德會 興會
子 致甲 치갑
未生卒墓贇壙
配延安車氏榮玉女癸
宇致彦甲戌一月十七日生墓元頭谷下壬坐

婦尚州周氏
子 有錫 유석
宇有成辛丑生壬辰十月二十九日卒墓元頭谷艮坐

婦盆城裵氏
一九三八年八月十六日生
子 漢局 한국
一九三二年一月四日生

子 漢時 한시
一九三八年一月四日生

婦金海金氏
在漢女一九三○年十五日卒墓坐
一名亨道
一九二三年六月十日生
子 相德 상덕 一九五年十一
子 点根 점근 十二月二
子 海根 해근 一九五七年十一月
子 海根 해근 二八日生
子 相龍 상룡 一九六三年十月二
子 海龍 해룡 一九六六年二月十
女 相今 상금 一九五二年十二
女 相今 三日生
一九五二年二月二

子 英洙 영수
一九六七年七月九日生
女芬錦 분금
一九五年五月二
一九五年

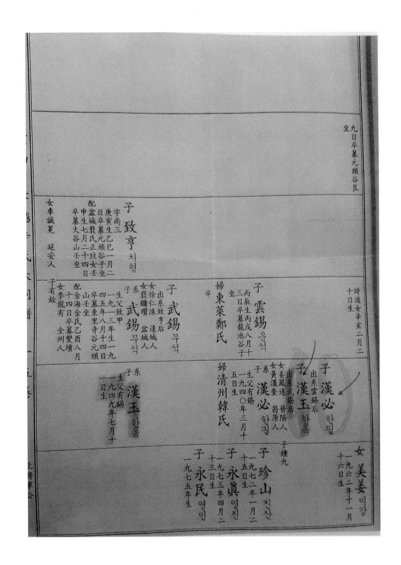

九日卒墓元頔谷民
坐

時適女辛亥二月二
十日生

子致亨 지형
字尚三
配
盆城襄氏
庚寅生乙巳一月二
日生卒墓元頔谷壬
坐申生七月二十四
日卒墓大谷山壬坐
女車誠晃 延安人

子雲錫 운석
婦東萊鄭氏 卒
丙辰生戊八月十
三日卒墓龍池谷子坐

子武錫 무석
女徐仁洙 達城人
出系致亨后
一九一三年一九
一四年八月生
卒墓里寺谷元頔
山壬坐

子漢錫 무석
女裵鑽瑣 盆城人

子有益
女李有龍 全州人
配金海金氏乙酉八月
四日生卒墓嬰墳

婦清州韓氏

子漢必 한필
系父有錫 昌原人
一九四〇年三月十
五日生
女美鳳遠
女黃漢奎

子漢必 한필
出系雲錫后
子漢玉 한옥
出系雲錫后

子系
漢玉 한옥
生父有錫
一九四九年七月十
一日生

女美姜 미강
一九六二年十一月
十六日生

子鍾九
子珍山 지산
一九七二年一月二
子永眞 영진
一九六三年四月二
十三日生
子永民 영민
一九七五年生

A CHALLENGING LIFE

발행	2024년 01월 17일
저자	Shin Hanok
펴낸이	한건희
펴낸곳	주식회사 부크크
출판사등록	2014. 07. 15(제2014-16호)
주소	서울특별시 금천구 가산디지털1로 119 A동 305호
전화	1670-8316
E-mail	info@bookk.co.kr
ISBN	979-11-410-6730-4

www.bookk.co.kr